FOLLOWING JOSEPH CAMPBELL'S LEAD IN THE SEARCH FOR JESUS' FATHER

William P. Frost

Texts and Studies in Religion
Volume 58

The Edwin Mellen Press
Lewiston/Queenston/Lampeter

Library of Congress Cataloging-in-Publication Data

Frost, William P.
    Following Joseph Campbell's lead in the search for Jesus' father /
William P. Frost.
        p.   cm. -- (Studies in the psychology of religion ; v. 5)
    Includes bibliographical references.
    ISBN 0-88946-249-6
    1. Jesus Christ--Rationalistic interpretations. 2. Jesus Christ-
-Family. 3. Jesus Christ--Psychology. 4. God--Fatherhood.
5. Campbell, Joseph, 1904- --Contributions in Christology.
I. Title. II. Series.
BT304.95.F76 1990
232--dc20   90-37934
                                                                   CIP

This is volume 58 in the continuing series
Texts and Studies in Religion
Volume 58 ISBN 0-88946-249-6
TSR Series ISBN 0-88946-976-8

A CIP catalog record for this book
is available from the British Library.

The author gratefully acknowledges the opportunity to use exceprts from
THE POWER OF MYTH by Joseph Campbell and Bill Moyers.
Copyright © 1988 by Apostrophe S Productions, Inc. and Bill Moyers and
Alfred Van der Marck Editions, Inc. for itself and the estate of Joseph
Campbell. Used by permission of Doubleday, a division of Bantam
Doubleday Dell Publishing Group, Inc.

Territory U. S.

The Edwin Mellen Press   The Edwin Mellen Press
        Box 450   Box 67
Lewiston, New York   Queenston, Ontario
        USA 14092   CANADA L0S 1L0

The Edwin Mellen Press, Ltd.
Lampeter, Dyfed, Wales
UNITED KINGDOM SA48 7DY

Printed in the United States of America

TABLE OF CONTENTS

Chapter One

Why This Study and Research Began

Most studies are, of course, made to gain general understanding about the matter in question. But the real issue here is to develop more insight regarding "ultimate meaning." That is a heavy concept, but it is truly the overall purpose of this scholarly effort. Ultimate meaning, not in terms of cosmology, physics, or the origins of our species. It is the basic religious dimension, that transcendent quality by which existence, happiness, and human suffering, hopes and expectations, heroic sacrifice and the affirmation of life, love and death receive some perspective.

Within this general quest for ultimate meaning I traveled roads which started out as avenues commonly journeyed by others in great numbers. Later I left the main roads and arrived at untrodden territory. This I want to explain in the following pages.

Here is an opening statement: Raised as a Roman Catholic Christian I am very much rooted in a personal identification with Jesus. The Christian and Catholic teachings which I received covered more territory than I had questions. Robert Bellah signifies Christianity (as well as Judaism and the Islam) as a "historic religion" in "Religious Evolution" in the *American Sociological Review*. Such religions, according to Bellah, provide those in pursuit of salvation relevant information. They perceive reality and its course of existence in terms of salvation events. Christianity in particular developed a salvation history, according to which the believer learns what went wrong, and when and how, and what went right in response to the wrong. Thus the connection with salvation can be made because one learns . what happened in the development of salvation in the course of history.

My personal interpretation of a "salvation history" mentality is that such an enterprise became a "know-it-all" religion. They know who was before the beginning of this creation, what happened during the process of creation (creationism), they know what is significant in the history of humanity (original sin is overcome by Christ's sacrifice on the cross; baptism into Christ's church offers the participation in this salvation), and they know what to expect at the end of time (doomsday, last judgment, heaven, hell, purgatory, and possibly limbo).

As a boy I was indoctrinated into such a triumphant (know-it-all) religious worldview, but personal learning also came into play. At an early age (ca. eight years old) I came to appreciate that other Christians, who were not members of the only true Roman church, were also alive in Jesus. I had to recognize that the life of Jesus ("I am the vine, you are the branches. Whoever remains in me, and I in him, will bear much fruit; for you can do nothing without me." John 15:5) is also true beyond the walls of Roman Catholicism. My Protestant playmates displayed virtues of Christian life which were obvious to me. So I was forced to make a judgment beyond the orthodox teachings which I received.

My Catholic teachers were not fundamentalists. They had ways of being interpretative. Somehow, the creation of the world in six days was never imagined as an exact six-day event. Moreover, it was understood that the history of humanity extended far and beyond the 4,000 years BCE, as the Old Testament seems to suggest. Of course, Noah (Gen 9:28) did not really live 350 years, and Adam (Gen 5:3) could not possibly have his son Seth when he was 130 years old, and he did not finally find death at the age of 930. Seth could not have lived 912 years (Gen 5:8). The readings in Genesis suggested that there were cities coexisting outside the immediate environment of Adam and Eve. Thus there was life beyond the accounts of the biblical stories.

Simply growing up and integrating common sense created the awareness that God was not responsible for changing the weather. But still, when someone in the family became sick, I prayed fervently to God to show his healing power and to keep alive such a dear one.

Because I believed in the saving power of being baptized in Jesus, I went to the seminary at the age of fourteen. There was a truly open Catholic mentality. I became a student of history, literature, languages, mathematics, culture, music and the arts. I experienced this as a continuous integration of human life and its memorable learning. The "know-it-all" attitude prevailed, but it became more and more complex by further refinements, sophisticated distinctions, and the unfolding of insight. I wanted to become a missionary. Possibly, I would go to Africa and baptize black souls into the shining light of God's grace so that they would be saved.

In the novitiate (a year of introduction into the religious life of this particular missionary society) I further developed the substance of prayer life and personal piety. My relationship with God was active all hours of the day. Morning prayers were followed by meditation in the celebration of the Holy Mass (not yet commonly known as Eucharist). Morning classes in Scripture and spiritual life were ended by lunch. In the afternoon all kinds of chores had to be done: cleaning halls, bathrooms, and yard work. Then again there were meditation and prayer till supper time and in the evening still some more spiritual readings till night prayers ended the day. So it went on, day after day, for a whole year. It was truly a monastic life. I was most serious in these matters and became a real member of this religious society. My life with God had substance, personal identification, and was rooted in the rituals and doctrines of the Roman Catholic. tradition.

When I entered the halls of higher learning, the seminary system offered courses in philosophy and theology. I was introduced into what the most celebrated minds of Western civilization had recorded about their thoughts on God humanity, and the physical reality. The difference between Aristotle and Plato, the integration of Aristotelian thought by Thomas Aquinas, the upheavals in the history of Christianity (Roman Catholic church) and also modern thought (Nietzsche's atheism, the Enlightenment and the birth of the sciences, resulting in positivism, empiricism, skepticism, alternated by idealism, humanism and existentialism), were summarized to be attacked and refuted.

The courses in theology gave me the basic insights in Roman Catholic doctrine regarding God, the Trinity, Christ, Church, Sacraments, the Holy Spirit, and the end of time (Eschatology). So I was readied to be an educated spokesman of the Roman hierarchy and serve the church as its priest.

My superiors requested me to pursue doctoral studies in moral theology to function as a professor in the seminary system. One of my teachers was Edward Schillebeeckx. Eminently learned in Catholic thought as a Dominican priest, this author of many Catholic books was spirited by an anthropological concern. He focused on the human side of the Christian reality. He spoke in the name of "common sense" and reason, and was critically interpretive of standardized traditions of the Roman hierarchy. Such an approach had become rather needed by others who had leaned more about life than the Roman Catechism did cover. That is why the writings of Schillebeeckx were so readily published, translated, and sold all over the Catholic world.

This mentality culminated in the ecumenical council, Vatican II. It was fathered by the *Nouvelle Theologie* (French theologians who promoted a return to the primary sources in Patristics and Scripture), e.g. Yves Congar, Jean Danielou, the rebirth of liturgy in Germany with the leadership of Romano Guardini, and the updated and relevant theology of Karl Rahner and Edward Schillebeeckx. The Documents of Vatican II express an affirmation of the goodness of God in His creation. One of the most revealing statements of this council was a declaration that God's Spirit is alive in the hearts of all living human beings. This superseded Augustinianism, which demanded the right baptism in the right church to obtain salvation and entrance in God's Kingdom. Thus my need to go as a missionary and baptize black souls became highly relativized.

All this had a great impact on my church identity, because now we were to embrace all of humanity. (Vatican II called the former Protestant heretics "our brothers and sisters in Christ.")

Philosophically, a major breakthrough occurred with the posthumous publication of the writings of Pierre Teilhard de Chardin S. J.. *The Phenomenon of Man* offered me a synthesis, which integrated the evolutionary dynamics of divine creativity in reference to physics, biology and anthropology. This invited me to truly appreciate the research and studies of scientists. They touched and analyzed the physical reality and produced insights which opened my mind to a beyond the "know-it-all" religion. It was the beginning of a mystical religiousness for me.

Later studies brought me in contact with the Process Thought of Alfred North Whitehead. He integrated the physical reality and the evolution dimension in terms of the divine creativity. I began to see that everything was in an ongoing dynamic flow where the more complex emerges from the less complex. Whitehead concluded that this could only make sense if one postulated a divine source, which is historically active in the productive process of such a greater intensification of the divine within reality.

In short, the visions of Theilhard had received a systematic and ontological account, theorized and formulated by a famous scientist, Whitehead. The scientist began to make sense out of the religious aspect of existence, and the responding theologians began to make sense out of the physical reality. An eminent example is Ralph Wendell Burhoe, the founding editor of *Zygon: Journal of Religion and Science* (beginning 1966 at the University of Chicago).

For me it was all coming together, and I personally testified to these insights in my first professional publications as a Professor of Religious Studies at a Catholic university.

But the quest for meaning goes on, and there is always more to be recognized and integrated. In the sixties (Time cover, April 8, 1966) God was declared to be dead. Thomas Altizer, Paul Van Buren, and William Hamilton provided the voices explaining why the traditional God had become culturally irrelevant. Especially Altizer communicated that one is better off to divest oneself of God-concepts because then the divine may have an opportunity to demonstrate its own presence in its own way. The naming of God obscures the life of the divine. Theologically I integrated this approach by specializing in the new trend, the Theology of Hope, fathered by Jurgen Moltmann and Wolfhart Pannenberg. Both at Tubingen, West Germany, they became enchanted with and inspired by Ernst Bloch. He was the Philosopher of Hope, and provided a true heuristic focus for those who wanted to speak meaningfully about the ambiguity of existence.

In short, Bloch writes that "S is not yet P." It means: nothing is what it is, because everything is characterized by the vacuum of the "not yet" of the future. That is, the meaning of things cannot be assessed in terms of the present. What they are to become to mean will occur in the perspective of a finalizing future. The vacuum places everything in a unknown openness and provides the needed space for creativity and energetic dedication.

Especially Moltmann made this meaningful for Christian theology. He argues that the Christian doctrines and declarations about reality cannot be verified because they are not true yet. They are tentative expressions about reality in reference to a divine future. The language is an expression of hope and is religious in nature. As such it is a language of expectation about what we, in the very divine core of our souls, project what reality may become.

That sounded convincing to me, because it took care of the discrepancies between what reality is and what religious teachings said it to be. Thus God may appear to be dead, but that is because he is not yet as significant as Christian theologians and the Church's doctrines make Him out to be.

Again, the quest for meaning is always restless. In my case I became involved in the study of Eastern religions, especially Hinduism and Buddhism. They offer an immense amount of wisdom, and the mystical awareness is enormously substantial. But I discovered a discrepancy between the Eastern spirituality and the biblical religiousness. The Eastern tradition speaks from the depth of human experiences as embodied in the mystery of existence. No particular revelation is needed. Just meditation, commitment to inner truth, and purity of heart and mind will guide one to a high sophisticated enlightenment. This liberates the soul from anxiety, prejudice, narrow-mindedness, and fear, and allows it to sense the eternal divine within a mystical wisdom. Reality is not to be taken seriously. It is simply a momentary emergent enveloped by its boundaries in space and time. Enlightenment reaches beyond space and time.

The biblical tradition is very much concerned with space and time, and the things which happen in the course of history. This creation and the events happening here and now are of interest to this religious tradition.

So, I learned to value existence as an invitation to actualize it in a unique way. Ernest Becker's *The Denial of Death* for (which he received a Pulitzer Prize) affirmed Paul Tillich's *The Courage To Be*. Life is not to be lived according to a pre-arranged set-up according to a presumed architect. Life has no prescribed meaning and has no pre-ordained value. There are no preset answers to our general quest for meaning. The quest itself, if lived well, is the value of life. This existentialistic embrace of human courage with genuine openness to what one is to make out of life's meaning comforted me in the very core of my bones. For quite a while I had sensed that all the answers and speculations about the "whatness" of life are in some respects always too limited to say it all. They may be inspiring, refreshing, and very informative in certain ways. But life is always greater than what we say about it.

In this context I followed Altizer's insight that there comes a time in our personal growth when the divine is not served by our theologies and doctrines. However lofty they may be, they still do not make the divine present. The moment came in my life that I started to laugh out loud when I began to pray. It simply dawned on me that the religious focus of my prayer language was too small and thus ridiculous. I did burst out laughing because this revelation hit me suddenly. It is like the pun at the end of a story which makes it all a true joke.

The arrival at the ridiculousness (not absurdity) was also brought on by my new interest: I became a reader of Gary Zukav's *The Dancing Wu-Li Masters: An Overview of the New Physics*. I learned to understand the philosophical insights resulting from the new physics, the study of subatomic particles. In general I identified with this new way of looking at reality. If some of it is to be summarized, then here are a few insights:

a) Physical reality, in its core, does not operate according to physical laws but according to dynamics of probability.

b) The physical reality is not an objective pile of matter out there, but is known to us according to our subjective way of seeing, hearing, and measuring things.

c) The way we perceive reality can be called "illusion."

d) What we call real is our interpretation.

e) Our universe is not created out of nothingness, but emerged out of an ocean of fullness.

f) Outside our understanding of order is not an empty chaos, but a greater and more encompassing order.

g) Nothingness does not exist, but there is only the fullness of being.

All this led Gary Zukav to write:

"Reality" is what we take to be true. What we take to be true is what we believe. What we believe is based upon our perceptions. What we perceive depends upon what we look for. What we look for depends upon that we think. What we think depends upon what we perceive. What we perceive determines what we believe. What we believe determines what we take to be true. What we take to be true is our reality. (313)

I can identify with Richard Feynman's attitude about meaning. He was the recipient of the Nobel Prize in Physics for his discovery of the "Feynman diagrams" which describe the dances of sub-atomic particles. In *"Surely You're, Joking, Mr. Feynman!" Adventures of a Curious Character*, Richard Feynman Ralph Leighton reports:

You see, one thing is, I can live with doubt and uncertainty and not knowing. I think it's much more interesting to live not knowing than to have answers, and possible beliefs and different degrees of certainty about different things. But I'm not absolutely sure of anything and there are many things I don't know anything about, such as whether it means anything to ask why we're here, and what the question might mean. I might think about it a little bit and if I can't figure it out, then we go on to something else. But I don't have to know an answer. I don't feel frightened by not knowing things, by being lost in a mysterious universe without having any purpose, which is the way it really is, so far as I can tell possibly. It doesn't frighten me.

This is an important statement for understanding the motivation of this intended study about the Father of Jesus. It expresses my concern with being responsive to a unique quality of Jesus' religiosity. It is not a search about meaning in an absolute sense, but a heartfelt curiosity about the uniqueness of this amazing man. He defies explanations in so many ways, and I hold that approaching the life of His Father would somehow explain more than what has been documented so far.

A few more pieces of information will complete this statement of purpose. While delving into the views of the new physics, I learned to particularly appreciate the writings of an eminent student of Einstein, David Bohm. We will return to him later. In this context he shall be known for his vision and theory of the implicate order. (See *Wholeness and the Implicate Order*.)

Bohm substantiated his insights as follows: Forms of being are not separate from each other in space and time. They are interrelated by a communality. Whatever exists belongs to an underlying and all-pervasive order. This implicate order, from which everything emerged within its own way, directly and dynamically influences the whole, of which everything is a part. This implicate order constitutes the interconnectedness of everything with everything else, not in a line within space and time but immediately insofar as each being is participating in the whole of being and as such receives its constitution.

In theological tradition this implicate order could have been called "creative energy" as an indication of a divine energy. But Bohm cautions us by remarking that the implicate order is not God or divine, because it can be presented as a mathematical formula. Bohm holds that God or the divine is beyond all that, because for him these words signify the eternal, which is beyond measurement.

It dawned on me that the reasons why we talked about God, Creator, and divine energy, were what Bohm identifies as the implicate order. There was no reason left for me to appeal to God, knowing that my appeal was really upon the transcendental and immanent implicate order. My awareness of the mystical was not an awareness of the divine but an awareness of the implicate order. The fact that Bohm could translate this aspect into a mathematical formula was for me the clincher which totally evaporated my need for a God in my life.

Nevertheless, as a Roman Catholic and a Christian, I had learned to appreciate the person Jesus. Through the years of my life this eminent man continued to amaze me. He so much impressed my attitude about life that I did not find Eastern religions satisfactory (I even wrote and published an article against Buddhism for that reason, ("Buddhism: Progress and

Regression?," in *The American Ecclesiastical Review*. I argued that the Christian view as espoused by Berdyaev criticizes Buddhism for being afraid of suffering and wanting to return to the pre-conscious stage (paradisiacal). He praises Christ for his courage to accept suffering and his death on the cross. In the cross, humanity has received the understanding of redemptive suffering, which does not submit to the negative forces of existence. On the contrary, it expresses a true resistance because it is based on a hope for a better life in the future (super-conscious wholeness that comes after freedom, reflection, and evaluation). Another adversary of Buddhist doctrine is Thomas J. J. Altizer, especially in his *The Gospel of Christian Atheism*. Altizer contends that Buddhism is correct in its negative evaluation of this world's existence. However, he rejects the Buddhist world-negation, as a backward movement which wants to return to the paradisiacal origin. From this viewpoint the Buddhist is comparable to a person who faces the frustration and harshness of the struggle for life. Then he experiences that he cannot stand the heat and wants to return to the womb. In psychological theory this attitude is recognized as an illness, and its dynamic is called regression.

In his observation of the world and its sufferings and darkness, Altizer proposes that we must not shy away or retreat. He sees this negative condition of existence as a "fallen" situation. It implies that the creative intentions which promoted the birth of life and reality are initially very good and contain a tremendous amount of potential. But the situation has turned sour because viciousness and evil obscure the basically positive perspectives of creation. The fallen situation is not hopeless if we commit ourselves with all our efforts to the positive future of this world. We are invited to leave our sheltered and sacred fortresses and enter the darkness of this world, so that we become totally part of this weary condition. By emptying ourselves we may develop the correct empathy for the fallen situation and then we may hope that goodness will begin to sprout, take root and grow into impressive and relevant forms.

It is significant in this context to refer to Sri Aurobindo, who left a revolutionary movement in India, because he had become enlightened. Although he was part of the Hindu tradition, his divine visions were of a different nature. Instead of self-annihilation and a radical world negation, Aurobindo's belief is based on the idea that humans as creatures want, by their very nature, to develop themselves and widen the boundaries of consciousness. The crises of this world are not to be evaluated as signs of sickness but as symptoms of growth. These developments need integration and guidance so that a new humanity may emerge.

It is imperative for humanity to affirm this world, which is not the prey of the devil or a self-delusion of the soul. This world is the soil where we can bring about the significance of the divine by being committed to creative potentialities. Our total efforts are needed, but in addition, we should be open to higher forces which are present in this world and desire to enter our consciousness. When this dynamic interrelation with the higher forces is established more substantially, we will arrive at supramental consciousness. By this supramental consciousness, this world will find its future, and evolution will progress ever more.

Somehow my religious identity is in this direction. These developments divested me of traditional Christian theological language and concepts. I learned to float more and experience life as a great force in which we participate passively and responsively. I learned that my moral identity, a sense for valuing existence, remained dedicated to earthy things. It means, I continued to appreciate the creative forces at work in reality in general and particularly in life. Moreover, stories like the Good Samaritan, where one becomes committed to the urgency of a situation rather than to principled truths, hold a great awe. (In that parable the priest and the Levite continued their ways to perform their services in the temple rather than assist the poor victim of the robbery along the road). Yes, Eastern religions and the related new physics philosophies provided me with the mystical awareness about the illusionary character of reality. But my being alive wants more than such a wisdom. I need a core, an inroad into life by which the appreciation of our personal uniqueness becomes sincere. I see this in the person Jesus, and that is my immediate delight in him. He ranks above the mystical, above wisdom when he is bleeding on the cross. Philosophers do not bleed on the cross, mystics do not get crucified. What motivated this man, Jesus, to be so powerfully dedicated to the quality of life?

The Jesus of the Gospels explains that it is the life of His Father which inspires him. Moreover, he and the Father are one. Remarkable feats are told about the healing power of Jesus. Blind, deaf, and crippled people are restored to health. In addition, some of those who had died (his friend Lazarus, the daughter of Jairus, and the young man of Naim) were called back to the life of the living.

Jesus himself faced the challenge of crucifixion and death in a mysterious obedience to his Father. Theological speculations try to unravel such a strange course of events in terms of sacrifice, atonement for our sins, and redemptive grace. Such theories are logical but do not touch the nerves of my heart. So, at this moment, here I am:

a)   without a need to believe in a God,

b)   impressed by the mystical wisdom espoused by the Eastern religions and the related theories of the new physics,

c)   dissatisfied with an enlightenment about the mystical in respect to truly becoming dedicated to individuals in space and time.

d)   thoroughly amazed about this man, Jesus, and wondering about who his Father possibly can be.

The last item is the focus of the forthcoming study. It will not be a theological endeavor, although some theology will emerge at the end. The road to be taken is inspired by the life-work of Joseph Campbell. Seeing this man in a six-week series on Public TV, being interviewed in a most intelligent fashion by Bill Moyers, became a delight for millions of viewers in the summer of 1988. The accompanying book, *The Power of Myth* (New York: Doubleday, 1988) is a quality product. The text is truly readable and the life of Campbell sparks in the spoken word as well as in the printed text. *Newsweek* calls him "the rarest of intellectuals in American life: a serious thinker who has been embraced by popular culture." Accordingly, this study wants to address this tremendous audience. They heard, saw, and read Campbell's repeated references to the Father of Jesus. It is done in a truly original fashion, which is worthy of further specification to make his insights more definite.

In my preliminary studies of Campbell's statements about Jesus' Father, I already sensed that his interpretations bring into play depth-psychology dimensions vocalized in mythological stories from a wide variety of cultures. As such, the Father of Jesus receives unexpected ways of recognition. But somehow, I hold that there is a particular character in Jesus' Father which was left untouched by Campbell's interpretations.

I am convinced that there is a uniqueness in the biblical tradition which supersedes cultural anthropological categories in general. Thus I will explore the Hebrew and Judaic documents to discern at least two major points. First, the uniqueness of the biblical way of relating to their God is of interest here. (Obviously the biblical way of relating to God is distinctly different from philosophical God-talk, e.g., Aristotle. This philosophical approach has become embodied in the tradition of western Christian theology.)

Second, of real importance is the significance of "Father" as a reference to God's presence. I already have found a most amazing study (rather unnoticed in related publications) by Saul Levin, *The Father of Joshua/Jesus*. Much more will be said about this remarkable book, but at this stage I want to share why I like Levin's study. First it is philology, and not philosophy or theology. We are being informed by someone who can analyze all the languages related to this kind of study (languages of the Ancient Near East, and also Latin and Greek) and he does this with great skill and spunky insight.

Second, although the name, Saul Levin, indicates that the author is Jewish, he is totally open in the discussion of the Jewish and biblical tradition.

Third, like Campbell, Levin is an extremely well-educated person who speaks from a multitude of information with great wisdom. Thus his theories and opinions are not just flimsical. On the contrary, they are surprising. Levin takes the reader beyond the traditional and shows all kinds of refreshing ways for a discussion of the Father of Joshua/Jesus.

Thus, I want Levin to be included so that our search for Jesus' Father will receive much drama and depth. This will help us tremendously in assessing in what way and why early Christian theology (especially Trinitarian theology of the first major ecumenical councils) produced such an abstract and lofty way of Father talk. Personally, I am not moved by the highly refined Trinitarian theology of the Christian orthodoxy. This is not because I lack the knowledge in these matters. I am sufficiently exposed to these doctrinal products to understand their concerns. But my heart does not feast on such information. For a while it did, because there is intellectual delight in such speculations. But then, other intellectual feats had similar effects. Expressions about God should be intended to embrace the whole person.

Nevertheless, when my need for a God faded, so did traditional theology lose my interest. If God is not needed, then one certainly does not respond to a monumental treatise of three divine persons, the Father, the Son, and the Holy Spirit. For me, Jesus is not the Trinitarian Son of the Trinitarian Father. New Testament scholars generally agree that Jesus had no idea about such theological extrapolations. But the Jesus of the Gospels had a definite awareness of his Father. Only in-depth studies of such a Father-awareness in human religiosity (Campbell) and a thorough study of biblical tradition (Levin) in regard to the Father of Jesus, will produce the materials to which my heart can respond.

I wrote these introductory remarks to indicate why this journey has begun. Some readers may not share the same need for explorations about Jesus' Father, and they may lack the motivation to meet the Father of Jesus somewhere. They may have an intellectual curiosity about the insights, sources, methodology, and what may constitute the major bulk of this product. However, I will remain faithful to my personal motivation as described above and look for religious conclusions relevant to people like me. Thus this research may not produce significant results in terms of academic expectations in philology, biblical studies, and historical accuracy. Perhaps I will fail to demonstrate that the Father of Jesus is definitely unique. Of course, that will be my disappointment, because I have great expectations that something highly relevant can be found about Jesus' Father, which is generally not recognized. This expectation, I am sure, will persist in me, no matter what this journey will proffer.

Chapter Two

On the Nature of Language:
How to Read This Information

In the introductory pages I stated my presuppositions, opinionations, prejudices and cultural biases. A psychoanalyst may conclude what is revealing of me in psychiatric terms. A structuralist in anthropology may dissect these statements according to his understanding of the human imagination and find which stories constitute the specific mental matrix operating in me. A philologist will quickly identify that my language belongs to a particular tradition where certain things are said in certain ways for certain reasons. A neurologist will observe that my brain is functioning substantially well and has integrated much of information that is in need of reshaping or reintegration and has a particular motivating focus which seems very important.

All these and similar disciplines can relativize whatever a person says about the meaning of life. My awareness of such a relativity is substantial. Nevertheless, my preoccupation with the Father of Jesus is a fact, and this well-founded preoccupation is to be subjected to scrutiny here. It is to be done in terms of established knowledge and sophisticated insights in these matters. It will be interesting to see what such a scrutiny may produce in this case. A whole flood of publications on the nature of language exists. Ludwig Wittgenstein (1889-1951) may have started the modern awareness about the relativism of language. But Wittgenstein was part of a cultural development within Western civilization, which was stirring up such waves of self-reflection in many ways. In the fifteenth century William of Ockham cracked open the bastion of medieval metaphysical thought by asserting that we cannot verify the beautiful metaphysical constructs produced by the minds of scholastic philosophers and theologians. He concluded that we can only give names to things which signify how we use these objects. The name does not describe the essence of the object but simply our use and understanding thereof. That is the core of nominalism. Sigmund Freud's psycho-analysis launched the idea of word-association, indicating that words are rooted in psychic constellations and are not just intellectual products.

Strongly reacting against the abstract metaphysical monumental construct of Hegel's worldview, where everything is understood according to its place in this conceptual universe, Soren Kierkegaard ventured into the privacy of his own experiences and uttered words which communicated the life of his soul. They were his words, not universal terms. And people interested in existentialism read his words with great eagerness because they could identify with this soul talk. Similarly existentially speaking, Martin Heidegger reflected with great tenderness about "das Wort" and recognized that the spoken word has a soul on its own and cannot be evaluated as a fragment of a spreadsheet in a computer. If all these developments express a form of skepticism, then this human awareness about the relativity of language is ancient. One finds such insights in the pre-Socratic philosophy of the Hellenic tradition; it is part of the wisdom in Taoism, Hinduism and Buddhism. There language is valued in an ambiguous sense. On the one hand, language is recognized as a valid means of communication. On the other hand, language is also known as being quite inadequate in conceptualizing and grasping what it wants to say, which is beyond language and transcends language. Moreover, that which one wants to communicate (the beyond language) is itself superseded by underlying motives, unconscious dynamics, and dimensions beyond our awareness. Thus language about the Father of Jesus, and my interest in such pertinent language, needs to be placed in such wider contexts.

Here, I prefer not to lose sight of the forest because of the trees. Thus I do not want to get lost in a thorough discussion of language from a philological, linguistic, philosophical (analytic philosophy of Wittgenstein and Ayer), neurological, anthropological, and psychoanalytical point of view. There is even no true space for an inclusion of the New Hermeneutics as introduced by Paul Ricoeur and George Gadamer. It suffices to know that all these approaches exist and are very well established. They all relativize language in their distinct ways. Nevertheless, the following is my wisdom in these matters. As stated above. whatever I will say can be analyzed according to those qualified to discern my biases, prejudices, assumptions, and the cultural and psychological categories which characterize my thought.

First, it is of no importance to concentrate on the Father of Jesus if one holds that life is essentially an illusion. In that case there is no need to say anything meaningful because one does not believe in expressing meaning.

Although I hold that much of what these "illusionists" are saying is substantially valid (i.e., is validly substantiated), I also hold that more can be said.

Why do I want to say anything anyway? Because I sense that what the illusionists say is not the whole story.

Why is it not the whole story? Because, I sense that illusionists, like Buddhists, are reductionistic, i.e., they leave too much unrecognized which makes the discussion less complex and their conclusions more easily acceptable.

Why do I feel this way? What follows will be quite a long answer, not to cover up my weakness (not to protest too much) but to allow the core of my sentiment to be pure and uncovered (naked). Basically, one can say that I value life beyond or in spite of the reductionism of the illusionists or nihilists. Notice that I agree with their arguments. Moreover, I disagree with the standard opponents of illusionism and nihilism. Generally, the opponents argue from positions which are less tenable than the illusionist view.

The illusionist, however, will tell me, that I believe in life, and that's why I value the Father of Jesus, because, as demonstrated in Jesus, the Father very much promotes life and is divinely faithful of it. The illusionist will try to point out that I start somewhere in the middle, without recognizing the deeper levels of awareness (without seeing that the emperor has no clothes).

Yes, I know, I am a product of life, and life uses me as a messenger to politically speak on behalf of life, which finds its culmination in making the Father of Jesus my focus.

I grant all this, and I know that life itself is originated in the universe (which is theorized to be more than twelve billion years old) about four billion years ago. Carl Sagan in his 1983 thirteen-week Public TV series, *Cosmos* demonstrated a very effective didactic way of making this understood by a wide audience. He proposed that in a twelve-month calendar each month were to represent about one billion years. Then our earth emerged in early September, and life later in the same month. In this perspective, life is very accidental and does not mean much in terms of the immense and overwhelming vastness of space and time in the universe.

Moreover, our universe means hardly anything at all in terms of dimensions which we can extrapolate from cosmological findings. The Big-Bang theory (now challenged by Guth's "pfff" theory) has been extended into an oscillating Big-Bang theory. There the universe emerges, grows to full proportions, and then returns to an primordial form of condensed energy, to again burst into a new universe, again, and again, and again, etc. (Guth's theory leads to the conclusion that other universes must coexist with our universe, and also, that our universe exists within a wider and more encompassing universe.) So, why should I be interested in the Father of a person, who became significant for some followers of two thousand years ago who have kept their association alive for some millennia, or, for that matter, till the end of time, when we all disappear at the end of this universe? Indeed, that is ridiculous, i.e., a source of laughter – a big laugh.

Here is the key, the heuristic moment. Yes, we may start to laugh at our assumption that our beliefs about the Father of Jesus are significant in any way within the dimensions of the supra-cosmological awareness, i.e., an awareness beyond this cosmos, beyond anything in particular. The fact that we can laugh is my awareness of the divine. Whatever we hold important becomes ridiculous in terms of "the far-beyond". The fact that we recognize "the far-beyond" indicates that we can relativize whatever we hold important. Our laughing is of a divine nature, because it relativizes everything. A reflection of this humorous moment allows me to say: I am laughing at my own ridiculous assumptions. Obviously, my own ability to know some things about "the far-beyond" and the resulting insights made me, indeed, burst out in laughter about my beliefs and whatever I stated to be true about the meaning of life. I, a living creature, have the potential, and actualized this potential, to laugh about the meaning of life. In me, life is laughing about itself. That is remarkable. Life laughing about itself in me is a true and spontaneous happening of life. Illusionists may hold with me that my laughing about life expresses exactly what they wanted to say. The illusionists and I have a common ground. We hold my laughing to be a true expression of that which is greater than life, greater than the universe, greater than existence. Where the illusionists and I may go separate ways is in the conclusions we derive from this basic awareness.

Some illusionists may say, "Thus life is absurd!" I and other illusionists may say, "I laughed about life and its absurdity!" This laughing bespeaks something which I hold to be precious somehow. It defies absurdity as an conclusion. In the way I laugh about life, I also am at awe about this person Jesus and his reference to his Father. In his life Jesus declared an awareness of that which is greater than life. The beyond, which made me laugh, was translated by Jesus into his accepting of the cross, as the story goes.

Let me retrace my steps for a moment, and start again with the reflection on language. In the light of the ridiculous, and by the authority of my laughing about life, I also sense that all language is political. We say something because we want something. We ask for food because we are hungry; we affirm people because we want to connect; we speak about ourselves or listen to others, what they have to say about themselves, to create a bonding of the personal.

However, all these political intentions which motivate us to speak operate on different levels. To quickly demonstrate this, a reference to Abraham Maslow's famous hierarchy of needs will suffice. He holds that we operate most basically to meet the needs of survival – food and shelter. When that is somewhat secured we can enter the levels of associating with others. Finally, we can allow ourselves to enter the realm of self-actualization. Similarly John Adams, one of the Founding Fathers who wrote the United States Constitution, reportedly said, that he had to fight wars, so that his sons could plough the fields and establish commerce, so that their sons could become philosophers and artists. These insights are quite obvious. Their story becomes more sophisticated in the discussions of stages of moral development according to Lawrence Kohlberg. (See *Zygon: Journal of Religion and Science*, Kohlberg's article, "Moral Development, Religious Thinking, and the Question of a Seventh Stage.") His experimental studies substantiated that, universally, the development of people's morality occurs according to six or seven stages. There are three basic groups: the pre-conventional, the conventional, and the post-conventional. Each of these three can be divided into two steps. At the beginning is the fear of punishment (and the liking of reward). This is followed by "I'll scratch your back if you'll scratch mine." The third stage (the first person in the conventional category) is characterized by "wanting approval." The fourth stage is entered by the awareness that the system will be good to you if you are good to the system. The last two stages, the post-conventional, deal, first with self-defined principles, and finally with an awareness of universal values.

From this summary one may conclude that my need for identifying the Father of Jesus is for reasons found on the higher levels. Moreover my pursuit to learn more about the Father of Jesus is in the name of universal values, insofar as I can tell. It means, I have no vested interests insofar as I do not want to promote any religion, any philosophy, and worldview. I am not a member of organizations which want to save the wilderness, the whales, or traditional family life. I have no soapbox from which to speak on behalf of anything. In the way I burst out laughing when I started my prayers, I experienced a sense of awe for the religiosity of Jesus, who claimed to be spirited by his Father.

The nature of the language used here is "religious". It means that it pertains to what Kohlberg identifies as the post-conventional stage. It also means that this language is different from what mathematicians talk about in reference to numbers and formulas. Chemists talk about the world of chemical components, and sociologist about categories of social behavior; psychologist use language to communicate insights about the emotional makeup of life.

Religious language has some aspects in common with philosophical language. Philosophers too, will speak about the meaning of life, but are committed to reason and the formulation of meaning in universal concepts. Religious language is by its very nature interested in ultimate meaning, but is not limited by universal concepts. It wants to communicate religious dimensions, which can be expressed in different forms: e.g., poetry, myths, symbols, metaphors, and concepts. In this context, we want to learn from Joseph Campbell's perception of metaphor and myth, because his book, *The Power of Myth*, will be one of the main references.

Joseph Campbell's Understanding of "Metaphor and Myth"

This is not an exhaustive study of all the works published by Campbell. His dialogue with Bill Moyers in *The Power of Myth* focuses on these concepts, metaphor and myth, repeatedly and with great spontaneity. This spontaneity, however, is rooted in Campbell's years and years of study, writing, and teaching. Especially the teaching may have given him the opportunity to express himself about such matters in a direct and common sense language. I have written about myths in varied ways and am acquainted with publications about myths: (e.g., my book, *Roots of American Religiousness* and *Visions of the Divine*.) I hold Campbell's statements about the metaphor and the myth to be delightfully genuine and honest. Moreover, he demonstrates his personal identifications with these dimensions of human language, i.e., he personally values metaphor and myths very much.

Instead of discussing metaphor separately from myth, it is more conducive to the flow or the treatise to deal with both of them together.

Before going into specifics, it is helpful to see where Campbell and I basically connect. In terms of my associating partly with "illusionist," the following reference to Campbell will establish a certain common ground.

MOYERS: and yet we all have lived a life that had a purpose. Do you believe that?

CAMPBELL: I don't believe life has a purpose. Life is a lot of protoplasm with an urge to reproduce and continue being.

MOYERS: Not true – not true.

CAMPBELL: Wait a minute. Just sheer life cannot be said to have a purpose, because look at all the different purposes it has all over the place. But each incarnation, you might say, has a potentiality, and the mission of life is to live that potentiality. How do you do that? My answer is, "Follow your bliss." There's something inside you that knows when you're on the beam or off the beam. And if you get off the beam to earn money, you've lost your life. And if you stay in the center and don't get any money, you still have bliss.

MOYERS: I like the idea that it is not destination that counts, it's the journey.

CAMPBELL: Yes. As Karlfried Graf Durckheim says, "When you're on a journey, and the end keeps getting further away, then you realize that the real end is the journey." The Navaho have the wonderful image of what they call the pollen path. Pollen is the life source. The pollen path is the path to the center. The Navaho say, "Oh beauty is before me, beauty behind me, beauty to the right of me, beauty to the left of me, beauty above me, beauty below me. I'm on the pollen path."

MOYERS: Eden was not. Eden will be.

CAMPBELL: Eden is. "The kingdom of the Father is spread upon the earth, and men do not see it." (229-230)

This exchange is reported on the last pages of the book, and it states very well what is at the heart of Campbell's life. The immediate focus now is Campbell's understanding of metaphor and myth.

MOYERS: What is the metaphor?

CAMPBELL: A metaphor is an image that suggests something else. For instance, when I say to a person, "You are a nut," I'm not suggesting that I think the person is literally a nut. "Nut" is metaphor. The reference of the metaphor in religious traditions is to something transcendent that is not literally anything. If you think that the metaphor is itself the reference, it would be like going to a restaurant there, and starting to eat the menu.

For example, Jesus ascended to heaven. The denotation would seem to be somebody ascended to the sky. That's literally what is being said. But if that were really the meaning of the message, then we have to throw it away, because there would have been no such place for Jesus literally to go. We know that Jesus could not have ascended to heaven because there is no physical heaven anywhere in the universe. Even ascending at the speed of light, Jesus would still be in the galaxy. Astronomy and physics have simply eliminated that as a literal, physical possibility. But if you read "Jesus ascended to heaven" in terms of its metaphoric connotation, you see that he has gone inward – not into outer space but into inward space, to the place from which all being comes, into consciousness that is the source of all things, the kingdom of heaven within. The images are outward, but their reflection is inward. The point is that we should ascend with him by going inward. It is a metaphor of returning to the source, alpha and omega, or leaving the fixation on the body behind and going to the body's dynamic source.

MOYERS: Aren't you undermining one of the great traditional doctrines of the classic Christian faith – that the burial and the resurrection of Jesus prefigures our own?

CAMPBELL: That would be a mistake in the reading of the symbol. That is reading the words in terms of prose instead of in terms of poetry, reading the metaphor in terms of denotation instead of connotation.

MOYERS: And poetry gets to the unseen reality.

CAMPBELL: That what is beyond even the concept of reality, that which transcends all thought. The myth puts you there all the time, gives you a line to connect with that mystery which you are.
　　Shakespeare said that art is a mirror held up to nature. And that's what it is. The nature is your nature, and all of these wonderful poetic images of mythology are referring to something in you. When your mind is simply trapped by the image out there so that you never make the reference to yourself, you have misread the image.
　　The inner world is the world of your requirements and your energies and your structure and your possibilities that meets the outer world. And the outer world is the field of your incarnation. That's where you are. You've got to keep both going. As Novalis said, "The seat of the soul is there where the inner and outer world meet." (56-57)

It was necessary to keep this long quotation into one piece, because it immediately reveals how radical Campbell's thought is. It also interrelates the concept metaphor with symbol and myth. Before turning to explicit statements about symbol and myth in the text, one more reference to metaphor can be included.

MOYERS: Is reincarnation also a metaphor?

CAMPBELL: Certainly it is. When people ask, "Do you believe in reincarnation," I just have to say, "Reincarnation, like heaven, is a metaphor."

The metaphor in Christianity that corresponds to reincarnation is purgatory. If one dies with such a fixation on the things of this world that one's spirit is not ready to behold the beatific vision, then one has to undergo a purgation, one has to be purged clean of one's limitations. The limitations are what are called sins. Sin is simply a limiting factor that limits your consciousness and fixes it in an appropriate condition.

In the Oriental metaphor, if you die in that condition, you come back again to have more experiences that will clarify, clarify, clarify until you are released from these fixations. The reincarnating monad is the principal hero of Oriental myth. The monad puts on various personalities, life after life. Now the reincarnation idea is not that you and I as the personalities that we are will be reincarnated. The personality is what the monad throws off. Then the monad puts on another body, male or female, depending on what experiences are necessary for it to clear itself of this attachment to the field of time. (57-58)

In what way is symbol different from metaphor? Metaphor is a figure of speech where one word or phrase "literally denoting one kind of object or idea is used in place of another to suggest a likeness or analogy between them." (Webster's description.) Symbol is "something that stands for something else by reason of relationship, association, convention, or accidental resemblance." (Webster's description.) For example, shaking hands is a symbol of agreement, and is not a metaphor. Saying that someone is a dove, is metaphor used in a symbolic way. Dove is the symbol of peace, and calling a person a dove is a metaphoric use of the word dove. Moyers and Campbell have a good discussion of symbol.

MOYERS: When I read your works – *The Masks of God,* or *The Way of the Animal Powers,* or *The Mythic Image* – I often come across images of the circle, whether it's in magical designs or in architecture, both ancient and modern; whether it's in the dome-shaped temples of India or the Paleolithic rock engravings of Rhodesia or the calendar stones of the Aztecs or the ancient Chinese bronze shields or the visions of the Old Testament prophet Ezekiel, who talks about the wheel in the sky. I keep coming across this image. And this ring, my wedding ring, is a circle too. What does that symbolize?

CAMPBELL: That depends on how you understand marriage. The word "sym-bol" itself means two things put together. One person has one half, the other the other half, and then they come together. Recognition comes from putting the ring together, the completed circle. This is my marriage, this is the merging of my individual life in a larger life that is of two, where the two are one. The ring indicates that we are in one circle together.

MOYERS: When a new pope is installed, he takes the fisherman's ring – another circle.

CAMPBELL: That particular ring is symbolic of Jesus calling the apostles, who were fisherman. He said, "I make you fishers of men." This is an old motif that is earlier than Christianity. Orpheus is called "the Fisher," who fishes men who are living as fish in the water, out up into the light. It's an old idea of the metamorphosis of the fish into man. The fish nature is the crudest animal nature of our character, and the religious line is intended to pull you up out of that.

MOYERS: A new king or new queen of England is given the coronation ring.

CAMPBELL: Yes, because there's another aspect of the ring – it is a bondage. As king you are bound to a principle. You are living not simply your own way. You have been marked. In initiation rites, when people are sacrificed and tattooed, they are bonded to another and to society.

MOYERS: Jung speaks of the circle as a mandala.

CAMPBELL: "Mandala" is the Sanskrit word for "circle," but a circle that is coordinated for symbolically designed so that it has the meaning of a cosmic order. When composing mandalas, you are trying to coordinate your personal circle with the universal circle. In a very elaborate Buddhist mandala, for example, you have the deity in the center as the power source, the illumination source. The peripheral images would be manifestations or aspects of the deity's radiance.

In working out a mandala for yourself, you draw a circle and then think of the different impulse systems and value systems in your life. Then you compose them and try to find out where your center is. Making a mandala is a discipline for pulling all those scattered aspects of your life together, for finding the center and ordering yourself to it. You try to coordinate your circle with the universal circle.

MOYERS: To be at the center?

CAMPBELL: At the center, yes. For instance, among the Navaho Indians, healing ceremonies are conducted through sand paintings, which are mostly into the mandala on the ground. The person who is to be treated moves into the mandala as a way of moving into a mythological context that he will be identifying with – he identifies himself with the symbolized power...

MOYERS: There is some effort, apparently, to try to center one's life with the center of the universe –

26

CAMPBELL: – by way of mythological imagery, yes. The Image helps you to identify with the symbolized force. You can't very well expect a person to identify with an undifferentiated something or other. But when you give it qualities that point toward certain realizations, the person can follow. (216-217)

I allowed this discussion to go on for quite a while for at least two reasons. First, one becomes aware of the learned preparedness by which Campbell is qualified to reflect on these issues with much knowledge, but also with great interest and sensitivity. That makes his presence so precious.

Secondly, one observes how the symbolic and the mythological really intertwine. Campbell holds that many symbols are rooted in a mythological context. On the other hand, the mythological context has embodied many natural symbols which are quite universal for the human psychological experience. Thus our interest shall be moved to the focus on myth and the mythological, again, within Campbell's words. After a selection of some major pieces of the discussion by Moyers and Campbell, a summarized list of definite aspects of the mythological will be composed.

MOYERS: Why myths? Why should we care about myths? What do they have to do with my life?

CAMPBELL: My first response would be, "Go on, live your life, it's a good life – you don't need mythology," I don't believe in being interested in a subject just because it's said to be important. I believe in being caught by it somehow or other. But you may find that, with a proper introduction, mythology will catch you. And so, what can it do for you if it does catch you? (3)

MOYERS: I came to understand from reading your books – *The Masks of God* or *The Hero with a Thousand Faces*, for example – that what human beings have in common is revealed in myths. Myths are stories of our search through the ages for truth, meaning, for significance. We all need to tell our story and to understand our story. We all need to understand death and to cope with death, and we need help in our passages from birth to life and then to death. We need for life to signify, to touch the eternal, to understand the mysterious, to find out who we are.

CAMPBELL: People say that what we're seeking is a meaning for life. I don't think that's what we're really seeking. I think what we're seeking is an experience of being alive, so that our life experiences on the purely physical plane will have resonances within our own innermost being and reality, so that we actually feel the rapture of being alive. That's what it's all finally about, and that's what these clues help us to find within ourselves.

MOYERS: Myths are clues?

CAMPBELL: Myths are clues to the spiritual potentialities of the human life.

MOYERS: What we're capable of knowing and experiencing within?

CAMPBELL: Yes.

MOYERS: You changed the definition of a myth for the *search* for meaning to the *experience* of meaning.

CAMPBELL: Experience of *life*. The mind has to do with meaning. What's the meaning of a flower? There's a Zen story about a sermon of the Buddha in which he simply lifted a flower. There was only one man who gave him a sign with his eyes that he understood what was said. Now, the Buddha himself is called "the one thus come." There's no meaning. What's the meaning of the universe? What's the meaning of a flea? It's just there. That's it. And your own meaning is that you're there. We're so engaged in doing things to achieve purposes of outer value that we forget that the inner value, the rapture that is associated with being alive, is what it's all about.

MOYERS: How do you get that experience?

CAMPBELL: Read myths. They teach you that you can turn inward, and you begin to get the message of the symbols. Read other people's myths, not those of your own religion, because you tend to interpret your own religion in terms of facts – but if you read the other ones, you begin to get the message. Myths help you to put your mind in touch with this experience of being alive...(3, 5-6)

This exchange sets the stage for some reflection for the sake of identifying some definite aspects. First, one notices that Campbell is not just the educated teacher of myths. He is not just a connoisseur par excellence. Basically, Campbell couldn't care less because his real interest is in the religious dimension of myths.

This needs further specification otherwise it might not receive the proper understanding. In "Religion as a 'Damn Interesting Subject'" (*The Christian Century*, October 22, 1975), Martin E. Marty maintains that not everything is to be placed under the umbrella "religious," because then nothing is religious in a definite sense. Those who argue that "religious" deals specifically with transcendence face the problem that Zen Buddhism as a form of religiousness does not focus particularly on transcendence. Marty suggests that "It might be better to speak of 'attracting' or 'magnetic' zones that exert pressure and pulls but do not even produce complete and neat coherence." (922)

That is a very intriguing statement, indeed, because it refers to three important characteristics. First, the religious should be able to motivate (attracting). Second, there should be something by which this motivation is substantiated (the magnetic zones). Third, it should not be an ideology where reality is interpreted and understood in one particular theory or theology (Never produce complete and neat coherence.) Obviously, Campbell's understanding of why myths are important coincides remarkably well with Marty's promotion of the word "religious." The language spoken by Campbell is religious, his very presence is religious because his delight is religious. He is aware of magnetic zones which attract him tremendously, and do not put him in boxes of complete and neat coherence.

This open approach to religiousness is not just arbitrary, but finds significant substantiation in the findings by Jean Piaget. By means of meticulous observations, conducted over long periods of time, he made his insights scientifically respectable. Thus we learn about aspects which characterize the development of children and their growth into more mature adult behavior.

Within the specification of developmental variables, Piaget discusses imagination in terms of assimilation and accommodation in *Play, Dreams and Imitation in Childhood*. Assimilation denotes that the child lives very much in its own world and does not respond to the demands of living in a realistic way. Imagination on this level is called creative, because it is less determined by facts and more characterized by a subjectivistic concern. Accommodation is regarded as a development, because the child learns to encounter reality in terms of facts and objectivity. Imagination in this context is called reproductive because the outside world is being perceived in its own right.

Piaget held that maturation is the growth from assimilation toward a balance with accommodation. Note this is not a shift from assimilation toward accommodation, but the emergence of a balance between a subjective and an objective way of valuing life. It is a balance between interpretation and verification. During my first reading of Piaget I had the impression that he denounced creative imagination as a subjectivistic and unreal perception of life. Upon closer examination, it appears that Piaget very much promoted the necessity of creative imagination because it preserves the personal identity of the individual:

> Creative Imagination, which is the assimilating activity in a state of spontaneity, does not diminish with age, but, as a result of the correlative progress of accommodation, is gradually reintegrated in intelligence, which is thereby correspondingly broadened. (289)

Thus Piaget held that intelligence is indeed helped by the subjective tendency of creative imagination. The importance is significant for operational thought. Operations are characterized by the interchange of assimilation and accommodation. Subjective interpretation of reality and an objective knowledge are both necessary to help the person become operational.

One should recognize that Piaget remained the psychological theorist and did not turn philosopher to explain abstractly some transcendental aspect of his insights. History praised Piaget for being such a precise observer of phenomena. Those who would like to speculate on the philosophical implications of Piaget's observations do this at their own risk.

It is not daring, I assume, to make the following conclusive comments. Piaget clearly indicated that creative imagination solely within the realm of assimilation is dangerously subjectivistic. It prevents the child from maturing (becoming more realistic). In a true agreement with accommodation, however, creative imagination will be able to supersede its initial location. It may have grown into the realm of facts, figures, and verifiable measurements. What is to be assimilated (subjective concern) is out there. Consequently, the imagination is called into action to make something personal out of the given reality. Not only is this the case with Joseph Campbell, but also with all the myths he admired so deeply and personally. This excursion about the creative imagination establishes the floor for truly appreciating his creativity and his disdain for boxes and the clinging to so called facts.

The reference to Piaget's affirmation of assimilation (subjective aspect) also makes clear that Campbell's personal identification with the mythological makes those stories come alive again in him and those who are hanging on his every word when he tells the stories. In him musea of anthropology come alive. It is telling that as a boy he visited the Museum of Natural History in New York, and he was "transfixed by the totem poles and masks." (Bill Moyer's introduction in *The Power of Myth*, sv). The interview, "Masks of Eternity," was taped in the museum to mark the birthplace of Campbell's career. This reincarnation of the mythological is a very important feature for understanding Campbell correctly. Let me explain.

In my previous publications on myths I stated that they are stories about the basic make-up of life. They include significant realms of nature, e.g., the sky, ocean, sun, rivers, the earth, the seasons, thunder and lightning, draughts, and the delight of "a clear day." Also included are the stages of human development, and the major emotional demons, such as love, hate, jealousy, revenge, sacrificial self-giving, sense of harmony and peace. In this way one has a description of the mythological. But it does not demonstrate the spirited life which is at the heart of myths. In his book, *Myth and Reality in the Old Testament*, Brevard Childs focuses on this "being alive" dimension of myths. He refers to Malinowski's perception of myth in its living primitive form, and he quotes:

> Myth as it exists in a savage community, that is in its living primitive form, is not merely a story told but a reality lived. it is not the nature of fiction...but it is a living reality. (18)

This was perfectly clear to me when I read it more than a decade ago. But the full impact of myth being "living realities" occurred only when Campbell was featured in the TV-series, *The Power of Myth*. He personally lived the mythological, and he talked about myths with so much conviction only because they were for him sources of life. It is not the story, not the myth, but the life contained in the myth which is valuable. The life Campbell senses and is excited about is also recognized by Julian Huxley in his book, *Essays of a Humanist*.

> Though gods and God in a meaningful sense seem destined to disappear, the stuff of divinity out of which they have grown and developed remains. This religious raw material consists of those aspects of nature and those experiences which are usually described as divine. Let me remind my readers that the term divine did not originally imply the existence of gods: on the contrary, gods were constructed to interpret man's experiences of this quality. (222)

One more reference shall be made to understand Campbell's language. At times he refers to the realm of the divine as "ground of being" and "ultimate reality." The first is definitely a term ushered into modern theology by Paul Tillich. In that respect he also used "ultimate reality." Campbell's use of ultimate reality comes very much from the Hindu tradition and its awareness of Brahman. But "ground of being" has connotations with Tillich's publication.

The following is a list of those aspects about myths recognized by Campbell in his discussion with Moyers:

a) The themes of the myths are timeless, "and the inflection is to the culture." (11) One should be alert to the parallel themes present in the different stories. (11)

b) Myths are not other people's dreams, but they are the world's dreams, archetypal dreams which deal with great human problems. They tell how to respond to certain crises of disappointment, delight, failure, and success. (15)

c) One of the myths' powers is the strength not to submit to the powers from outside, but to command them, which is the message of *Starwars*. (18)

d) Myths are metaphorical of spiritual potentiality in humans, and the same powers that animate our life animate the life of the world." (22)

e) "There are myths and gods that have to do with specific societies" (22) This is different from myths that relate one to one's nature and to the natural world. The mythology that is strictly sociological links one to a particular society (23) (This insight will become important in our discussion of the Biblical tradition.)

f) Myths serve four basic functions:

1) Realizing an amazement about our existence in the universe.

2) Creating a sense of mystery about the universe.

3) Supporting a particular social group.

4) Educating us to live "a human life time under all circumstances." (31)

g) Myths are the eyes of reason. (32)

h) Myths are different from dreams. Dreams are personal experiences "of the deep, dark ground that is the support of our conscious lives, and a myth is the society's dream." (40) The two may coincide or clash. Visionaries, leaders, and heroes may move a society into a new myth.

i) Archetypes are "elementary ideas what could be called 'ground ideas'" (51) They have appeared all over the world in different costumes and traditions. As such, myths are true "in different senses." (55)

j) The idea of life as an ordeal through which you become released from the bondage of life belongs to the higher religions. I don't think I see anything like that in aboriginal mythology. (58)

k) "The sanctification of the local landscape is a fundamental function of mythology." (91) One needs "a center of transformation, the idea of a sacred place, where temporal walls may dissolve to reveal a wonder." (92)

l) Differing approaches to myth are indicated by the "way of the animal powers," the "way of the seeded earth," the "way of celestial lights," and the "way of man." "These have to do with the symbolic systems through which the normal human condition of the time is symbolized and organized and given knowledge of itself." (102)

m) In the myths about the heroic, the beyond is experienced, and this awareness is communicated to the group by the hero's return. (129)

n) "A key difference between mythology and our Judeo-Christian religion is that the imagery of mythology is rendered with humor. You realize that the image is symbolic of something. You're at a distance from it. But in our religion everything is prosaic, and very, very serious. You can't fool around with Yahweh." (220)

o) Myths are full of the desire for immortality. It does not mean immortality of an everlasting body. It is an identification with that which is eternity in one's own life. (228)

This constitutes a very substantial awareness of the mythological. It should be noted that Campbell's language is mythological in nature for reasons stated above. They are not philosophical or theological, but religious statements in a mythological sense. My search for the Father of Jesus will be of a similar nature. It will not be a theological endeavor, but a religious one.

Before moving to the real theme of this search, the Father of Jesus, more thought should be given to the level of imagination on which this information and these insights are communicated. This is to prevent misunderstanding.

Chapter Three

Levels of Religious Imagination and Its Heroic Intensity

In "The Hero's Adventure" (Chapter V in *The Power of Myth*) Campbell refers to Otto Rank's book, *The Myth of the Birth of the Hero*. (124) What did this Freudian student, Rank, think about the development of the human psyche? For him the trauma of birth is the basic experience. Campbell describes this in his own words:

> ...everyone is a hero in birth, where he undergoes a tremendous psychological as well as physical transformation, from the condition of a little water creature living in a realm of amniotic fluid into an air-breathing mammal which ultimately will be standing. That's an enormous transformation, and had it been consciously undertaken, it would have been, indeed, a heroic act. (124-125)

What is Rank's story? This birth trauma is the key to his personality theory. The fact that we are suddenly forced out of the protective security of the mother's womb and find ourselves in a strange environment where we are to breathe and crawl, signifies the experience which is at the foundation of human lives. The birth trauma is explained as the universal source of primal anxiety.

Human life shows a desire for the security of the embryonic state and carries within itself a willingness to return figuratively to the womb. *Life fear* represents the aspect whereby people are afraid to set themselves apart and be counted. The latter is called individuation. Because a person cannot go back to the womb, a certain unity with the immediate environment is pursued for security's sake. The person will not welcome the challenge of sacrificing this self-made realm of safety, and the call toward greater independence will find deaf ears. (This is also recognized by Erich Fromm in his book, *Escape from Freedom*. He discovered that people basically want only a little bit of freedom; not too much, otherwise they become afraid in their need for security and leadership by which they enjoy a sense of common identity.)

On the other hand, there is the fear of losing one's newly obtained individuality, and this is called *death fear*. *Death fear* makes the person avoid dependency on others, and thus the drive for individuation and independency becomes a reality.

These two aspects, *life fear* and *death fear*, constitute the primal anxiety which is the basic conflict in each personal life. Rank hold that cultures and civilizations are enterprises which pursue the integration and balance of these two opposing aspects so that human life can become possible.

Within the human psyche the process of individuation is sometimes rough. In a child, the will to become independent expresses itself by showing a negative attitude toward the parent. Such a negative assertion against the parent is called counterwill. Of course, this crisis causes uncomfortable emotions, especially guilt. The person will seek to resolve these ill feelings by developing a more balanced unity where the individuality as well as dependency find an acceptable compromise.

In his global evaluation of humanity, Rank discovered three categories of people. First, the *average* person who has given up the will to self-assertion and has submitted to the parental and other authority figures of society. The pain of guilt is avoided and the easiest way toward comfort is preferred over the challenge to grow and develop as a person. The tension between separation and union is annihilated. Of course, when the social authority crumbles or fails, this person becomes devastated as a victim of insecurity.

Second, the *neurotic* person, who is in the crisis of self-assertion and is not yet quite capable of becoming successful. He/she is the victim of the two opposing dynamics of individuation and the need for dependency or union. The neurotic operates more with the counterwill, the negative and rejective approach, and suffers from guilt feelings and hostility which is built up in the relationship with others. Rank perceived the counterwill and the related hostility as a positive force which could be used constructively for the purpose of helping the person become more successful in her/his search for integrity.

The third category is the *artistic* person, who has allowed the pain of separation to enter the psyche. Unlike the neurotic, the artistic person is able to develop a level of understanding where the need for separation and union becomes integrated within a creative dynamic which promotes personal lifestyles within the human reality. The artistic person can transform the realm of freedom into personalized freedom. That would be Campbell's key to the true hero.

In the normal use of language, an artist is someone who specializes in one of the arts with taste and imagination. Taste signifies the special quality contained within the concept of beauty. Rank's own interpretation of the word artist places the aesthetic enterprise within the basic concern for union. The artist is the person who has arrived at that level where she or he can respond to reality and its demands in a positive manner. The neurotic symbolizes the breach between the situational context and the particular individual. The characteristics of this condition are: counterwill, separation, hostility, and the feeling of being out of place with reality.

Rank proposes the artist as the life style where reality has become acceptable in a decisive and challenging way. There is an underlying morality implicit in Rank's theory. The *average* person is criticized for a total submission to the authority of the establishment. The *neurotic* person is praised because of the courage to break with this submission in favor of self-assertion. Here we find the promotion of individuation and the birth of the heroic. The final goal, however, is the artist, the exemplary type who has found a creative agreement with reality. This is the dynamic involved in Campbell's description of the hero's return (to be explained later).

Rank's wisdom about the artistic character implies that finally, after enough individuation has occurred, a positive appreciation of the existing reality should follow. This development receives more understanding in the following references to James Fowler and William James O'Brien.

In his article, "Moral Development, Religious Thinking, and the Question of the Seventh Stage, Kohlberg refers to the work of James Fowler, a Protestant theologian and a developmental psychologist. Fowler used Kohlberg's six stages of moral development and applied them to describe stages of faith development. His research is not based on substantial data as in the case with Kohlberg. Still, Kohlberg held that Fowler's applications are valid. He refers to the work of F. Oser, "Stages of Religious Judgment," in the book, *Toward Moral and Religious Maturity*. The stage description can be summarized as follows:

Stage 1:   Moral judgment is based on a sense of obedience to parents and other authorities. God is perceived as a parent on whom the child depends.

Stage 2:   Moral fairness is understood in terms of equal exchanges. The religiousness on this level reads, "You be good to God, and he'll be good to you."

Stage 3:   Morality is interested in receiving much approval. Fowler finds that God on this level is "a personal deity" who acts as a shepherd, or even a friend. This God sees everything and keeps score of your good deeds which are worth of rewards.

Stage 4:   The system is perceived as very important. Morality consist of trying to operate within the system. On this level God becomes a supreme being. Religion is the institution where we pay homage to God who is the Creator of everything and who deserves our reverence.

Stage 5:   The morality acts out of individualized principles by which the system is evaluated, receives criticism, and possibly some corrections. God is seen as the true prophet who brings about a new kingdom. People feel called to creative activity for a better tomorrow.

Stage 6:   The morality on this level is inspired by perspectives of ultimate dimensions which consider the whole of being to be more important than a particular form. The religiosity on this level is a mystical nature which perceives the divine presence in everything. It is an awareness of the basic goodness which permeates all of reality. God has become less particular, and one senses an inability to conceptualize God.

If one evaluates the importance of these stages in terms of one's own religious convictions, the challenge may prove to be dramatic. For example, children are taught that God is a final judge. At the day of judgment there will be a division between the good and the bad people. Those on the right side will be invited to enter Heaven, the place the Father has prepared from the beginning. Those on the left side are condemned to Hell for all of eternity. According to the six stages presented above, one may conclude that such a religiousness is of the first or second level. There is a religiosity which supersedes those initial stages. Does that mean there is no heaven or hell? The answer depends on why one wants to cling to these concepts of final justice. Heaven and hell can be symbols by which the sincerity of life can be dramatized. Such interpretations may reveal reasons which indicate the level of religiousness of the interpreter.

No doubt Joseph Campbell in expressing his religiousness uses language, concepts, and ideas which pertain to Stage 6. One would note that his inability to conceptualize God, heaven, and hell does not refrain him from telling inspiring stories about God, heaven and hell as metaphors.

To understand better how the meaning of heaven, hell and final justice can be interpreted in various ways, William J. O'Brien's book *Stories to the Dark: Explorations in Religious Imagination* is truly helpful. The author distinguishes five stages of the human imagination: innocence, fallen, alienation, purgation, and sanctification.

At the innocent stage, a person hears a story and becomes part of it, as in a dream. Reality in that moment is perceived and experienced by the power of the story, its images and its drama. It does not attempt to offer explanations. (10)

The fallen stage makes doctrines out of stories. For instance, stories about hell dramatize the human psychological need for punishment. As such, hell-talk serves a definite purpose. But to conclude that there is a hell is a fallen way of interpreting the story. Campbell would say that the metaphor has been taken as a fact. O'Brien says that the fallen imagination projects an inner reality onto a world of objects. (25)

The third stage, alienation, occurs when one recognizes that all interpretations of life are forms of imagination and that there is no true center of objection knowledge. Such an experience can confuse people when they wake up to this awareness. O'Brien writes:

In approaching imagination in its alienated mode, imagination in the modern context, we need to discover what transpired within the human spirit between the time of the ancients and the time of the moderns. Most notably we need to recall the advances in science which signalled a shift in the human spirit; then we need to consider the salient features of the philosophies that emerged to account for those advances. The point is not that alienated imagination was a product of modern philosophy. Rather precisely because modern philosophers attempted a central role, they forged a particularly useful language and conceptual framework with which to display imagination in a new role. (48)

In the TV production, "Profile of Joseph Campbell," Campbell explains how his studies in biology demolished the belief about creation which had been taught him in the Roman catholic church. In that context he expresses that such a state is very painful, because it hurts in the very core of your being. This agony of alienation is also described in *The Power of Myth*.

I don't know what's coming, any more than Yeats knew, but when you come to the end of one time and the beginning of a new one, it's a period of tremendous pain and turmoil. The threat we feel, and everybody feels – well, there this notion of Armageddon coming, you know. (17)

This applies not only to the breakdown of cultural periods, but also the psychological development within a person. At least, Campbell recognized that there is life beyond alienation – the beginning of a new one [a new time]. According to O'Brien, this is purgation, the fourth stage. It may develop in a person, after being alienated, and silence enters the heart. In such a silence one may learn that reality has its own voice, which should be allowed to speak to us while we remain silent. The fullness of dynamic dimensions, as they surround and permeate us, is then invited to invade our psyche and our imagination. This may be the beginning of a rebirth of one's appreciation of life.

Stage five, sanctification, emerges from a true purgation. A person is aware of a story without necessarily changing it into a doctrine. Moreover, one may have learned to affirm the fact that there is no absolute knowledge, and our ideas are based on an imaginative interpretation of what we see, hear and intuit. Because purgation and its silence prepared us for becoming inspired by forces greater than our own little prejudices and boxed-in theories, we may show a; personal willingness to become motivated by such ultimate dimension. Our fear of flying may diminish. At the stage of sanctification, a person may have learned to enjoy an awareness about the basic wholeness and goodness of life without truly knowing the how, why, and the what of it all.

Obviously, a person at the second stage, fallen, will speak differently about heaven and hell than a person at the fifth stage. Sanctification recognizes that there is truth in the story about heaven and hell and final judgment but that is sensed and intuited. It is not based on a factual heaven and hell.

The difference between the fallen stage and the sanctified stage is in the quality by which a person may operate. It is likely that a person who is on the second (fallen) stage, will try to be moral out of fear for eternal damnation and the torment of hell. The sanctified person may sense the dignity of moral goodness and its importance for all of humanity. Then the moral good is perceived as a source which will bring a heavenly peace within one's heart. The moral evil may produce situations in which people become victimized and suffer pain. Then the story of heaven and hell becomes symbolic of dimensions of life which we hold important. The moral then does not depend on punishment and reward only, but is rooted in the creative concern which is at the heart of a true human responsibility. In Campbell's words it reads:

> Heaven and hell are within us, and all the gods are within us. This is the great realization of the Upanishads of India in the ninth century B.C. All the gods, all the heavens, all the worlds, are within us. They are magnified dreams, and dreams are manifestations in image form of the energies of the body in conflict with each other. That is what myth is. Myth is a manifestation in symbolic images, in metaphorical images, of the energies of the organs of the body in conflict with each other. This organ wants this, that organ wants that. The brain is one of the organs. (39)

We will return to a discussion of the brain and our imagination in a separate chapter. Here it shall be noted that according to the information gathered above, one must conclude that the insights and the life as perceived by Campbell is developmentally of a high level. In terms of Otto Rank, it is the stuff of the artistic person. According to Fowler's stages of faith development Campbell belongs to Stage six. And by O'Brien's account of the development of the human imagination, it is the level of sanctification, where one has worked through alienation and purgation, expressed in the language of metaphors and not by knowledge of facts.

Obviously, Campbell's perception of life energy is focused by the mythological image of the hero. The book most characteristic of his work is *The Hero with a Thousand Faces*. It is not just something he became excited about at the beginning of his writing career. On the contrary, it is also the focus of his last book *The Inner Reaches of Outer Space: Metaphor as Myth as Religion*. In the first, he already is into gathering the mythological varieties into one characteristic umbrella, which he called "The Monomyth." The Table of Contents of *The Hero with a Thousand Faces* reveals significantly the way Campbell viewed and approached the world of mythology:

The theme of the Prologue, "The Monomyth," is at the heart of Campbell's life's work. He held that all major myths contain an "ancient meaning" which is wrapped in symbolic language. The art is to discern this ancient and universal human sense of meaning in these culturally conditioned texts.

The interpretation of myths and the understanding of their basic meaning is greatly helped by psychoanalytic theory and its focus on the reading of dreams. Books on dream-analysis, of course, assume that the language of dreams is symbolic. Moreover, these symbols have a universal meaning, and those books instruct readers about the general aspects and dimensions of this life energy.

Campbell was the editor of *The Portable Jung*. As such he was well aware of archetypes and their presence in the collective unconscious. This provided him with the vehicles to develop a "monomyth" of the hero. It means he developed a definition of "hero" in general or he explained "hero" in universal terms.

> The standard path of the mythological adventure of the hero is a magnification of the formula presented in the rites of passage: separation – initiation – return: which might be named the nuclear unit of monomyth.

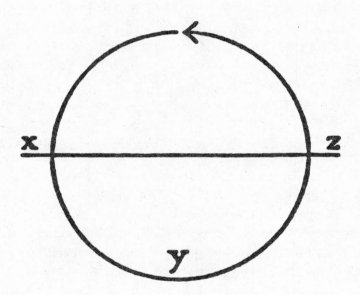

> A hero ventures from the world of common day into a region of supernatural wonder: fabulous forces are there encountered and a decisive victory is won: the hero comes back from this mysterious adventure with the power to bestow boons on his fellow man. (30)

With this key perception in mind Campbell composed Part I of *The Hero with a Thousand Faces*. Part II, *The Cosmogonic Cycle* features aspects of birth, maturation, death, or the cycles of descent and ascent, or the cycle of Spring, Summer, Fall, and Winter. In astronomy it would pertain to the oscillating Big Bang, where the universe emerges and expands and then contracts within itself so that a new universe emerges to continue this ongoing and everlasting aspect of cosmic energy. In this context Campbell places such topics as "space, life, emanations which are manifestations which evaporate into dissolutions." This vision of a cosmic consciousness is very aware of the dynamic energy within the universal cycles.

The same cosmic energy is viewed in Campbell's description of the hero. Life is placed in the significance of emanations unfolding within an awareness of elevated and greater dimensions. With such an enlightened awareness the hero is to bring about the needed determination to become involved in the adventure of creative living. The heroic act is more significant than its accomplishments. For example, the building or creation of a free city is an exciting venture. The city itself will dissolve in due time because the microcosmos and the macrocosmos will find their appropriate endings on doomsday. The celebration of the creative awareness is at the heart of it all. This vision of the complexity of energies constitutes the core mentality of vital mythologies.

Campbell applies this monomyth of the hero in his interpretation of Christ in many ways (e.g., in reference to Albrecht Durer's woodcut, "The Great Crucifixion"). All this will be encountered in the chapter dealing with Campbell's understanding of Jesus and his Father. In this chapter it may be helpful to elaborate on the "heroic" as a dynamic in the human imagination, the heroic intensity of creative imagination.

The Protagonist View

Wolfhart Pannenberg speaks explicitly about the importance of the productive imagination in his article, "Appearance as the Arrival of the Future." While discussing how the appearance itself came to be understood as contingent in nature according to Aristotelian philosophy, Pannenberg refers to Immanuel Kant, who explained that the content of the appearance is "to be conditioned through the forms of our faculty of knowledge." One of these faculties is our productive imagination which holds something to be sensibly given without truly being present in the appearance itself. The productive imagination supersedes what is given to the experience of the appearance itself. Pannenberg understands this productive imagination to be meaningful if it functions as the anticipation of what possibly may become the substantial future of the appearance. For example, when the Pilgrims came to this country, their imagination saw in this land simply a place to live out their lives till the coming of the Lord. Soon thereafter, they reinterpreted their new homeland in terms of opportunities and new possibilities. The epitome of such a productive imagination can be found in the resolve of the Founding Fathers in 1776 and 1787, by writing the Declaration of Independence and, consequently, by creating the Constitution of The United States of America.

Thus truth is not solely determined by a correspondence between the perception and the present form of a thing. The not yet (the future) may function as the core meaning of the appearance. Its true realization may occur by the power of the imaginative anticipation. Pannenberg warns that the anticipation may interpret incorrectly the future of the appearing reality.

Consequently, the imagination is not totally reliable in its perception of the anticipated fulfillment. Pannenberg does not elaborate on the virtue of such a productive imagination. His mentor, Ernst Bloch, is more forceful in describing the power of the future in the human imagination. Especially in the thought of Ernst Bloch, significant connections can be made with Campbell's views. Thus the insights into Bloch's religiousness will accentuate dimensions present in Campbell's affirmation of the religiosity of the hero.

Ernst Bloch was born in Germany in 1885 and was of a Jewish extraction. The American reader was introduced to his philosophy by the publication of *Man on his Own*. This book is a collection of significant essays, most of Bloch's recent writings. The first part, "Karl Marx, Death, and the Apocalypse," is taken from his book, *The Spirit of Utopia*, which was originally published in German in 1918. The majority of his essays are taken from his major work. *The Principle of Hope (Das Prinzip der Hoffnung)*, written in exile while living in Philadelphia, and first published in East Berlin in 1955; then in Frankfurt in 1959. The selected part bears the title "Man's Increasing Entry Into Religious Mystery."

Bloch begins with the observation that all major religions have been founded by exceptional people. Of special interest to him are Moses and Jesus, because both men asserted themselves as leaders in the identification of religious promises. Other founders became absorbed by the greatness of the religious dimensions which they signified, and they did not really challenge people to stand up and start on the road to something new. The history of humanity did not mean much in their religious experience. But Moses and Jesus spoke words which placed the people in the light of a longed-for future. Their admonitions contained images which are to an extent illusions of what ought to be real and is not yet a fact. The most important aspect of those images is that the inner dynamic wants to include hope for everything – "the *totum* of hope that relates to the whole world to a whole perfection." (151)

In the context of hope, Bloch explains Jesus as a person who is not conciliatory toward the existing form of reality. Jesus represents a central change for the totality of existence. He initiates a total hope which is of eschatological significance.

Bloch noted that religious feelings teach us greater dimension, and we learn from them not to take our immediate selves as the all-decisive measure of what is or ought to be. The concept, "God," symbolizes that which is greater than our immediate being. He is the Other. But the Other is very much unknown – *Deus absconditus* (the hidden God.) Because our self-interpretation depends very much on God as the central point of reference, we will discover that we too are rather unknown – *homo absconditus*. The quality of being covered (*absconditus*) should also apply to whatever we project about the ultimate future of humanity. To be human is a mystery in the light of the total otherness which signifies the religious aspect of our existence. Religion should be the enterprise wherein people are constantly called to a leap into that unknown.

To help ourselves develop the courage needed to respond to the unknown, some understanding of God may appear to be useful. The more we learn to grasp the unknown quality of God, the more we incorporate the awareness of otherness, the less we will fear the aspect of infinity which permeates the core of our being. The discovery of our own infinity in the context of Otherness puts us on the road toward seeing ourselves as being godlike in mentality. Bloch's favorite religious founders were those who forged this religious otherness into the human consciousness. There is thus a religious dimension in life which seeks realization. Although this religious dimension exists, it also speaks of what-is-not-yet.

These insights are, of course, not noticed by mechanical materialism. But dialectic materialism has a trace of them because it promotes the perfect – *ens perfectissimum*. Because its religiousness does not acknowledge a God, it is atheistic. Bloch identifies himself with those who see the going belief in a God as an essential obstruction to human religiousness or fundamental infinity. He assumes that the concept, God, implies an all powerful Creator of Heaven and Earth. In the light of this super-being the human is just a little, inconspicuous particle. Such a God has foreknowledge or preknowledge and holds everything according to his predetermined plans. If we want to follow Moses or Jesus, then this God has to be dismissed. ("without atheism there is no room for messianism." [162]).

Bloch recognized that the history of God-talk is a history of formulations of our radical longings and anticipation of what-is-perfect. Radical longing is the context where images of God are being created. Bloch wants to promote a going on the road toward transformation where the perfect will become significantly true. This is messianism which aims at keeping the human personally interested in the infinity aspect of reality.

The history of God-talk has produced a God who is too far away and has become insignificant. Thus, people seek their salvation in what they can control and measure. Bloch believed that the abolishment of that God will help people return to taking themselves more seriously in a challenging creation of the what-is-not-yet. Moses is then the prototype of what could be done. The killing of the slave-driver is the first act of rebellion which signifies the Mosaic mentality. The Exodus from the slavery in Egypt is the beginning of the road away from suffering and suppression. In his theology Moses sees God's presence in a cloud and pillar of fire. The God of Mount

Sinai becomes a traveling God – the Exodus God. The people who placed themselves under Moses' leadership lived according to communal ethics, and their hopes were group-oriented. As a community they had received the inspiration of the promise. Their justice was infiltrated by the ideas of what should become just, according to the promise mentality.

This is the justice by which they questioned the God-images which had emerged in their minds. Consequently, when Yahweh becomes imagined as an established God, then there is a need for reinterpretation of the divine.

Cultural environments favor one particular God-image over others. The Hebrews learned that their God is not Baal, is not an established God. The famous self-revelation of Yahweh, *Eh'ye asher eh'ye*, (Exodus 3:14) should read, according to Bloch, "I shall be Who I shall be." (172) The emphasis is on the not-yet or futuristic aspect of God – *Deus Spes* (the God of Hope).

Further biblical interpretations are brought to the attention of the reader so that Bloch can continue to communicate his understanding of messianism. David is projected as a national revolutionary leader, and from the house of David a new Moses or messiah will emerge. Because the image of God becomes more and more a sanctity on its own, the messianic ideas of Yahweh as the cloud and the fiery pillar go over into the authority of the messiah himself. "There shall come forth a rod out of the stem of Jesse." (Isaiah 11:1)

Although messianic thought developed in historically related cultures as well, only the Jews had the necessary makeup for bringing hope and strength out of suffering. This resolve for the improvement of life became the center of the Israelite religiousness, and its messianism became devoted to the aspect of otherness. Consequently, his messianism could challenge any establishment, social or religious. The need for liberation became the guiding force of identification.

Bloch refers to Thomas Munzer as the exponent of a revolutionary preacher who exemplified what Christ's incarnation meant. Munzer took his Christian commitment seriously and wanted to change reality accordingly. Jesus, too, is not just an idea, but really lived and contributed to the change of history. "Thus Christian faith lives by the historical reality of its founder as no other faith" (184). The imitation of Christ is then a historical experience where we place ourselves in community with him, Jesus, who identified with the poor and the oppressed. Jesus initiated an upward movement, or rebellion, where the last shall be first. Poverty itself is not a virtue, but being able to lay down your life for your neighbor is an expression of the spirit of poverty. This spirit declares communality with the least of humanity. In this process of rebellion, Jesus was killed. He did not seek the cross, but it was imposed on him because of circumstances. The political leaders sensed that Jesus was promoting a totally different hierarchy. As an immediate and essential threat, this uncommon messiah had to be eliminated.

However, the spirit of Jesus lives on. Christians believe that the Kingdom will not drop from Heaven unexpectedly. It has to be wrought out of present conditions. Kingdom – ethics is eschatological in nature because the people feel responsible for what is to become real. In this striving for what-is-not-yet, the Kingdom idea implies that something totally new (otherness) will be essential for this paradise. Moreover, Jesus himself will be the center and the living light of this apocalyptic future. Jesus will be one in substance with God, *homo-ousia* (the Greek term used by the Council Fathers of Nicaea and Constantinople – 4th Century C. E. – to indicate the oneness (*homo*) in being (*ousia*) of the divine Persons in God. Jesus was defined as the Son of the Father, and one in being with the Father.) Then the hidden aspect of God will receive a center. Jesus replaces the centrality of Yahweh because as messiah he personifies the aspect, "I shall be Who I shall be."

In this context Bloch refers to interpretations where the serpent in Paradise is the symbol of the deepest desire in the human to become like God. Exactly this longing for the divine is explained as personified in Jesus, the Messiah. Before his departure Jesus emphasized very much his total interest in the spirit of the divine, and he promises the Paraclete as the Second Comforter. This lifts Jesus' messianism above his own death. But in the end Jesus will return as the very center of divine glory. The dramatization of the Parousia (second coming) in terms of fire falling from Heaven, trumpet blasts in the sky, indicates the total otherness where we shall experience the new and we will be God-like.

Bloch places messianism in opposition to fatalism, where only the inevitable is expected to happen. Consequently, the coming reality of Jesus as the Messiah is not something that is ordered from on high by the God Almighty. (That is how Christian theology understands salvation history.) Jesus' future glory will be the result of human effort and creativity.

Bloch makes a distinction between spatial and temporal distances which separate us from all that we hope for. In the spatial distance we have a tendency to magnify the object of our hope extensively; in the temporal distance we seem to project a more ideal picture of (idealize) what we want. Bloch applies this observation to our imagery of God. If God is far out there (spatial), then we magnify Him as the almighty, omniscient sovereign of all cosmic powers. If God is understood in terms of "I shall be Who I shall be," (temporal) where the future realization of God becomes part of our reflections, then we will project in our God-talk, aspects which are very attractive and ideal, according to the deepest essence of our longing. This, of course, brings to mind Feuerbach's thesis that God is a projection of our highest ideals. Because we humans cannot easily agree on what is ideal, God-talk is open to the floor. Feuerbach's thesis implies an open-ended form of God-talk, because people themselves do not know what is decisively ideal for them. This observation signifies again the *homo absconditus* (the hidden nature of being human) quality of our existence. The fact that we are not yet determined in the understanding of ourselves liberates us from fatalism. The process of self-creation becomes the essential dynamic in our search for meaning. Self-creation can occur because reality is open and free.

In his comments concerning Feuerbach's wisdom, Bloch observes that God is not merely a projection of our wish fulfillment. Bloch adds that this God also represents our anticipation of better conditions to emerge. Anticipation, of course, is more dynamic than wish fulfillment, and Bloch favors enterprise over merely dreaming.

Religion as the concentration of a significant identification of and with God is then a very creative undertaking. Especially when Feuerbach signals God-talk as the discovery of the best in ourselves. The *homo homini lupus* (man is a wolf to his fellowman) of some pessimistic existentialists changes into the hopeful *homo homini Deus* (the human is a god to his fellow human beings). In such a sanctimonious evaluation of people the appreciation of ourselves becomes the beginning of a transcendental actuality. Not Heaven remains the transcendental realm of our quests, but the understanding of our transcendental perspectives becomes the horizon of our ultimate concern. Christ becomes very important in this process of self-appreciation, because he personifies the willingness to seek these transcendental aspects of our lives. This willingness may not suffice and the enterprise itself may fail. That would signify the existence of Hell. But the success in truly attaining these transcendental forms of being is also a possibility. We have the opportunity to consider ourselves as being on the way toward becoming divine.

If that means that we have to give up a certain belief in an already existing God, then atheism will liberate us from a fear which impedes our deepest longings from becoming viable. Atheism does not take away our search for the transcendent significance of reality. Atheism dethrones that which is considered to be already perfect, and it creates an open space – a vacuum. The search for transcendence continues, but the center receives a different understanding.

Bloch interprets Jesus as the one who became what the Father symbolized. Thus, Bloch's atheism is not anti-Christ nor of the Anti-Christ. Although Bloch's tidings are bad news for the powers above, they are regarded as good or glad tidings for us here below. We learn to perceive that the natural, social, and historical forces are not inevitably determining our fate. On the other hand, the way to the Promised Land is not a way toward what is totally undetermined either. Bloch, in his discussion of miracles, points at aspects within the existing reality (nature, society, and history), which show signs of internal openness. In this openness, newness has emerged in the course of time and by the creative workings of participants. If the new evokes in us a sense of wonder and joy, then this is welcomed as progress toward the object of our deepest hope.

These insights allow us to become stimulated and inspired by a hopeful faith which has its roots in the present sense of wonder. Prophets are needed to help us find ways in which more goodness can be realized. Bloch believes that the higher religions have given history such prophets who inspired people to seek "a land in which milk and honey flow actually as well as symbolically" (240).

Some Clarifications

It is rather obvious that Bloch refers to religious language and concepts as media by which he intends to communicate his own philosophical interests. Bloch is not a professional theologian who researches the religious tradition for the sake of informing a religious community, denomination, or church about the basic makeup of their sources and their pasts. Philosophically, Bloch shows that he is inspired by the fundamental message of Marxism, and the insights which motivated founders of religious traditions and those who initiated religious revolutions.

Religious language, concepts, and symbols have an archetypal significance. They appeal to a primordial consciousness which is at the foundation of cultures and the overall religious awareness from which specific traditions emerged. On the other hand, because of his special promotion of Moses and Jesus, Bloch supersedes these collective archetypal aspects. Moses and Jesus are praised for their original initiation of something unique; the calling into movement of a religious enterprise which lets itself be guided by transcendental dynamics. The ever-receding horizon becomes the context according to which the motion of life finds perspectives.

In the following section we will see how Bloch understands the appealing pull of the future to direct our actions. His perception of the apocalyptic future is permeated with ideas which are yet to be realized. Because these ideas are at the core of our human longings, they will be able to inspire us and set us into action. Bloch sees in Karl Marx an example of such a dynamic leadership. But his own insights and aspirations reach far beyond the dialectic materialism of Marxism.

Bloch's Apocalyptic Future

Significant for the understanding of Bloch's visions of redeemed and glorious future is his article, "Karl Marx, Death and the Apocalypse." It is the opening unit in his *Man on his Own*.

Bloch identifies himself with the cultural crises where societies seemed to have lost their ability to organize economic efficiency. People crave for social solutions, and courageous persons are needed to bring about change, instead of waiting for things to get better. The significance of ideas for the sake of creating new possibilities, and the decisive importance of the human will to realize these improvements, are illustrated in the life and work of Karl Marx. Then Bloch moves beyond this hero. He criticizes Marx for placing the focus of interest on the economic centrality. Bloch believes that people do not live by bread alone, and that human life is primarily characterized by the dynamic forces of the spirit or soul. (We will learn that Bloch has a very viable awareness of soul, which is really the heart of the matter and all that matters.) Karl Marx does not have much to offer to those who want to know about his intended "heaven on earth." Ernst Bloch made it his task to elaborate on the importance of the spiritual or divine aspect of life for the promotion of an attitude which is called hope. This attitude is interested in the creation of perspectives which signify a future life. He faces the problem squarely by taking the harshness of death seriously.

> We dwindle as we mature. Very soon we shall turn yellow and
> lie rotting far beneath. (43)

Then he observes that our fear of death is very much based on our theoretical interpretation of what death appears to be in terms of the physical. Our minds work according to what we can see and measure as concrete objects. If the concrete is the all-decisive point of reference, then death is, of course, the final destruction and nothing can be expected.

However, and here Bloch relates his personal and mature experiences of religiousness, humans are not merely concrete objects. They have in themselves a center of soul, which Bloch regards as an indestructible gem. It is the ground and substance of all our self-appreciation. As the center of our being, it drives us far beyond the immediate boundaries of the body. In the face of death we sense that the imminent destruction of the body will become real. However, because of that destruction, we sense that greater forces than we are at work. Death is one of those greater forces, but it is not the only one. There is a multitude of greater dynamics, and one of them is the experience that our center or soul contains an indestructible aspect. Bloch calls this aspect the "metaphysical." From this awareness of the metaphysical, people allow themselves a belief in metempsychosis or transmigration of souls.

It would not be correct to conclude that Bloch preaches the re-incarnation doctrine. He is a very sophisticated philosopher who wants to relate insights by which we can understand how the idea of transmigration may have emerged. The vision of the theory, not the definite conclusions, are of importance in his writings. For Bloch, the transmigration of souls means that the mystery of ourselves may be open to greater developments in the course of creative reality (56). The dynamic by which such theories come into the human mind is recognized as day-dreaming. Bloch favors this journey of the psyche for the sake of letting people become creative about life and its unknown possibilities. The opposite of such creative efforts is experienced as evil, because as fatalism and weariness take hold of us, we cease to be interested in opening ourselves to our selves. The veil of sadness and hopelessness will continue to conceal deeper aspects of ourselves. We become victims of the situation instead of rising above the immediate boundaries. Here we locate Bloch's interpretation of original sin, which is described as the contentment within ourselves as we are and the acceptance of this world and its mundane mentality. Evil and original sin are explained as our unwillingness to be like God (62). Thus, in the end we are in the power of the Anti-God who does not want us to grow as God-like beings. Evil is when we understand death and dying in terms of the physical or unfeeling aspect of reality, instead of referring to other, long-ignored forces.

Bloch indicates the stultifying aspect of physical nature by describing the Second Law of Thermodynamics as the process by which everything will end finally in a frozen state or eternal chill. However, entropy is not the only force at hand. Bloch refers to emergents in nature which represent the aspects of discontinuity. (He mentions the process of radio activity. At that time the theories of "negative entropy" for which Prigogine received a 1973

Nobel Prize, were not well publicized. They hold that life itself is a monument of forces which somehow defy entropy significantly. Especially the evolutionary process within life allows for such an insight.) The point is that we should not become single-minded about reality by accepting only one view of the physical, e.g., entropy. Bloch communicates his belief in forces which may become more significant and powerful. He mentions the Cabbala, according to which "God shattered the deathly-clear rubble heap of worlds because man did not occur in them" (64). (The latest scientist who speaks to the human imagination regarding perspectives beyond entropy is Rupert Sheldrake. He theorizes about reality where he observes "morphogenetic fields" fields where forms are born into greater complexity. He argues that there is a special creativity which is at the origin of forms and their multi-variety of appearance. See Chapter 4 of *Dialogues with Scientists and Sages: A Search for Unity* by Renee Weber.)

Bloch favors a dualistic worldview in which the creative power of God opposes the "monstrous, headless stage prop" of physical nature. Apocalypse is the expectation that the shell of our security, our physical environment will be demolished, and we must face ourselves naked. In the light of that earth-destroying end we will have nothing else to rely on than that which we wrought in the purity of our hearts and the gentleness of our minds. (The purity of our hearts and the gentleness of our minds constitute our nakedness. It is the truly genuine presence of the divine which expresses itself in our soul most decisively in our search for justice and fairness. Our anger, our frustration, our hurt and pain because of the injustices in this world is the divine spirit in its most radical concern.) What was once important in terms of wealth and physical possession shall become worthless. Some see the promise of the apocalyptic end-time as is characterized by a quotation from Dostoevsky's *The Brothers Karamazov.*

> Oh, Alyosha, I do not want to blaspheme! I do understand what an upheaval of the universe it will be when all things in heaven and earth and under the earth blend in one song of praise, when all that lives and has lived cries out: "Thou art just, O Lord, for Thy ways are revealed!" When the mother hugs the friend who threw her child to the dogs, and all three of them sing with tears in their eye, "Thou art just, O Lord"–then, of course, the crown of all knowledge and all

cognition is reached and everything will find its explanation. (66-67)

However, if the Lord is praised as being just because he can justify the fact that the child was thrown to the dogs, then, with Iwan Karamazov, Bloch refuses to worship Him. He wants to promote a God who cures the world and cures us of the world (67). For that purpose he brings into discussion "the God of the future Ascension," who is different from the mundane God who tries to pacify and appease. As in our souls, so in God, there is a spirit of rebellion which does not tolerate that certain things are reconciled. Bloch promotes the divine germ of the Paraclete as the conqueror, who is different from the divine mediator. Bloch, in a fashion, interprets Christ's saying that he who loses his life will find it, and he who seeks his life will lose it. Only those who are willing to follow the life of the soul which vibrates beyond the body are made free for an immortality which is more real than the existing reality.

The vigorous and virtuous life can be found in the soul. It is the spirit of hope which can become the father of innocence and inconceivable thoughts. These thoughts may produce the birth of things to come, which alone will be truthful. However, this truth is not-yet-being and has a utopian (not-being-anywhere) character. Hesitation and doubt are part of this context, and in the face of the overall ambiguity Bloch asserts his insights and sums them up prophetically.

> But that we shall be saved, that there can be a kingdom of heaven, that an evident insight into dream contents establishes them from the human soul, that correlatively confronting them is a sphere of reality, no matter how we define it–this is not only conceivable, that is, formally possible; it is downright necessary, far removed from all formal or real indication, proofs, allowances, and premises of its existence. (700)

At the time we really experience suffering and seriously long for redemption we should accept the invitation of our soul to let go of our eternal securities and go into the core of our soul where the will of goodness is located. The good will has no limits, and as a consequence its projections may be felt to be utopian. Bloch advises us that certain projections of this driving goodness inspire our imagination for the sake of creating distinct ideas about what should be done concretely in our trials at fashioning the good life.

But he warns us not idolize these ideas as being all good themselves That would constitute false objectifications. The purity of goodness, the object of the virtuous soul (as well as the essence of the soul itself), should be our ever-present guide in our world of actions. Thus we are in need of prayer to place our works in an upward movement. Bloch refers to this religiousness to complement the work-oriented philosophy of Marx. The final sentences of this inspiring chapter epitomize Bloch's prophetic concern:

> For we are powerful; only the wicked exists by virtue of their God. But as for the just – there God exists by their virtue, and in their hand lies the sanctification of the name, the very nomination of God who stirs and moves within us as a door we sense, as the darkest question and inmost rapture, who is no fact but a problem laid into the hands of our God-conjuring philosophy, and of truth and prayer. (72)

Comment

Bloch's apocalypse is not described in terms of fictitious visions. Bloch is not a science-fiction writer who projects what the future will bring. His poetic and religious mind is inspired by the source of human hopes and expectations. It is the human heart where the longings for the good, the beautiful, and the truth are pure. Within this source we have to refresh and recreate continually our images of the divine. Moreover at times of disillusionment and possible despair, we should let ourselves become re-invigorated by the soul of our being so that we will be able to face again the challenge of forging the good out of the hard and irresponsible surface of the concrete.

Bloch's writings are deeply involved in the religious dynamics of life. In Bloch's particular approach, classical religious themes are integrated according to personal insights, which are so significant for his convictions. Bloch is not a philosopher who merely concerns himself with problems of language analysis of the epistemological debates concerning empiricism or positivism. He stays within the celebrated tradition of really outstanding philosophers who allowed their minds to roam creatively over the vast planes of truly ultimate perspectives.

As a philosopher Bloch was sincerely interested in the discovery of wisdom. He has been received as a visionary of respectable depths and heights which can be explored in the basic dynamics of life's processes. Bloch allowed himself to become involved in reflective observations of reality which speak through the voices and appearance of many cultural phenomena. In this way he developed a distinct grasp of life's wisdom, and his words contain a prophetic message.

Although Bloch used a terminology which is well known to Christian theologians (e.g., sin, Paraclete, God, Christ, Apocalypse, and Heaven), all these concepts are not affirmed in a traditional sense but received a highly personal and very different interpretation. We should not forget that it was Bloch as an atheist who promoted prayer and a relationship with the divine. He did not want to believe in a God who is the all masterful creator of everything and who knows from eternity what will happen next. Bloch was inspired by the divine aspect, or soul, within the human. He urged people to become reflective and assert creatively their divine potential. This may explain why Bloch's first translated publication for the American reader is entitled *Man on His Own*.

Bloch expressed in many ways his Jewish affiliation and voiced a faith formed in the history of the Hebrew culture. This will be specified later on. For now it shall be said that, also because of his association with Marxism, he was a kingdom-oriented philosopher, who placed great emphasis on energetic leadership and planning. He believed in revolutionary movements.

Regarding his writings, they are definitely poetic insofar as they are visionary, agile, forceful, and creative. He uses language in a spontaneous fashion. His sentences communicate a divine drift. The developmental stages of his maturation and personal growth can be indicated by the journeys he made in this world in search of a proper environment. After his studies at different German universities and his encounters with colleagues in the field, he moved to Switzerland in 1914. He did not want to become involved in wars between nations. In ever-neutral Switzerland he wrote his *The Spirit of Utopia*. The work reveals a sense of alienation from God and a struggle to affirm the meaning of life within himself.

Back in Germany he became a free-lance writer and a social critic. His "The German High School Composition" was a satiric attack on the Third Reich which had established itself as the governing power of Germany. The reaction left him no choice but to flee his native land. There he wrote his famous *Das Prinzip Der Hoffnung* (*The Principle of Hope*). He stayed in Philadelphia but did not experience the brotherly love for which he longed.

Following World War II he returned to Germany but preferred the communist territory. He became a professor in Leipzig. There, authorities did not approve of his unorthodox interpretations of Marx's philosophy. They forced him into retirement. While visiting West Germany he heard the news about the building of the Berlin Wall, and he decided not to return to the "homeland of the proletariat." The University of Tubingen offered him a teaching position, and many young scholars in philosophy and theology learned to appreciate this man's wisdom and spirituality.

Bloch's recognition resulted in the movement of hope. Philosophers and theologians began to apply Bloch's insights in their writings. Especially Wolfhart Pannenberg and Jurgen Moltmann have benefitted tremendously from Bloch's teachings. They extended his creative thoughts into their books and publications. Thus the visions of Bloch permeate much of contemporary religious thought. Two significant poles of the divine are emphasized. One is to be found in the human core of longing – the soul. The other is responsive to the human imagination and enterprise – the future. The future inspires the human heart and mind to believe in things unheard and unseen. This dynamic field between the two poles constituted for Bloch the divine reality.

Here again, is Campbell's description of the monomyth:

> A hero ventures forth from the world of common day into a region of supernatural wonder: fabulous forces are there encountered and a decisive victory is won: the hero comes back from his mysterious adventure with the power to bestow boons on his fellow man.

It is evident that Bloch described hope in terms of the heroic as understood by Campbell. The protagonist is not just present in the written word but also the life of the author. A discussion is needed to make clear the similarities and the differences between Campbell and Bloch.

Discussion

If we take Otto Rank's theory of personality development, then both Campbell and Bloch represent very well the third stage, the artistic person. They do not suffer from life fear, they do not seek to be isolated, and they very much understand the balance between separation and union. They lived lives of highly personalized freedom.

Also according to O'Brien's five developmental stages of the human imagination, both authors represent the fifth level, sanctification. Both Campbell and Bloch were very much into the symbolic language and the mythical. They did not make doctrines out of the stories (fallen stage). They were alienated by the close-mindedness of ideologies and theologies. They creatively produced a personal identification with the power of the stories. They spoke in metaphors in the name of the life forces.

In applying Fowler's six stages of faith development, however, some differences begin to occur. One may say that much of Bloch's writing is prophetic, which is a characteristic of the fifth stage. A dedication to, and total emphasis on, creative activity for a better tomorrow is far more prevalent in Bloch than in Campbell. Campbell's approach represents more the mystical, an awareness beyond this world. This becomes dramatically clear at the end of Chapter II, "The Journey Inward," of *The Power of Myth:*

> Once in India I thought I would like to meet the major guru or teacher face to face. So I went to see a celebrated teacher named Sri Krishna Menon, and the first thing he said to me was, "Do you have a question?"
>
> The teacher in this tradition always answers questions. He doesn't tell you anything you are not ready to hear. So I said, "Yes, I have a question. Since in Hindu thinking everything in the universe is a manifestation of divinity itself, how should we say no to brutality, to stupidity, to vulgarity, to thoughtlessness?"
>
> And he answered, "For you and for me – the way is to say yes."
>
> We then had a wonderful talk on this theme of the affirmation of all things. And it confirmed in me the feeling I had that who are we to judge? It seems to me this is one of the great teachings', also of Jesus.
>
> MOYERS: In classic Christian doctrine the material world is to be despised, and life is to be redeemed in the hereafter, in heaven, where our rewards come. But you say that if you

affirm that which you deplore, you are affirming the very world which is our eternity at the moment.

CAMPBELL: Yes, that is what I'm saying. Eternity isn't some later time. Eternity isn't even a long time. Eternity has nothing to do with time. Eternity is that dimension of here and now that all thinking in temporal terms cuts off. And if you don't get it here, you won't get it anywhere. The problem with heaven is that you will be having such a good time there, you won't even think of eternity. You'll just have this unending delight in the beatific vision of God. But the experience of eternity right here and now, in all things, whether thought of as good or as evil, is the function of life.

MOYERS: This is it.

CAMPBELL: This is it. (67)

Bloch promoted the here and the now in terms of the unknown future. As such, reality was taken with an ultimate sincerity by the authority of the human soul. The human soul is the seat of the divine which looks at reality and senses in the very depth of its being that there is so much injustice, suffering, malaise, which cries out for our creative involvement. This is the prophetic character of Bloch's vision.

For Campbell, the soul is the meeting-point between the internal and the external. So reality is viewed by an internal awareness of the external. The here and the now is simply an emanation of the eternal. We view reality with the eyes of eternity. Consequently, the dedication to the here and the now is relativized by the mystical. The mystical supersedes the formed and that which is shaped.

When Campbell, in this context, refers to Jesus, then it is certainly true that in John's gospel Jesus announces that he did not come into this world to judge or to condemn (3:17; 12:47). But John's gospel is full of paradoxes. Jesus says also that he has come into the world for judgment (9:39). The texts themselves do not exclude judgement, and there is a definite dedication to this world. A discussion of John's gospel regarding this matter of judgement will initially separate Bloch from Campbell. But the underlying spirituality of John will supersede such a division. First, a look at a succession of pertaining texts:

For God did not send his Son into the world in order to judge the world, but that the world might be saved through him. He who believes in him is not judged; but he who does not believe is already judged, because he does not believe in the name of the only-begotten Son of God. Now this is the judgment: The light has come into the world yet men have loved the darkness rather than the light, for their works were evil. For everyone who does evil hates the light, and does not come to the light, that his deeds may not be exposed. But he who does the truth comes to the light that his deeds may be manifest, for they have been performed in God. (3:17-21)

Amen, amen, I say to you, the Son can do nothing of himself, but only what he sees the Father doing. For whatever he does, this the Son also does in like manner. For the Father loves the Son, and he shows him all that he himself does. And greater works than these he will show him, that you may wonder. For as the Father raises the dead and gives life, even so the Son also gives life to whom he will. For neither does the Father judge any man, but all judgment he has given to the Son, that all men may honor the Son even as they honor the Father. He who does not honor the Son, does not honor the Father who sent him. Amen, amen, I say to you, he who hears my word, and believes him who sent me, has life everlasting, and does not come to judgment, but has passed from death to life. (5:19-24)

And they who have done good shall come forth unto resurrection of life; but they who have done evil unto resurrection of judgment. Of myself I can do nothing. As I hear, I judge, and my judgment is just because I seek not my own will but the will of him who sent me. (5:29-30)

The Jews therefore in answer said to him, "Are we not right in saying that thou art a Samaritan, and hast a devil?" Jesus answered, "I have not a devil, but I honor My Father, and you dishonor me. Yet I do not seek my own glory; there is one who seeks and who judges." (8:48-50)

Jesus answered and said, "Not for me did this voice come, but for you. Now this is the judgment of the world; now will the prince of the world be cast out. And I, if I be lifted up from the earth will draw all things to myself." (12:30-32)

"And if anyone hears my words, and does not keep them, it is not I who judge him; for I have not come to judge the world, but to save the world." (12:47)

It seems that when Campbell read these texts, he favored that aspect where Jesus emphasizes that he did not come to judge. Indeed, the text can be interpreted in this direction. But, on the other hand, other aspects are underplayed or left out. For Campbell, as we will see, the Father is the inner presence of eternity within Jesus. It is inspiring to read John's statements on judgement that way.

For Bloch too, the Father of Jesus is the inner spiritual force within Jesus. He took it to mean that this inner source of the divine is the very core of our sense of justice by which the world is to be judged.

For the sake of a juxtaposition, one may say, that Campbell sees the eternity within Jesus as the source of enlightenment by which judgment is relativized. Within the light of eternity the judgment is that judgments are to be taken less seriously. The awareness of eternity supersedes the death of the dead and the destruction of evil. One is enlightened about the more and the beyond.

Bloch's view is less tranquil and regards the presence of the Father within the soul as the source of judgment. One is not allowed to forgive and to forget in the name of an eternal peace. Bloch refuses to praise the Lord, if he is the one who can justify that the child was thrown to the dogs. The Father in us points at the imperfections and evil, and we are to make judgments which are the beginning of creative action for the sake of a divine future.

So, we have two different perceptions of the Father of Jesus. It is proper to return to John's gospel and see how the paradox is to be understood. First, John is not as advanced in Hindu religiousness as Campbell. Nevertheless, there is in John a definite awareness of the mystical. But this is experienced within the Jewish tradition, which is definitely committed to the here and the now. The degree or intensity of such a commitment, of course, depends on one's religious views or ultimate concern. Whatever such speculations may project, in regard to judgment talk, John has one major concern. This is stated by John L. McKenzie in his *Dictionary of the Bible*:

> Yet there is a unity of thought in these paradoxes, and it lies in the nature of the judgment, which is peculiar to Jn. In Jn the judgment is always present and is, so to speak, the act of man himself. The believer is not judged, but the unbeliever is already judged by his very unbelief (3:18; 5:24). The unbeliever has his judge on the last day, and the judge is the word which Jesus has spoken (12:48). The spirit will not judge the world but will demonstrate that there is a judgment by showing that the prince of the world, the spirit of evil, is already judged (Jn 16:11). And Jesus affirms that the judgment of the world is *now*, when the critical hour of his rejection by

his own people is near (Jn 12:31). It seems clear, then, that in Jn the judgment is the rejection of faith in Jesus Christ. Those who refuse faith will rise to the resurrection of judgment, which is opposed to the resurrection of life (Jn %:29). Jesus is judge in the sense that He presents Himself as the object of decision, and it is thus that the Father judges no one but has committed judgment to the Son. He comes not for the judgment of unbelief but to save those who believe. (468)

Thus McKenzie explains how John's view on judgment shall be understood. He does not help us in our deliberation about apparent differences between Bloch and Campbell, which offer us two interpretations of Jesus' Father in terms of the divine presence in the human soul. Both situate the spirit of the Father within us, but each interpretation accentuates a different emphasis. Bloch promotes a dedication to this world, the future of the here and the now. Campbell's mystical awareness supersedes the here and now in the presence of eternity, which is beyond.

Is the difference really that simple – one versus the other, and the other versus the one? Both authors produced a very personalized attitude about existence. Without doubt, Campbell recognizes that the life of the soul, where the external and the internal meet, is also present in all life and in all of existence. It is the dynamic energy which is dramatized in the stories of the myths. This sense of oneness within reality evokes a pertinent sense of awe for the mystery of reality. The underlying oneness can be experienced in many ways; the dance, meditation, recognizing the simple fact of one's existence as a mystery, the ecological awareness of the American Indian, the mystery of human love. But Campbell offers a very dramatic story in this respect.

> There is a magnificent essay by Schopenhauer in which he asks, how is it that a human being can so participate in the peril of pain of another that without thought, spontaneously, he sacrifices his own life to the other? How can it happen that when we normally think of as the first law of nature and self-preservation is suddenly dissolved?
>
> In Hawaii some four or five years ago there was an extraordinary event that presents this problem. There is a place called the Pali, where the trade winds from the north come rushing through a great ridge of mountains. People like to go there to get their hair blown about or sometimes to commit suicide – you know, something like jumping off the Golden Gate Bridge.

One day, two policemen were driving up the Pali road when they saw just beyond the railing that keeps cars from rolling over, a young man preparing to jump. The police car stopped, and the policeman on the right jumped out to grab the man but caught him as he jumped, and he was himself being pulled over when the second cop arrived in time and pulled the two of them back. Do you realize what had suddenly happened to that policeman who had given himself to death with that unknown youth? Everything else in his life had dropped off – his duty to his family, his duty to his job, his duty to his own life – all of his wishes and hopes for his lifetime had just disappeared. He was about to die.

Later, a newspaper reporter asked him, "Why didn't you let go? You would have been killed." And his reported answer was, "I couldn't let go. If I had let that young man go, I couldn't have another day of my life." How come?

Schopenhauer's answer is that such a psychological crisis represents the breakthrough of a metaphysical realization, which is that you and that other are one, that you are two aspects of the one life, and that your apparent separateness is but an effect of the way we experience forms under the conditions of space and time. This is a metaphysical truth which may become spontaneously realized under the circumstances of crisis. For it is, according to Schopenhauer, the truth of life.

The hero is the one who has given his physical life to some order of realization of that truth. The concept of love your neighbor is to put you in tune with this fact. But whether you love your neighbor or not, when the realization grabs you, you may risk your life. That Hawaiian policeman didn't know who the young man was to whom he had given himself. Schopenhauer declares that in small ways you can see this happening everyday, all the time, moving life in the world, people doing selfless things to and for each other. (111)

No doubt, with this story Campbell comes very close to Bloch in dramatizing what kind of life inspires the hero. The spirit of the soul is the basic awareness of oneness with others. This awareness is fundamental and it is the life of the Father who spirited Jesus to preach brotherly love, because the neighbor and I are one. This promotion of this oneness is at the heart of our souls.

A look back into history will clarify the origins of Bloch's approach. The biblical tradition is rooted in the Semitic cultures. There we find the beginning of historic civilization in the context of powerful cities and their struggle for existence. The mythical imagination will cross over into the integration of human effort for the sake of making life work. Life is not just a given, but demands a creative activity for establishing an order of security and possibility. This recognition of an established order as necessary for the maintenance of life became a decisive model by which the concept of a Father god was fashioned.

Chapter Four

The Historical as Transformation of the Mythical

The difference between Bloch and Campbell will receive more understanding if one learns about the particular nature of the Jewish and also biblical tradition. It is rather unique and therefore less universal than Campbell's presentation of myth. This uniqueness is more complex than Campbell's assessment as reported in the chapter on the nature of language. It is #5 in the list of aspects about myth as stated by Campbell.

> #5. "There are myths and gods that have to do with specific societies." (22) This is different from myths that relate one to one's nature and to the natural world.
>
> The mythology that is strictly sociological links one to a particular society. (23)

In many aspects this applies to the Biblical tradition in general and the Jewish tradition in particular. However, more should be said. This is done by John F. Priest in "Myth and Dream in Hebrew Scripture." He emphasizes that myths are expressions of universal human experiences because they deal with the totality of people's existence (51). However, when a particular group experiences the mystery of life and its creativity in a particular way, perhaps because of certain majestic happenings, then their mythology will be characterized by such events.

> It is thus possible to say that the central position in Israelite thought is occupied by history rather than myth, and that such survivals of myth as exist are controlled by the historical sense. (53)

Thus myths are controlled by the historical sense. Original nature festivals have been transformed into feasts in memory of great happenings in history.

> Thus Yahweh's biography and the resultant Yahweh myth was indistinguishable from the history of Israel itself. *One can say that the history of Israel is the biography of Yahweh* and this insight provides the justification for the contention that the history was in fact the mode of the Israelite expression of myth. (56)

This insight reveals that the religious language in the biblical tradition is mythical in a particular sense. The mystery of life is not celebrated in universal terms but in reference of historical events. Nevertheless the language itself can be understood as metaphorical, i.e., the Bible is not history. It is a book filled with religious language. When Bloch became highly interpretative of the biblical material, he touched upon the mythical dimension of this partiuclar language. It is of no use to argue about the historicity of the biblical events, because in the Bible they are narrated in religious statements. Thus the Father of Jesus is not a historical reality, but a reality experienced in history and as reported in reference to great events.

This places the mythical of the biblical tradition in a particular dimension. This is signified by Priest.

> But when the Israelite was able to redefine myth in historical terms and to desacralize nature without a total loss of wonder, he was able to move toward participation in the new myth, the myth of the will of God which was the articulation of the highest aspiration of a humanity willing to risk disintegration for the sake of wholeness. (58)

Thus Israel committed itself to divinely revealed laws and legal codes. Sometimes the revelations were given by dreams and visions. The focus of such experiences was not creativity but "the will of God."

> Thus we see that dream in the Old Testament tradition hardly turns out to be dream at all. The primary and ultimate preoccupation is with what God is saying and doing with respect to human affairs. (Priest, 65)

This biblical tradition is extended into the New Testament. The focus on history receives the following characterizations.

a) With the coming of Christ, the end-time has arrived

b) All of reality is placed within an ongoing course toward its divine completion – eschatological perspective.

In his "Myth and Dream in Christian Scripture," Amos N. Wilder in *Myths, Dreams, and Religion* concludes:

> We made a fundamental observation here when we say that "myth and dream" in Christian Scripture are shaped by the eschatological consciousness. All the creative symbol is governed by the sense of the world-transformation in course and ultimate goals within reach, and these are social and cosmic goals as well as individuals. (71)

Toward the end Wilder concludes:

> The myth and dream of Jewish and Christian origin is unique in its nexus with man's social experience and his historical life. This is a commonplace in all study of comparative religion. the most radical discontinuity we have had to recognize was that in which Hebraism historicized the older mythos of the ancient Near East. The new myth and ritual of Israel was oriented to time, to the birth of the people in time, and to its promise and obligation in time. The mythology of natural cycles was largely overcome. The Christian mythos, indeed, looked to the end of history but in such a way that the historical experience of man was still validated. (87)

Such a conclusion clarifies why Bloch presented the heroic in terms of creative activity in the here and now – to bring about the fulfillment of the divine in history. Although Mesopotamia and Babylon are also regarded as Semitic cultures, and they identified strongly with a divine creativity, they kept their wisdom within the realm of the non-historical myth. In our context it is important to recognize that they too speak about God as Father, but it is more metaphorical than historical. One experiences this easily when reading the Babylonian Genesis summarized as follows.

The story is about the birth of the universe, where in the beginning everything was water. Three aspects of the watery mass are mentioned: Apsu, the primeval sweet water; Tiamat, the salt-water ocean; and Mummu, representing the mist and clouds rising from the waters. The elements were mingled into one, and they gave birth to separate centers of powers or gods. Some of them were Anshar, a paternal authority, and Anu, the sky-god. Anu gave birth to Ea, a god of exceptional wisdom. These three gods are basic in the story as fatherly spirit, the spaciousness of the sky, and the power of wisdom in other myths.

Other gods were born, and they were less fundamental. Their ways of life were more noisy than significant. Apsu, in his primordial slumber of the waters, was disturbed by the trivial busy ongoings of the younger gods. He deliberated with Tiamat and considered their destruction. The only reply coming from Tiamat was one of maternal instinct: "Why should we destroy that which we ourselves have brought forth?" Apsu was determined to restore the eternal quietude of primordial peace: "I will destroy them and end their way, that silence be established, and then let us sleep."

It seems as if the myth wants us to see that the primeval dynamics are somewhat creative but do not really care to sacrifice themselves for the sake of future developments. They are conservative and do not desire change in favor of the new. A generation gap emerged, and the struggle between the new and the old began. The story promotes the protection and organization of the new and its future.

When Anshar, Anu, and Ea heard of the destructive plans of Apsu, they convened and discussed possible ways which would bring help in this hour of gloom. Ea emerged in the conference as the powerful one who would stand up against Apsu. The primordial strength of Apsu was countered by "the one of supreme understanding," who was skillful and wise. Ea possessed great intelligence and knew how to manipulate powers to the advantage of life. He was the god of magic, and he placed a protective magic circle around the young gods. He also composed a holy incantation by which he put Apsu in a very deep sleep.

Then Ea took away Apus's crown which had supernatural radiance, and placed it on his own head. Now all might and splendor was bestowed on him. He destroyed Apsu, the father of the gods. Over the slain Apsu he formed a spacious realm and called it "Apsu." It became the place for shrines in honor of himself and other gods (Hall of Fame). Ea lived there with his wife, Damkina, and they had a son, Marduk who was destined to become the wisest of the gods. His parents instilled in him their greatness. As a baby, he drank from the breasts of goddesses to obtain additional divine powers. While growing up, Marduk became an impressive young man, with flashing eyes and an awe-inspiring majesty. Later, when the young man was mature enough, Ea elevated him to the stature of a god. This was done by magical power, which is the fruit of divine wisdom and supreme skillfulness.

Tiamat, the wife of the slain Apsu, bitter over her husband's death, was restless and sought revenge. This became known to Kingu, the leader of the rebellious gods. He offered Tiamat help to avenge Apsu's death. A coalition was formed, and a war against Ea and his gods was planned. Tiamat gave birth to monster serpents and dragons, which would help her in the destruction of Ea's reign. Kingu received a lot of privileges and magical powers, and he became a ferocious demon.

These developments became known to Ea, and he was shocked by the dangerous threat which was being prepared. He went to his grandfather, Anshar, to discuss a strategy by which he could save their kingdom. Had not Ea defeated the majestic power of Apsu? Would not he, again, be able to assert his might against the primeval forces of Tiamat? These thoughts made him decide to let Ea lead the battle in defense of his established creation.

The fight began and Ea failed. Then Anu, the sky-god, was prepared for a confrontation with Tiamat. He would try to soften her anger and break down her bitter hate. However, Tiamat could not be influenced by any magic. Anu failed to succumb her into a letdown of her revengeful determination. He returned and was terrified.

A great silence came over the gods. Tiamat had to be destroyed by physical force; otherwise, everyone would be slain. The gods realized the hopelessness of the situation. The crisis was extremely serious.

In the dark moment, the fatherly god, Anshar, remembered the young and promising Marduk, the son of Ea. Would not he be strong enough to stand up against Tiamat? They sent for him, and when Anshar saw the young Marduk in his radiant strength, "his heart was filled with joy; he kissed his lips, his fear was removed."

Marduk immediately showed the cunning quality of his excellence and demanded a high price for his special services. He wanted to advance his own importance while the opportunity placed him in an extremely favorable bargaining position. Marduk asked to be installed as the supreme authority among the gods, so that he would be the most powerful in the battle against Tiamat.

The gods deliberated, and in their fear of a terrifying destruction, they unanimously decided to confer upon Marduk the "kingship over the totality of the whole universe." There was a celebration and an official ritual by which Marduk received all these extraordinary powers. The gods vested him with the insignia of his supreme importance. Then they gave him their mandate and mission, "Go and cut off the life of Tiamat."

Marduk isolated himself to begin a period of preparation for the decisive battle. He made magical weapons a bow, and arrows of a special kind, which would cause lightning to precede him. He filled his body with a blazing fire; he made a net carried by the four winds, and he improved his irresistible storm chariot, drawn by four overwhelming creatures. For his protection he designed a layer of metal rings which would cover his body.

The day of battle arrived. Marduk appeared in his dazzling might, which shocked Kingu and his rebellious gods. But Tiamat was less easily impressed, and she welcomed Marduk with a terrifying roar. The young god was strong in his determination to destroy Tiamat and challenged her to a duel. Tiamat felt terribly insulted and anger boiled inside of her. Almost beyond herself in frustration, she began to attack. Marduk was prepared and he threw the net over her. "When Tiamat opened her mouth to devour him, he drove in the evil wind, in order that she would not close her lips." The wind inflated Tiamat's body. Marduk shot an arrow through her open mouth; it struck her heart and she died.

The rebellious gods saw that their leader was dead. They tried to flee, but all of them were captured. Marduk took all the privileged powers from Kingu, especially the tablet of destinies, which he now sanctioned with his own seal. From now on, Marduk would be the lord and master of history.

As final act of battle, Marduk divided the immense body of Tiamat into two parts to form the universe. With one half he created the sky; with the other he modeled the earth. The gods were then assigned their particular domains. Only Marduk would reign over the total cosmos. He made his rule felt by instilling order into reality. The calendar was installed by the organization of the stellar and planetary constellations. (Constellation itself reveals such a rootage. *Stella* is the Latin word for star, and *con* means with. So it is an organization in reference to star formations.) The years, months, weeks, and days were destined by the motions of the sun, moon, and stars.

The story of the victorious Marduk implies, without any doubt, that might and power will be obtained by the person who responds courageously to the inspiration of the creative sources. Moreover, the hero is one who can even destroy of subdue primordial forces with great cunning (magic) and excellence, for the sake of the maintenance and enhancement of life and its basic structure. Order means a distribution of powers so that security and harmony can be enjoyed. Marduk portrays such a hero, and his bravery is an inspiration for civilized life. Does that mean that the Babylonian culture wants its citizens to be like the god, Marduk? The last part of this Genesis suggests otherwise.

The imprisoned gods, who had joined Tiamat in her destructive plans, were condemned to become the servants of the gods in Marduk's kingdom. They really suffered in this slavery, but their godlike aspirations were still vital, and they pleaded with Marduk to be relieved from this degrading burden. Apparently, Marduk understood their basic hurt, and he decided to create true servants, who would take over the menial works of the rebellious gods. At the same time this action would made the rebelliousness of those gods quite impotent. Marduk created the human race by killing the leader of the rebels, Kingu. The spilled blood became the seed which gave birth to the first humans.

This story reveals the basic philosophy about human life contained within the Babylonian Genesis. In his heart, the human has a rebellious power which has been killed by the victorious Marduk, the supreme god of the universe. There is nothing else left for the human than to serve the gods of Marduk's cosmos. The human is too little and too insignificant to rely on his/her own basic drifts. The human is destined to be servant of the gods.

Consequently, the priests of Babylon invited the citizens to erect and maintain a temple in honor of Marduk. The temple would be the reminder of this god's majestic powers, which were truly victorious and which should be worshipped. The temple is also a monument to the deep human feeling of inferiority. There are divine powers within us, but they have been destroyed by the one who is greater. By worshipping Marduk, the citizens expressed a basic sentiment; "Let us be good losers and give glory and recognition to him who excelled so supremely. Our security and destiny are in his hands." The last paragraphs are my personal interpretations and demonstrate how one can respond to this mythical account of the beginning of civilization and why humans sense that they are in a fallen situation.

Historically, there have been different versions of this Babylonian Genesis. The account rendered here is supposedly an edition from the time of King Hammurabi (1728-1686 B. C. E.) He is famous for having established the Babylonian civilization on a very sound footing by the writing of his legal codes, which became a cultural breakthrough. From now on, people would not be victimized at random by those more powerful and cunning. The little people and weak had some recourse by calling upon "justice" as a divine institution of organized and civilized life. The written word became a source of security, hope, promise, and fairness. These developments are at the root of biblical origins, and they help us in the identification of the Father of Jesus.

In reference to King Hammurabi one may say that the wisdom of life of a particular culture was only to be found in its myths. The institution of civilized life demanded that people learned to appreciate its significance. Not just the powers of nature and the human psyche constitute the makeup of life as told by myths. The mythological also had to integrate those stories which clarified the life of civilization, which is a particular order within the outer world. The outer world is dominated by a multivariety of power-plays among the gods and goddesses. Civilization cuts into such a haphazard existence. It regulates in the name of what is understood to be fair and just. This is the religiousness underneath the birth of written legal and moral codes. To live in such a civilization, one has to be educated in various ways. An indoctrination into the established tradition along with learning certain skills helps the individual to find a place in the established order and become productive accordingly. Productivity is celebrated as that enterprise which will bring prosperity to the people. Thus one creates the foundation for future developments. The future becomes impregnated with possibilities. Life receives an invitation to become more than presently is the case. Not just wisdom, but also the learning of significant skills, is needed to maintain the established order and provide it with perspectives of projection and planning ahead. Part of the maintenance of such an order is the resolve to defend and protect it against outside forces. One learns to become defensive in a professional and artful way. Without such a defense one is weak and becomes an easy prey for those who want to overpower in the name of their selfish interests. All that is part of life's reality. Civilization is an expression of such a determination. (Determination itself indicates that one is willing or capable of drawing the lines, knowing the boundaries and limitations.) This is somewhat present in the divine character of Marduk. The Babylonian hero is of such a spirit.

Again, for the sake of juxtaposition, let us place some of Campbell's discussion of the hero in this context.

> MOYERS: That's what intrigues me. If we are fortunate, if the gods and muses are smiling, about every generation someone comes along to inspire the imagination for the journey each of us takes. In your day it was Joyce and Mann. In our day it often seems to be the movies. Do movies create hero myths? Do you think, for example, that a movie like *Star Wars* fills some of that need for a model of the hero?

> CAMPBELL: I've heard youngsters use some of George Lucas' terms—"the Force" and "the dark side." So it must be hitting somewhere. It's good sound teaching, I would say. (143-144)

> CAMPBELL: The fact that the evil power is not identified with any specific nation on this earth means you've got an abstract power, which represents a principle, not a specific historical situation. The story has to do with an operation of principles, not of this nation against that. The monster masks that are put on people in *Star Wars* represent the real monster force in the modern world. When the mask of Darth Vader is removed, you see an unformed man, one who has not developed as a human individual. What you see is a strange and pitiful sort of undifferentiated face.

> MOYERS: What is the significance of that?

> CAMPBELL: Darth Vader has not developed his own humanity. He's a robot. He's a bureaucrat, living not in terms of himself but in terms of an imposed system. This is the threat to our lives that we all face today. Is the system going to flatten you out and deny you your humanity, or are you going to be able to make use of the system to the attainment of human purposes? How do you relate to the system so that you are not compulsively serving it? It doesn't help to try to change it to accord your system of thought. The momentum of history behind it is too great for anything really significant to evolve from that kind of action. The thing is to learn to live in your

period of history as a human being. That's something else, and it can be done.

MOYERS: By doing what?

CAMPBELL: By holding to your own ideals for yourself and, like Luke Skywalker, rejecting the system's impersonal claims upon you.

MOYERS: When I took our two sons to see *Star Wars*, they did the same thing the audience did at that moment when the voice of Ben Kenobi says to Skywalker in the climatic moment of the flash light, "Turn off your computer, turn off your machine and do it yourself, follow your feelings, trust your feelings." And when he did, he achieved success, and the audience broke out into applause.

CAMPBELL: Well, you see the movie communicates. It is in a language that talks to young people, and that's what counts. It asks, Are you going to be a person of heart and humanity – because that's where the life is, from the heart – or are you to do whatever seems required of you by what might be called "intentional power?" When Ben Kenobi says, "May the Force be with you," he is speaking of the power and energy of life, not of programmed political intentions. (144)

Throughout *The Power of Myth* Campbell emphasizes that this "intentional power", which is "the Force", resides in us. The juxtaposition with the Marduk account provides the opportunity for a relevant discussion. Campbell is very well aware that civilization is a monument which deserves our respect. (The momentum of history behind it is too great...) Campbell's statements are situated in a context where civilization is well established. Moreover, the land of opportunity and free enterprise is founded on a Constitution where individual rights form the core of its integrity. As such there is less need for serving the system, and a greater need for playing the game artfully, artistically, and creatively according to the Force within you. That is true wisdom.

The Babylonian Genesis and its hero, Marduk, originated in a time when civilization had to be forged out of a chaos of forces. There were multiple cities and multiple gods who were assigned to protect this town against the other god or goddess of another town. Wars were the talk of the town. Power-play was the basic requirement for survival. A god was only significant if it could be demonstrated that he was successful in protecting and guiding a particular group of people on roads to greater safety, prosperity, and greater power in numbers as well as in splendor. Stories are significant when they dramatize the process and dynamics of developments in fashioning a reliable social order. That is at the heart of the myths in the Semitic traditions, including Babylon and the Hebrew people. The biblical tradition is rooted within this need for establishing a reliable order, founded by a divine source, a god, may it be Marduk or Yahweh or Enlil or El.

That is why people in Latin America who are serious about creating a society of integrity where they will not be abused any more by a few powerful and rich elite, use in their liberation theology images and symbols from the biblical tradition. There they find encouragement and perspectives by which to look at their own predicament with hope and deliberation. The reference to the exodus of the Hebrew people out of the slavery in Egypt into the land of promise, gives focus to their own sentiments.

Bloch's presentation of hope is in the context of understanding that evil forces have names and faces, and they victimize too many people too often. Liberation is needed. Campbell looks at those people who are in the land of promise and do not know how to play the game creatively as liberated creatures. That is why Campbell refers to the source of creativity, the Force within. That is also why his interpretation of the Father of Jesus is characterized by his promotion of the inner life.

> CAMPBELL: It's important to live life with the experience, and therefore the knowledge, of its mystery and of your mystery. This gives life a new radiance, a new harmony, a new splendor. Thinking in mythological terms helps to put you in accord with the inevitable of this vale of tears. You learn to recognize the positive values in what appears to be the negative moments and aspects of your life. The big question is whether you are going to be able to say yes to your adventure. (163)

Thus we have specified Campbell's preferred way of portraying the hero. This will be also his preference when he speaks about Jesus and his Father, which will be our next topic.

Chapter Five

Joseph Campbell's Views
on The Oneness of Jesus and His Father

Besides the canonical biblical books (those officially approved by the hierarchy of Christianity and the Jewish authorities) there exists what is called "The Other Bible." Willis Barnstone edited *The Other Bible*; on the cover is printed, "For the first time in one volume ancient esoteric texts from: the pseudopigrapha, the Dead Sea Scrolls, the early Kabbalah, the Nag Hammadi Library, and other sources." This refers to the fact that orthodox Jews and Christians were very selective in picking those sources which promoted their own belief systems and doctrines. The other sources were regarded heretical, and some of the devil.

Campbell was not just a student of such non-canonical sources, he also was well at home with stories, myths, and texts of the Ancient Near East: Egypt, Mesopotamia, and the Semitic cultures, especially Babylon and the Hebrew tradition. In such comparative studies he learned to appreciate the similarities and the differences, as well as the historical developments by which such cultures became characterized. Such universal interpretations (recognition of common elements) were very much fostered by Carl G. Jung's understanding of archetypes, the collective unconscious (where all those archetypes find an umbrella existence) and the interpretations of dreams according to pertaining symbols. (Campbell was the author of *The Portable Jung*.) As such he could make comparisons between the biblical imagery and the images used in Greek, Persian, Egyptian, and Babylonian myths. Within the biblical tradition of the Old Testament there were political groups, which did not agree with each other and also opposed each other. In his book, *Wisdom in Israel*, Gerhard Von Rad, describes such a case.

Although part of the Hebrew culture, Judaism arose as a tradition during the Babylonian Exile, when the Babylonian King Nebuchadnezzar led a substantial portion of the Judaites into captivity. This occurred in the last part of the Sixth Century B. C. E. The temple of Jerusalem had been destroyed, and the circumstances did not allow for temple rituals, which were the center of identity. The cult was replaced by a stronger adherence to God's law, the Torah, which would hold people together in their tradition. The written word was portable; it was contained on scrolls of parchment. It was open for everyone to read, and as such one could take the word of God wherever one traveled. The synagogues became the religious gathering places, and the religious authority changed from priests to those laymen who studied God's laws, the Rabbis.

This Judaism became concerned with the regulations of the practical life and the interpretations of historical events. At its center is Yahweh. This God is very exclusive and benevolent to those who deserve his blessings. The dispute about the way in which the blessing would be bestowed upon people became the cause of internal debates and struggles.

One group simply maintained that the divine blessings will come as a consequence of being faithful to God's rules about their daily lives. This is the Deuteronomic tradition. Another group held that there was also a definite wisdom within the created reality, which needed to be discovered and studied more fully. This insight was held in various ways by the Wisdom literature. A segment of this Wisdom believed that divine blessings do not solely depend upon obedience to the Torah but may result from a reasonable response to the divine truth within creation.

The Deuteronomic tradition is the orthodox mentality within Judaism. The Wisdom approach is more enlightened in terms of reason, human philosophy, meditation, and forms of mystical experiences. It can be noted that the orthodox position contains a degree of Wisdom mentality insofar as they allow themselves on expectation of blessings as a result of a faithfulness to the Torah. They held it to be *reasonable* that God would reward his servants for having done good works. However, this *reasoning* was checked with the awareness that the hope for blessings is ultimately based on a revealed promise as part of the covenant. It does not refer to a causality as strongly as is the case in Wisdom literature. The latter holds that there is a certain order at the heart of God's creation. A life lived in accordance with this order can be expected to be a rewarding life. This reward is then understood in terms of cause and effect.

The two traditions were already present before the Babylonian Exile. The orthodox had acquired political power under the reign of King Josiah. He had been inspired by the discovery of scrolls, which contained regulations and were perceived to be God's law. Josiah awakened the hopes of his people by promoting their obedience to these divine rules, with the promise that God would bring his reward in the form of a much needed national stability and prosperity. It was a re-grouping movement of the people in Judah in their search for identity. They had allowed themselves significant communications with other cultures. This interchange had produced a syncretic mentality and a spirit of enlightenment. The traditional identity had suffered substantially. The resurgence of orthodoxy established a needed security. The political power was in the hands of the Zadokite priests, who organized a hierocratic order. The promotors of the Wisdom tradition came into discredit, although they remained a significant force in the historical development of Judaism.

With the Babylonian Exile, the two groups continued their struggle for power and acceptance. On the one hand there was a concern for the perpetuation of the nation which focused on a return to Jerusalem, their holy city, and the rebuilding of the temple. Quite different were the voices of the known prophets of those days, Jeremiah, Ezekiel, and Deutero-Isaiah. They were not against the rebuilding of the temple, but did not hold this to be the exclusive center of hope. Jeremiah and Ezekiel promoted aspects of an individualized religion where God speaks in the heart of people. They wanted to educate the exiled in an understanding of wider perspectives, which superseded their nationalistic beliefs. God's power was explained as being at work in all nations and in all of history. Redemption should not be expected exclusively from the temple cult.

After the exile, the orthodox tradition was victorious in the power struggle. The Wisdom-oriented group, which favored adaptation and openness to new perspectives, became more alienated. Initially, they maintained a certain hope for the future based on the dynamism of the wisdom within God's creation. This cosmic source would made goodness emerge as a distinct realm of God's realized glory, God's kingdom. (Thus the divine energy of the Father is within the cosmos and within the individual.)

Von Rad holds that the growing alienation of the Wisdom mentality resulted in a pessimism regarding the coming of God's kingdom, based on human efforts in response to wisdom within creation. Redemption came to be expected from God's dramatic intervention within history. God was to bring about the needed transformation. The proportions of these transformations became more radical and grew in scope. Visionaries described their cosmic dimensions which would pertain to all of creation. This was the origin of Apocalyptic literature. Von Rad believes the new emergent to be based on the Wisdom tradition.

It should be noted that the Wisdom as a dynamic energy within all of creation was never an independent power but was explained as an expression of God's created goodness. Von Rad phrased this insight well. "Indeed, it was precisely because this knowledge of Yahweh was so strong, so unassailable, that Israel was able to speak of the orders of this world in quite secular terms" (63).

As a summary, the following events describe the drastic cultural changes during the Exilic Age: a) deterioration of the Jewish nationalism; b) External cultural influences from Babylonian and Hellenic civilization promoted the development of rationality; c) The Prophets emphasized the significance of a personalized religiousness, which caused a metamorphosis, diminishing the nationalistic collectivity; d) The development of personalized religiosity gave rise to a concern for individual justice in the context of undeserved suffering of the righteous, e.g., Job.

Von Rad explains how Job's final solution to the problem was not merely a submission to God's will. This would have been the orthodox mentality. It was Yahweh's reference to the greatness and incomprehensible majesty of His creations, Wisdom's appreciation of creation, which made Job see that God can be trusted. Job's suffering was not the result of unfaithfulness to God's Law. The suffering was to be understood within the incomprehensible greatness of God, whose majesty supersedes our minute sense of justice and fairness. God's justice is greater than we ever will know, and it should not be subjected exclusively to our human criteria.

Although one of the last canonical books of the Old Testament, Daniel has a definite apocalyptic character, the real apocalyptic writings originated in the last two centuries before Christ. Generally they are products of the "intertestamental" period (between the Old and the New Testament). They are known as Jewish pseudopigraphs, that is, scriptures, usually from the intertestamental period, attributed to an assumed great name of the Old Testament. They are noncanonical and were composed mostly in Palestine and Egypt, where the Jews living outside their land (in the Diaspora) created Graeco-Jewish literature. They also belong to the apocryphal books or "hidden" books which claim divine authorship which is denied by Jewish and Christian authorities. They are extremely valuable for understanding the popular beliefs of Judaism and New Testament times and tracing those traditions which were declared "heretical" by the orthodox religions. What happened to the religious imagination of the Jewish tradition in those days is well summarized by Conrad L'Huereux in an unpublished paper, "Cultural Anthropology and the Death-Immortality Dialog."

> For a long time Israel clung stubbornly to the idea that God was just and so he must reward those who are faithful to him and punish sinners. Since, in the early period, there was effectively no belief in an afterlife, this reward and punishment must be found in the present life. Historical experience, however, did not support this belief in divine justice and retribution. For one could find just and pious men who suffered in life whereas there were wicked unfaithful men who lived long and happy lives. This contradiction between theological conviction and historical experience is the principle cause of the emergence of belief in reward for the just after death. So we see that from biblical perspectives, belief in a blessed afterlife is not a presupposition or first principle of

faith, but a conclusion arrived at because it was the only way to reconcile an apparent contradiction. (Department of Religious Studies, University of Dayton, Ohio, 1972.)

Wolfhart Pannenberg complements these insights by observing that, with the rise of individualism, the meaning of the individual's life on earth was not completely understandable. (See *Theology Digest*). He emphasizes how the fellowship with God expressed in Psalm 73 gives the worshipper an experience which supersedes his own mortality. Pannenberg concludes that hope for an afterlife has its origin in this religious fellowship with the immortal God.

> How good God is to the upright;
> the Lord to those who are clean of heart!
> But, as for me, I almost lost my balance;
> my feet all but slipped,
> because I was envious of the arrogant when
> I saw them prosper though they were wicked.
> For they are in no pain;
> their bodies are sound and sleek'
> they are free from the burdens of mortals,
> and are not afflicted like the rest of men.
> So pride adorns them as a necklace;
> as a robe violence enwraps them...(1-6)

> Because my heart was embittered.
> and my soul pierced,
> I was stupid and understood not;
> I was like a brute beast in your presence.

> Yet with you I shall always be;
> you have hold of my right hand;
> with your counsel you guide me, and in the end you will receive
> me in your glory.
> Whom else have I in heaven?
> And when I am with you,
> the earth delights me not.
> Though my flesh and my heart waste away,
> God is the rock and my portion forever....(21-26)

Additional insights pertain to the martyrdom of the righteous. Many scholars recognize the tragedy as a source of apocalyptic thought. In his book *Resurrection, Immortality, and Eternal Life in Intertestamental Judaism*, George W. E. Nickelsburg elaborates on this martyrdom aspect. He delineated developments within literature which deal with this theme. In the segment, "The Story of the Righteous Man and the Isaianic Exaltation Tradition" (170), he observes how initially the righteous, who is condemned to death, is rescued and exalted to a high position. In later literature (the Wisdom of Solomon), changes emerged. The protagonist was put to death but was vindicated and honored in the heavenly court, where he became a high ranking official.

The above references to the presence of the Wisdom tradition before and during the Babylonian Exile, and the development of the intertestamental Apocalyptic literature at the end of the Old Testament period, indicate the difference from the orthodox tradition. In the intertestamental period and especially in the first century C. E., there is the birth of a new Jewish tradition–Gnosticism. Although Gnosticism consists of a wide variety of schools and espouses at the times opposing ideas, still, they can be fitted under one umbrella. As such, Gnostics believe that salvation was to be achieved by a special or esoteric knowledge. Evil was explained in the belief that at the beginning, before creation, there were two opposing principles, light versus dark, or goodness versus evil. Creation is really an act by some dumb Creator who mixed those two together in the formation of reality. The only way to become liberated from such a captivity within the claws of the dark, is to obtain a special enlightenment, *gnosis*. It is rooted in the Wisdom and Apocalyptic tradition which had definite expectations about created reality and its future, but became frustrated. This frustration became amplified especially in the first century C. E. with the destruction of the temple. Everything went wrong; there was no way out of this predicament. Moreover, the tradition teachings about a Creator God did not make sense at all. The orthodox teachings proved to be irrelevant; moreover they deserved to be ridiculed and exposed as erroneous. Everything of the tradition, paradise, Adam and Eve, the serpent and the Tree of Life, the expulsion from Paradise, Noah's ark and the flood, the Creation of the world, the Messiah, Heaven, and Hell, Wisdom and righteousness needed to be interpreted anew according to this gnosis. This one finds in the early gnostic literature which is originally Jewish.

The first Christians were Jews, and many of them developed their Christian identity in gnostic terms. The orthodox church of Jerusalem reacted strongly against the gnostic interpretation of the Christian faith. They tried hard to keep gnostic ideas out of the scriptures which were to represent their beliefs. In this the orthodox church was not totally successful, because there are many gnostic ideas within the New Testament texts. The gnostic writings were considered among the apocryphal books, which were not inspired by God. For a long time orthodox Christianity was successful in suppressing these writings; that is why they were "hidden" (in Greek *apokryphos*). Shortly after World War II, the secret scriptures of the Gnostics were discovered near the Upper Nile city of Nag Hammadi in Egypt. They are now known as the Nag Hammadi Library. Most of the Nag Hammadi texts became available only in the mid-1970s.

Already in 1925 the renowned New Testament scholar, Rudolf Bultmann, concluded that early Christianity formed itself according to a Gnostic redeemer myth, where Jesus is a divine figure "sent down from the celestial light, the Son of the Most High coming forth from the Father, veiled in earthly form and inaugurating the redemption through his work." Here is John Dart's description in his book, *The Laughing Savior*:

> The Gnostic myth tells the fate of the soul, man's true inner self represented as "a spark of a heavenly figure of light, the original man." In primordial times, demonic powers of darkness conquer this figure of light, tearing him into shreds.
>
> The sparks of light are used by the demons to "create a world out of the chaos of darkness as a counterpart of the world of light, of which they were jealous." The demons closely guarded the elements of light enclosed in humans. "The demons endeavor to stupefy them and make them drunk, sending them to sleep and making them forget their heavenly home." Some people nevertheless become conscious of their heavenly origin and of the alien nature of the world. They [the Gnostics] yearn for deliverance.
>
> "The supreme deity takes pity on the imprisoned sparks of light, and sends down the heavenly figure of light, his Son, to redeem them. This Son arrays himself in the garment of the earthly body, lest the demons should recognize him. He invites his own to join him, awakens them from their sleep, reminds them of their heavenly home, and teaches them about the way to return.
>
> The redeemer teaches them sacred and secret passwords, for the souls will have to pass different spheres of the planets, watchposts of the demonic cosmic powers. "After accomplishing his work, he ascends and returns to heaven again to prepare a way for his own to follow him. This they will do when they die..."
>
> The redeemer's work will be completed when he is able to reassemble all the sparks of light in heaven. That done, the

world will come to an end, returning to its original chaos. "The darkness is left to itself, and that is the judgment" (45-46).

Obviously, much of the Gnostic myth is present in the gospel of John. It is certainly a challenge to read this gospel from a gnostic viewpoint rather than with the eyes of the traditional Christian worldview. The orthodox Christian worldview is very simple. There is one God, who is the creative principle of all existence. Initially everything was fine (Paradise). But the disobedience of the first man and his wife caused the birth of evil. In his goodness, the Creator God promises a messiah. The birth of Jesus and his death on the cross resulted in the bodily resurrection by which Jesus became the Christ. This Christ is the second person of the Divine Trinity – Father, Son, and Holy Spirit. One can become part of this divine life if one is baptized in the name of the Father, the Son, and the Holy Spirit, as demanded by Jesus. Creation is simply a temporary reality which will be superseded by Heaven, which the Father created since the beginning of time. Our sins are washed away by Christ's blood on the cross. The life of Christ is to be found in His true church, Christianity. The religion preaches an almighty God, Creator of heaven and earth, and everything is regulated and ruled by Him. Total obedience to His word will secure eternal life. Life itself is just one of those things that shall be subjugated to God's laws. Life itself needs to be redeemed because it is not yet sufficiently spiritualized. Plato's perception of the soul being incarcerated in the body has permeated much of Christianity. In fact, the doctrine of soul is typically Platonic. In the Bible, the soul is not an independent spiritual being. Even the inventor of Christianity, Saint Paul, did not believe in a soul. For him, death was like going to sleep. What awaits the dead is the resurrection of the body, which is a transformation. Not the life of the spirit, because that would be gnostic, and Paul fought against gnosticism, but the resurrection of the body is promised.

The above paragraph was intended to indicate that orthodox Christianity became a very particular form within the Christian reality. Some people assume that the first Christians were orthodox and that later the gnostic version emerged. This becomes highly debatable if one learns that one of the gnostic writings, The Gospel of Thomas, is considered as being older than the four gospels in the New Testament. This gnostic gospel is a compilation of Jesus' sayings which some of those sayings seem more original than similar ones within the canonical gospels. (See Dart's *The Laughing Savior*, 15, 91-96.)

Joseph Campbell refers repeatedly to The Gospel of Thomas. Before going into his interpretations and use of such a gnostic text, more needs to be explained about these writings.

John Dart devotes a number of chapters to making the connection between the gnostic writings and the Jewish tradition, and also a few chapters to indicate the Christian nature of this particular gnosticism. In Chapter Nine, "The Envious God," he discusses the Christian Gnostic work, "The Testimony of Truth." There is a retelling of the Genesis story. There the serpent is regarded as "wiser" (not "more cunning") than all the animals, and he promises Eve that the eating of the apple will open "the eyes of her heart." After the eating of the apple God asked "Where are you?" "The Testimony of Truth" ridicules this:

> What sort is he, this God?
> First, [he] envied Adam that he should eat from the tree of knowledge. And secondly he said, Adam, "where are you?"
> And God does not have foreknowledge: that is, since he did not know (it) from the beginning.
> [And] afterwards he said, "Let us cast him [out] of this place, lest he eat of the tree of life and live for ever."
> Surely he has shown himself to be an envious slanderer.
> And what kind of God is this? For great is the blindness of the commandments; and did they not reveal him? And he said, "I am the jealous God; I will bring the sins of the fathers upon the children until three (and) four generations" [see Exod. 20:5]
> And he said, "I will make their heart thick, and I will cause their mind to become blind, that they might not know nor comprehend the things he has said to those who believe in him [and] serve him! (Dart, 63)

Obviously, the author is very much interested in wisdom and turned off by the Creator God of the Genesis story. In this context, a reference can be made to Joseph Campbell's personal experience as told in the television program "Joseph Campbell: A Profile." Once, in Japan, he was at the entrance of a Buddhist shrine, with a Buddha seated under the Tree of Immortal Life. At the gate were statues of two guardians. At that moment

Campbell realized that they reminded him of the cherubim with the flaming sword, which God had placed east of the Garden of Eden to guard the way of the tree (Gen. 3:24). Campbell reflected further that this guard is our belief in a Creator God whom we make all important. Then the wisdom of life is obliterated and inaccessible. Campbell is well prepared to speak about God in terms beyond the Creator God. He definitely learned about this in the Hindu tradition, where the divine supersedes the God of creation in the eternal presence of Brahman. The creator is simply an expression of one of the innumerable divine possibilities. A mystical awareness of the Brahman, the eternal, goes beyond a creation-oriented concern. Here are two references from Campbell's *The Power of Myth*.

> And the cherubim at the gate – who are they? At the Buddhist shrines you'll see one has his mouth open, the other has his mouth closed – fear and desire, a pair of opposites. If you're approaching a garden like that, and those two figures there are real to you and threaten you, if you have fear for your life, you are still outside the garden. But if you are no longer attached to your ego existence, but see the ego existence as a function of a larger, eternal totality and you favor the larger against the smaller, then you won't be afraid of those two figures, and you will go through. We're kept out of the Garden by our own fear and desire in relation to what we think to be the goods of our life.
>
> MOYERS: Have all men at all times felt some sense of exclusion from an ultimate reality, from bliss, from delight, from perfection, from God?
>
> CAMPBELL: Yes, but then you have moments of ecstasy. The difference between everyday life and living in those moments of ecstasy is the difference between being outside and inside the Garden. You go past your fear and desire, past the pair of opposites.
>
> MOYERS: Into harmony?
>
> CAMPBELL: Into transcendence. This is an essential experience of any mystical realization. You die to your flesh and are born into your spirit. You identify yourself with the consciousness of life of which your body is but the vehicle. You die to the vehicle and become identified in your consciousness with that of which the vehicle is the carrier. This is the God. (107)

The other reference is from the chapter, "Masks of Eternity."

MOYERS: How does one have a profound experience?

CAMPBELL: By having a profound sense of the mystery.

MOYERS: But if God is the god we have only imagined, how can we stand in awe of our creation?

CAMPBELL: How can we be terrified by a dream? You have to break past your image of God to get through to the connoted illumination. The psychologist Jung has a relevant saying: "Religion is a defense against the experience of God."

The mystery has been reduced to a set of concepts and ideas, and emphasizing these concepts and ideas can short-circuit the transcendent, connoted experience. An intense experience of the mystery is what one has to regard as the ultimate religious experience.

MOYERS: There are many Christians who believe that, to find out who Jesus is, you have to go past the Christian faith, past the Christian doctrine, past the Christian Church –

CAMPBELL: You have to go past the imagined image of Jesus. Such image of one's god becomes a final obstruction, one's ultimate barrier...(209)

These references to Campbell illustrate why the Gnostic writings put down the Creator-God in the Genesis story. Another point of interest in Dart's book is the portrayal of the serpent as being "wise." This is explained according to two Gnostic writings: "The Nature of the Archons," and "On the Origin of the World." The first one starts as follows:

Above, in the infinite aeons, is Imperishability. Sophia, she who is called Pistis, wanted to make a work by herself, without her partner. And her work became the images of heaven. There is a curtain between those above and the aeons which are beneath. (Dart, 68)

In "The Origin of the World" we read:

Sophia sent Zoe, her daughter, who is called "Eve," as an instructor in order that she might rise up Adam, in whom there is no psyche [soul] so that those whom he would beget might become vessels of light. When Eve saw her companion-likeness cast down she pitied him, and she said, "Adam, live! Rise up upon the earth!"

Immediately her words became a work for when Adam rose up, immediately he opened his eyes. When he saw her, he said, "You will be called 'mother of the living' because you are the one who gave life to me." (70)

In "The Nature of the Archons," Sophia enters the serpent, who then acquires the name Instructor. "On the Origin of the World" holds that Sophia created the Instructor to teach Adam and Eve the truth about their origins. In the serpent one hears the voice of Sophia or wisdom.

Then the one who is wiser than all of them, one who was called "the wild beast," came. And when he saw the likeness of their mother, Eve, he said to her: "What is it that god said to you? – "Do not eat from the tree of knowledge?" She said: "He said not only 'Do not eat from it' but 'Do not touch it, lest you die.'"

He said to her, "Don't be afraid. You will surely not [die], for [he knows] that when you eat from it your mind will be sobered and you will become like the gods, knowing the distinctions which exist between the human evil and the good. For he said this to you, being jealous lest you eat from it." Then Eve was confident of the words of the instructor, and she peered into the tree...(71)

Dart explains that after the eating of the fruit, the archons questioned Adam and Eve and learned what the serpent had done. They tried to approach the serpent-Instructor, but he blinded their eyes. Then the archons cursed Eve and later Adam and everything that had been created.

It is obvious that the patriarchal orthodox tradition has discriminated against women in significant ways. The Gnostic writings try to counteract this sick fear of the feminine. The two sources mentioned above report stories of Eve being raped by the descendants of darkness but the wisdom of Eve superseded the evil of this act. In another story the wife of Noah, Norea, is refused entrance into the Ark by Noah. Dart writes:

Norea cries for help from the highest God, and a golden angel clothed in snowy white descends from heaven, causing the archons to withdraw.

"Who are you?" asked Norea.

"It is I who am Eleleth, Sagacity, the Great Angel who stands in the presence of the Holy Spirit. I have been sent to speak with you and save you from the grasp of the Lawless.

And I shall teach you about your Root," said the angel. (75)

Studies by George MacRae suggests that the Gnostic Sophia is very much influenced by the Jewish Wisdom as found in the Old Testament's Proverbs.

The Lord begot me, the firstborn of his ways, the forerunner of his prodigies of long ago, from of old I was poured forth, at the first, before the earth.

When there were no depths I was brought forth, when there were no fountains or springs of water; before the mountains were settled into place, before the hills, I was brought forth. (8:22-25)

The Gnostic Sophia is "a breath of the power of God, who breathes life into a shapeless mass to form Ialdabaoth (the Supreme Lord) and she breathes life into Adam. (Dart, 78) This is quite different from the male chauvinism of the orthodox biblical tradition. Still one more character is to be introduced to become aware of the main symbolic or mythical figures in the Gnostic writings. It is the son of Adam, Seth. In his *Patterns in Comparative Religion*, Mircea Eliade narrates the version which he considered the most widely accepted:

> When Adam had lived for 932 years in the Hebron valley, he was struck down with a fatal illness and sent his son Seth to ask the angel who stood guard at the gate of Paradise for the oil of mercy. Seth follows the tracks of Adam and Eve's footsteps, where the grass has never grown and, coming to Paradise, he imparts Adam's wish to the archangel. The archangel advises him to look three times to Paradise. The first time Seth sees the water from which four rivers flow, and a dried-up tree above it. The second time, a serpent coils itself round the trunk. The third time he looks, he sees the tree rise up to heaven; at its top is a newborn child (the Tree of Life stood at the centre of the universe and it passed as an axis through the three cosmic spheres). The angel tells Seth the meaning of what he has seen, and announces to him that a Redeemer is to come. At the same time he gives him three seeds from the fruit of the fatal tree of which his parents ate, and tells him to place them upon Adam's tongue; he says that Adam will die in three days. When Adam hears Seth's story he laughs (sign of Gnostic wisdom) for the first time since being banished from Paradise, for he realizes that mankind will be saved. When he dies, the three seeds Seth has placed on his tongue rise up in the valley of Hebron, three trees growing with a single span till the time of Moses. And he, knowing their divine origin, transplants them to Mount Tabor or Horeb (the "center of the world").
>
> The trees remain there for a thousand years till the day David gets an order from God to take them to Jerusalem (which is also a "centre"). After a great many further episodes (the Queen of Sheba refusing to place her foot on their wood, etc.), the three trees become one tree, and the cross of the Redeemer is made of it. The blood of Christ, crucified at the centre of the Earth, on the very spot where Adam was created and buried, falls upon "the skull of Adam", and thus, redeeming him from his sin, baptizes the father of mankind. (293)

Dart's book, *The Laughing Savior*, receives focus in Chapter Sixteen, "The Laughing Jesus." In the Gnostic writings, Jesus, when nailed on the cross, does not really suffer pain. Only the body knows pain. Jesus laughs about those who cling to his dead body, which is not the life-giving savior, the revealer of the true *gnosis*. In the "Second Treatise of the Great Seth" the speaker is presumably Jesus Christ:

> It was not I whom they struck with the reed. It was another who lifted the cross onto his shoulders – Simon. It was another on whose head they placed the thorny crown. But I was up above, rejoicing over all the wealth of the archons and the offspring of the error of their empty glory. And I was laughing at their ignorance. (Dart, 108)

These references to the Gnostic writings will make Campbell's interpretation of Jesus and his Father more understandable. A selection of some significant statements about Jesus expresses Campbell's delight in this heroic messiah.

In *The Power of Myth* references to Jesus and his Father include the following:

> The Christ story involves a sublimation of what originally was a very solid vegetal image. Jesus is on Holy Rood, the tree, and he is himself the fruit of the tree. Jesus is the fruit of eternal life, which was on the second forbidden tree in the Garden of Eden. When man ate of the fruit of the first tree of knowledge of good and evil, he was expelled from the Garden. The Garden is the place of unity, of nonduality of male and female, good and evil, God and human beings. You eat the duality, and you are on the way out. The tree of coming back to the Garden is the tree of immortal life, where you know that I and the father are one. (107)

> CAMPBELL: I live with these myths, and they tell me this all the time. This is the problem that can be metaphorically understood as identifying with the Christ in you. The Christ in you doesn't die. The Christ in you survives death and resurrects...(39)
> There is an equivalent scene described in the apocryphal Christian Acts of John, immediately before Jesus goes to be crucified. This is one of the most moving passages in Christian literature. In the Matthew, Mark, Luke and John gospels, it is simply mentioned that, at the conclusion of the celebration of the Last Supper, Jesus and his disciples sang a hymn before he went forth. But in the Acts of John, we have a word-for-word account of the whole singing of the hymn. Just before going out into the garden at the end of the Last Supper, Jesus says to the company, "Let us dance!" And they all hold hands in a circle, and as they circle around him, Jesus sings, "Glory be to thee, Father!" To which the circle company responds, "Amen."
> "Glory be to thee, Word!"
> And again, "Amen."

"I would be born and I would bear!"

"Amen."

"I would eat and I would be eaten!"

"Amen."

"Thou that dancest, see what I do, for thine is the passion of the manhood, which I am about to suffer!"

"Amen."

"I would flee and I would stay!"

"Amen."

"I would be united and I would unite!"

"Amen."

"A door am I to thee that knocketh at me...A way am I to thee, a wayfarer." And when the dance is ended, he walks out of the garden to be taken and crucified.

When you go to your death that was, as a god, in the knowledge of the myth, you are going to your eternal life. So what is there in that to be sad about? Let us make it magnificent – as it is. Let us celebrate it. (109)

Voluntary participation in the world is very different from just getting born into it. That's exactly the theme of Paul's statement about Christ in his Epistle to the Philippians: that Jesus "did not think Godhood something to be held to but took the form of a servant here on earth, even to death on the cross." That's a voluntary participation in the fragmentation of life.

MOYERS: So you would agree with Abelard in the twelfth century, who said that Jesus' death on the cross was not as ransom paid, or as a penalty applied, but that it was an act of atonement, at-one-ment, with the race.

CAMPBELL: That is the most sophisticated interpretation of why Christ had to be crucified, or why he elected to be crucified. An earlier one was that the sin in the Garden of Eden had committed mankind to the Devil, and God had to redeem man from the pawnbroker, the Devil. So he offered his own son, Jesus, as the redemption. Pope Gregory gave this interpretation of Jesus as the bait that hooked the Devil. That's the redemption idea. In another version, God was so offended by the act of impudence in the Garden that he became wrathful and threw man out of his field of mercy, and then the only thing that could atone man with God was a sacrifice that would be as great in its importance as the sin had been. No mere man could make such a sacrifice so the son of God himself became man in order to pay the debt.

But Abelard's idea was that Christ came to be crucified to evoke in man's heart the sentiment of compassion for the suffering of life, and to remove man's mind from blind commitment to the goods of this world. It is in compassion with Christ that we turn to Christ, and the injured one becomes our Savior. (112)

CAMPBELL: Yes, the idea of the Goddess is related to the fact that you're born from your mother, and your father may be unknown to you, or the father may have died. Frequently, in the epics, when the hero is born, his father has died, or his father is in some other place, and then the hero has to go in quest for his father.

In the story of the incarnation of Jesus, the father of Jesus was the father in heaven, at least in terms of the symbology. When Jesus goes to the cross, he is on the way to the father, leaving the mother behind. And the cross, which is symbolic of the earth, is the mother symbol. So on the cross, Jesus leaves his body on the mother, from which he has acquired his body, and he goes to the father, who is the ultimate transcendent mystery source. (166)

MOYERS: In *Star Wars*, Luke Skywalker says to his companions, "I wish I had known my father." There's something powerful in the image of the father quest. But why not mother quest?

CAMPBELL: Well, the mother's right there. You're born from your mother, and she's the one who nurses you and instructs you and brings you up to the age when you must find your father.

Now, the finding of the father has to do with finding your own character and destiny. There's a notion that the character is inherited from the father, and the body and very often the mind from the mother. But it's your character that is the mystery, and your character is your destiny. So it is the discovery of your destiny that is symbolized by the father quest.

MOYERS: So when you find your father, you find yourself?

CAMPBELL: We have the word in English, "at-one-ment" with the father. You remember the story of Jesus lost in Jerusalem when he's a little boy about twelve years old. His parents hunt for him, and when they find him in the temple, in conversation with the doctors of the law, they ask, "Why did you abandon us this way? Why did you give us this fear and anxiety?" And he says, "Didn't you know that I had to be about my father's business?" He's twelve years old—that's the age of the adolescence initiations, finding who you are. (166)

CAMPBELL: It happens when you awaken at the level of the heart to compassion, compassion, shared suffering: experienced participation in the suffering of another person. That's the beginning of humanity. And the meditations of religion properly are on that level, the heart level.

MOYERS: You say that's the beginning of humanity. But in these stories, that's the moment when gods are born. The virgin birth—it's a god who emerges.

CAMPBELL: And do you know who that god is? It's you. All of these symbols in mythology refer to you. You can get stuck out *there*, and you think it's all out *there*. So you're thinking about Jesus with all the sentiments relevant to how he suffered – out there. But that suffering is what ought to be going on in you. Have you been spiritually reborn? Have you died to your animal nature and come to life as a human incarnation of compassion?

MOYERS: Why is it significant that this is of a virgin?

CAMPBELL: The begetter is of the spirit. This is a spiritual birth. The virgin conceived of the word through the ear. (174)

MOYERS: Of course, the heart of the Christian faith is that God was in Christ, that these elemental forces you're talking about embodied themselves in a human being who reconciled mankind to God.

CAMPBELL: Yes, and the basic Gnostic and Buddhist idea is that that is true of you and me as well. Jesus was a historical person who realized in himself that he and what he called the Father were one, and he lived out of that knowledge of the Christhood of his nature.

    I remember, I was once giving a lecture in which I spoke about living out of the sense of the Christ in you, and a priest in the audience (as I was later told) turned to the woman beside him and whispered, "That's blasphemy."

MOYERS: What did you mean by Christ in you?

CAMPBELL: What I meant was that you must live not in terms of your own ego system, your own desires, but in terms of what you might call the sense of mankind – the Christ – in you. There is a Hindu saying, "None but a god can worship a god." You have to identify yourself in some measure with whatever spiritual principle your god represents to you in order to worship him properly and live according to his word. (210-211)

MOYERS: What do you think about the Savior Jesus?

CAMPBELL: We just don't know very much about Jesus. All we know are four contradictory texts that purport to tell us what he said and did.

MOYERS: Written many years after he lived.

CAMPBELL: Yes, but in spite of this, I think we may know approximately what Jesus said. I think the sayings of Jesus are probably pretty close to the originals. The main teaching of Christ, for example, is Love your enemies.

MOYERS: How do you love your enemy without condoning what the enemy does, without accepting his aggression?

CAMPBELL: I'll tell you how to do that: do not pluck the mote from your enemy's eyes, but pluck the beam from your own. No one is in a position to disqualify his enemy's way of life.

MOYERS: Do you think Jesus today would be a Christian?

CAMPBELL: Not the kind of Christian we know. Perhaps some of the monks and nuns who are really in touch with high spiritual mysteries would be of the sort Jesus was. (211)

CAMPBELL: ...There is an important passage in the recently discovered Gnostic Gospel According to St. Thomas: "'When will the kingdom come?' Christ's disciples ask." In Mark 13, I think it is, we read that the end of the world is about to come. That is to say, a mythological image – that of the end of the world – is there taken as a predicting an actual, physical, historical fact to be. But in Thomas' version, Jesus replies: "The kingdom of the Father will not come by expectation. The kingdom of the Father is spread upon the earth and men do not see it" so I look at you now in that sense, and the radiance of the presence of the divine is known to me through you.

MOYERS: Through me?

CAMPBELL: You, sure. When Jesus says, "He who drinks from my mouth will become as I am and I shall be he," he's talking from the point of view of that being of beings, which we call the Christ, who is the being of all of us. Anyone who lives in relation to that is as Christ. Anyone who brings into his life the message of the Word is equivalent to Jesus, that's the sense of that.

MOYERS: So that's what you mean when you say, "I am radiating God to you."

CAMPBELL: You are, yes. (213)

MOYERS: So, when a scripture talks about man being made in God's image, it's talking about certain qualities that every human being possesses, no matter what that person's religion or culture or geography or heritage?

CAMPBELL: God would be the ultimate elementary idea of man.

MOYERS: The primal need.

CAMPBELL: And we are all made in the image of God. That is the ultimate archetype of man. (218)

There is no way that Campbell's statements can be paraphrased. They have to be kept within the actual verbalization. Otherwise the interpretative wording will take away the spontaneity and the actual presence of the life which is contained in his words.

The main purpose of this chapter is to place Campbell's statements about Jesus and his Father within the context which he himself indicates: in sum, the Jungian analytic psychology and its awareness of archetypes and the collective unconscious, the Hindu tradition, the awareness of the wisdom in the Ancient Near East (Egypt, Babylon, and the Hebrew tradition), the wisdom of structuralism in cultural anthropology, which makes one aware of the common denominators in all cultural myths, and the difference between the Gnostic writings and the orthodox canonical books of the Old and the New Testament. Where does that leave Joseph Campbell in his affirmation of Jesus and his Father?

Campbell's affirmation of Jesus and the Father is in his acceptance and his personalized interpretation of the metaphor, Jesus, and the metaphor, Jesus' Father. Much of his integration of the wisdom and spiritual life within these metaphors is according to the Gnostic tradition. His stories and references to the Gospel of Thomas and the apocryphal Acts of John reveal a personal delight. Nevertheless, Campbell's background is so voluminous and so complex that it would be incorrect to simply call him a Gnostic. For him the story is not real but the life of the story is. As such Campbell cannot be categorized within the story of the Gnostic tradition, because the life of the story is greater than its form.

Because Campbell's book, *The Power of Myth*, devotes a separate chapter (VI, "The Gift of the Goddess") to the feminine aspect of the divine, it is proper to enlarge and broaden the metaphor, "the Father of Jesus," with the metaphor, "Our Mother." This will be the next part of this journey.

Chapter Six

Our Mother Who Art the Universe

Joseph Campbell's respect for, and celebration of, the feminine and womanhood is very well stated in the title of Chapter VI, "The Gift of the Goddess." He is not just saying the things one finds in political slogans such as "Women are equal to men." or "Equal pay for equal work." Campbell is not into equal rights issues or related social problems. He is, again, the person who receives his wisdom and personal convictions from the myths which speak to the heart. Campbell's heart responds beautifully in his great delight, when he interprets the cultural history with the focus on the Goddess. Here is the opening of Chapter VI:

> MOYERS: The Lord's Prayer begins, "Our Father which art in Heaven..." Could it have begun "Our Mother"?

> CAMPBELL: This is a symbolic image. All of the references of religious and mythological images are to planes of consciousness, or fields of experience that are potential in human spirit. And these images evoke attitudes and experiences that are appropriate to a meditation of the mystery of the source of your own being.
> There have been systems of religion where the mother is the prime parent, the source. The mother is really a more immediate parent than the father because one is born from the mother, and the first experience of an infant is the mother. I have frequently thought that mythology is a sublimation of the mother image. We talk of Mother Earth. And in Egypt you have the Mother Heavens, the Goddess Nut, who is present as the whole heavenly sphere.

> MOYERS: I was seized in Egypt upon first seeing the figure of Nut in the ceiling of one of those temples. (156)

Staying with the theme, "Our Mother," the discussion brings out Campbell's dislike for the warrior god of the Hebrews, Yahweh:

MOYERS: What would it have meant to us if somewhere along the way we had begun to pray to "Our Mother" instead of "Our Father"? What psychological difference would it have made?

CAMPBELL: It certainly has made a psychological difference in the character of our culture. For example, the basic birth of Western civilization occurred in the great river valleys – the Nile, the Tigris-Euphrates, the Indus, and later the Ganges. That was the world of the Goddess. The name of the river Ganges (Gangä) is the name of a goddess, for example.

And then there came the invasions. Now, these started seriously in the fourth millennium B. C. and became more and more devastating. They came in from the north and from the south and wiped out cities overnight. Just read the story in the Book of Genesis of the part played by Jacob's tribe in the fall of the city of Sechem. Overnight, the city is wiped out by these herding people who have suddenly appeared. The Semite invaders were herders of goats and sheep, the Indo-Europeans of cattle. Both were formerly hunters, and so the cultures are essentially animal-oriented. When you have hunters, you have killers. And when you have herders, you have killers, because they're always in movement, nomadic, coming into conflicts with other people and conquering the areas into which they move. And these invasions bring in warrior gods, thunderbolt hurlers, like Zeus, or Yahweh.

MOYERS: The sword and death instead of the phallus and fertility?

CAMPBELL: That's right, and they are equated.

MOYERS: There's a story you tell about the overthrow of the mother goddess Tiamat.

CAMPBELL: I guess that could be taken as the key archetypal event here.

MOYERS: You called it a critical moment in history.

CAMPBELL: Yes. The Semitic people were invading the world of the Mother Goddess system, and so the male-oriented mythologies became dominant, and the Mother Goddess becomes, well – sort of Grandmother Goddess, way, way back.

It was in the time of the city Babylon. And each of these early cities had its own protective god or goddess. The characteristic of an imperialistic people is to try to have its own local god dubbed big boy of the universe, you see. No other divinity counts. And the way to bring this about is by annihilating the god or goddess who was there before....(169-179)

CAMPBELL: Well, the interest turned to the interest specifically of the male governors of the city Babylon.

MOYERS: So the matriarchal society began to give way to a –

CAMPBELL: Oh, by that time – 1750 B. C. or so – it was finished. [King Hammurabi.]

In ch. II, "The Journey Inward," we find related insights. There Campbell refers to a historical explanation of the snake in Genesis. It is based on the invasion of the Hebrew into Canaan. They overpowered the inhabitants. The principal divinity of the people in Canaan was a goddess who was associated with the serpent, which is a symbol of the mystery of life. The Hebrew invaders were directed and guided by a male god. The story of the serpent in the tree, inviting Eve to eat from the apple, and Yahweh's rejection of her, indicated the male god mentality. (48)

MOYERS: It does seem that this story has done women a great disservice by casting Eve as responsible for the Fall. Why are women the ones held responsible for the downfall?

CAMPBELL: They represent life. Man doesn't enter life except by woman, and so it is woman who brings us into the world of pairs of opposites and sufferings. (48)

In ch. I, "Myth and the Modern World," Campbell described Yahweh in similar negative terms:

CAMPBELL: Yes, you see, this is a problem you get in the book of Kings and in Samuel. The various Hebrew kings were sacrificing on the mountaintops. And they did wrong in the sight of Yahweh. The Yahweh cult was a specific movement in the Hebrew community, which finally won. This was a pushing through of a certain temple-bound god against the nature cult, which was celebrated all over the place.

And this imperialistic thrust of a certain in-group is continued in the West. But it has to open up to the nature of things now. If it can open, all the possibilities are there. (21)

A very delightful and insightful criticism of the Yahweh mentality is stated in ch. II, "The Journey Inward." The discussion is about the word "God."

CAMPBELL:...Now you can personify God in many ways. Is there one god? Are there many gods? Those are merely categories of thought. What you are talking and trying to thing about *transcends* all that.

One problem with Yahweh, as they used to say in the old Christian Gnostic texts, is that he forgot he was a metaphor. He thought he was a fact. And when he said, "I am

God," a voice was heard to say, "You are mistaken, Samael."
"Samael" Means "blind": blind to the infinite Light of which he
is a local historical manifestation. This is known as the
blasphemy of Jehovah – he thought he was God. (62)

Campbell is a friend of myths which deal with the fullness of life as
found in nature. He compares two different orders of mythology. The one
that relates the person to the natural world, and the one that tries to box
people into a particular society. The socially-oriented systems are usually
nomadic, and group-centered. The nature-oriented order relates to earth-
cultivating people. Campbell regards the biblical tradition as "a socially
oriented mythology" (23).

When we want to compare Campbell's insights in the context of very
learned and scholarly interpreters, then Mircea Eliade's *Patterns in
Comparative Religion* provides such an opportunity. Chapter II, "The Sky and
the Sky Gods," intends to describe a certain development. First, the sky is
experienced as a sacred place (a place where our imagination senses the
transcendent, the immensity of a great power). For certain cultures, this
divinity within the realm of the sky is so far removed from our human daily
life that it was difficult to relate to a sky god or goddess. Such a divinity was
known but not worshipped directly ("Deus Otiosus"). Intermediate gods and
goddesses were imagined which would be relevant to the immediate
environment. The motif of a primordial pair – Sky (male) and Earth
(female) – became fairly common. (51) With the recognition that life
emerged from such a primordial mating of the male and female aspect, other
goddesses and gods were begging for their place in the pantheon insofar as
they were serving definite human concerns, e.g., the fertility of the land and
the management of wealth conducive to good crops and rich harvests.

The sky god is somehow the one who maintains the cosmic order.
Other gods are needed to promote historical futures for certain groups of
people. In the Babylonian Genesis that would be Marduk. There is a need
for gods and goddesses who are powerful and apply magic to have things
their way. Some of those magical gods live in the sky as thunder gods. They
are called "fecundators." (86) They were imagined in the form of a bull.
Although, sometimes these divine powers of fertility were goddesses, soon
they were replaced by a male god. (That is perhaps the case of the
replacement of El by Ba'al in the Phoenician pantheon. (90))

The thunder gods symbolize male fertility (which is different from the rainy sky which alludes to the Greek Goddess). Most of the thunder gods found their mates with whom they procreated. Yahweh, however, is regarded as one of the very few sky gods who maintained their independence. They indicate the laws of nature and the rules of social behavior.

> The "evolution" of the supreme God of the Hebrews is to be found on a plane that is in some parallel. Yahweh's personality and religious history are far too complex to be summed up in a few lines. Let me say, however, that his celestial and atmospheric hierophanies very early became the centre of those religious experiences which made later revelations possible. Yahweh displayed his power by means of storms; thunder is his voice and lighting is called Yahweh's "fire", or his "arrows". The Lord of Israel declares his presence: "...thunders began to be heard and lightning to flash, and a very thick cloud to cover the mount" (Exod. 19:16) while he was transmitting the Law to Moses. "And all Mount Sinai was on a smoke" because the lord was come down upon it in fire." (19:18) Deborah recalled with holy dread how at the Lord's footstep "the earth trembled and the heavens dropped water." (Judges 5:4) Yahweh warns Elias of his approach by "a great and strong wind...overthrowing the mountains and breaking the rocks in pieces: the Lord is not the wind. (3 Kings 19:11-12)...The fire of the Lord descends on the holocausts of Elias (3 Kings 18:38)...The burning bush in the story of Moses, and the pillar of fire and the cloud [which] leads the Israelites through the desert are epiphanies of Yahweh. And Yahweh's covenant with the descendants of Noe after his escape from the Flood is expressed by a rainbow: "I will set my bow in the clouds, and it shall be the sign of a covenant between me, and between the earth". (Gen. 9:13)
>
> These hierophanies of sky and weather, unlike those of other storm gods, manifest above all the "power" of Yahweh. "God is high in his strength: and none is like him among the lawgivers." (Job 36:22) (94-95)

In these words Eliade backs up Campbell's interpretations. However, Eliade is aware of the complexity, e.g., the reference is made to that group of the Hebrew traditions which is characterized by the Yahweh cult They pushed the other traditions aside. Mention should be made of El, the sky-god in the Canaanite pantheon. This El is not a divinity operating by power and magic. It is not a divine power interested in serving a particular city, tribe, or people. El is the divine source who brings unity within a multitude of private interests. El lords in the sky as the one who conserves the unity of the totality. Although El is known as the Father of the gods and the goddesses, nevertheless, the psychological character is one of the gatherer, whose primary concern is to keep everything within the boundaries of the cosmological order, the universe. How the Yahweh cult emerged from the El religion can be indicated by a reference to the development of Ba'al.

Recent studies have researched the status of El in the Canaanite pantheon: e.g., the "Harvard Semitic Monographs," Conrad E. L'Heureux *Rank among the Canaanite Gods* and E. Theodore Mullen, *The Divine Council in Canaanite and Early Hebrew Literature.* El is described as the supreme god, and all other gods are to serve him, and they are members of El's assembly. Ba'al is more an independent god who fights to conquer the cosmic forces. He is not emerging as the supreme god like El. Yahweh too is Lord almighty by his power and decisiveness to let every one know that he is in charge. El is not so much the conqueror as the one who unites by his very nature of a supreme authority.

The difference between Ba'al and Yahweh is that Ba'al will recognize the supremacy of El. Yahweh is portrayed as the one who is the same as El in terms of lordship, all sovereign power. In the Yahweh cult there is no place for anyone else but Yahweh. It is totally exclusive of other gods. While in the Ba'al tradition one remains aware of other gods, especially El.

For the sake of recognizing the complexity of the Old Testament, one should understand that there are many traditions in the first five books of the Bible, the Pentateuch. Each tradition portrays God in its own way. There is the J (Jahwist) tradition, the E (Elohist) tradition, the P (Priestly) tradition, and a combination of E and P. In W. Brueggeman's "David and His Theologian," he argues that the author of the J tradition must have understood who God was in the eyes and heart of David. Although still a little boy, David was elected by God to become king. Although Goliath was a giant and David only a boy, God guided the hand of David in shooting the rock at Goliath's head, so this enemy could be eliminated. David experienced God's mercy whenever he had committed sin. David sang songs (Psalms) about the greatness of God and his special concern for him and his people. This God showed consideration for Adam and Eve after they sinned and deserved to die. He promised a redeemer in the future to come. Thus

God is experienced as the merciful one. Obviously, the reading of the psalms makes one aware that here is a very deep personalized relationship between the biblical person and the biblical God. In general Campbell's description of Yahweh is valid also. And the jealousy of the warrior god, Yahweh, permeates the Old Testament in many ways. Such a masculine god is not conducive to an enjoyment of the divine as promoted by Campbell. He is far more delightful about the gift of the goddess.

> MOYERS: So it would be natural for people trying to explain the wonders of the universe to look for the female figure as the explanation of what they see in their own lives.

> CAMPBELL: Not only that, but when you move to a philosophical point of view, as in the Goddess religions of India – where the Goddess symbology is dominant to this day – the female represents *maya*. The female represents what in Kantian terminology we call the form of *sensibility*. She is time and space itself, and the mystery beyond her is beyond all pairs of opposites. So it isn't male and it isn't female. It neither is nor is not. But everything is within her, so that the gods are her children. Everything you can think of, everything you can see, is a production of the Goddess. (167)

Or

> We have found hundreds of early European Neolithic figurines of the Goddess, but hardly anything there of the male figure at all. The bull and certain other animals, such as the boar and the goat, may appear as symbolic of the male power, but the Goddess was the only visualized divinity at that time.
> And when you have a Goddess as creator, it's her own body that is the universe. She is identical with the universe. That's the sense of that Goddess Nut figure you saw in the Egyptian temple. She is the whole sphere of the life enclosing heavens. (167)

Discussion

From the above one easily concludes that the Father symbol remains limited and particular in the imagination of the myths. Father is the prototype of the masculine, the begetter, he who sows the seed, the one who stirs the waters. Campbell is not that happy with such father gods. He presents the mother goddess as a more encompassing, caring divinity, who is truly and totally dedicated to fertility, procreation, nursing and the nourishment of life in its multitude of forms. In the Greek mythology there is a good perception of the feminine versus the masculine as primordial sources of creation and procreation.

In the history of the Greek culture there have been many different traditions which tell about the births of the gods (theogonies). The one selected here is Hesiod's, which dates as early as 700 years B. C. E. A tension between primordial forces and the creative drift is expressed at the outset of the myth, which holds that in the beginning there was Chaos (vast and dark space) and Gaea (the fertile earth). Chaos gave birth to the night, while Gaea born Uranus, the sky. Out of the union between Gaea and Uranus emerged the first race, the Titans. Among them were Oceanus, Iapetus, Cronus, and Rhea. Uranus could not cope with having an offspring. As soon as Gaea gave birth, he locked the newborn in the underworld. Gaea was saddened and became angry. She developed a need for vengeance. Of her children, only the youngest, Cronus, was willing to help his mother carry out a plan. When it was evening Cronus hid himself in his parent's sleeping quarters. During the night, when Uranus was fast asleep, Cronus emerged and castrated his father, who became powerless. From that time on, Cronus was the powerful ruler among the gods.

It may be good to identify some of the underlying meanings which will be carried through most of the basic Greek myths. There is the idea that the primordial forces tend to obstruct the development of their offspring. Life and future opportunities are open only for those who assert themselves by outsmarting the primeval powers. If Uranus is the dimension of the sky, then nothing is of any great significance in the context of such an immense spacious vastness. The highest tower ever built by humans, the highest mountain ever climbed, look ridiculously small in the presence and height of the sky. However, the myth suggests that by means of time (Cronus), things may amount to something important. This interpretation does not claim to be authoritative, but it is authentic and it surely expresses the basic mentality of the Greek myths. The same theme occurs in the next episode of the theogony.

Cronus liberated his brothers and sisters, and under his government creation continued to be productive. Night gave birth to Doom (Mores) and to Death (Thanatos). Also, the Fates came into existence. They gave each mortal being his or her share of good and evil. Hesiod tells that under the dynasty of Cronus (time), Old Age, Forgetfulness, Hunger and Disease, Murder, Battles, Lies and Injustice emerged.

Cronus, in his primordial power, did not welcome the idea that someday he would be replaced by one of his offspring. Thus, he swallowed each of the children as soon as it was born. His wife, Rhea, became desperate and went to her parents for help. Uranus and Gaea provided a hiding place where Rhea gave birth to a new son, Zeus. He was saved by Uranus and Gaea, while Rhea wrapped a stone in some clothing and presented it to Cronus as the newborn child. Cronus swallowed it without any suspicion. As Zeus grew up under the care of Uranus and Gaea, he became strong and vigorous. He decided on a plan to punish his father. Cronus was thus driven from the sky and thrown into the depth of the world. He would have power only in the underworld. The Greek myth here implies that it is possible for a cunning and enterprising spirit, Zeus, to become victorious over the primordial forces of the firmament, and even of time.

The creation myth presents two characteristic insights:

a)   the female principle is life-nourishing in procreation, and

b)   in the end, Zeus is praised as the cunning, victorious Lord of the pantheon.

Campbell would prefer Gaea and Rhea over Uranus and Cronus. The myth itself is aware of the complexity of life, the paradox and the political struggles between the goddesses and the gods. Their cunning is a portrayal of the facts of life. The Greek mentality is well aware that cunning, scheming, maneuvering, strategic powerplays are needed in life to establish a place for oneself. One has to rise to the occasion; one has to assert oneself in order to reach some degree of quality life.

Nevertheless, a simple juxtaposition of the male god and the female goddess indicates that the latter is motivated by a deep appreciation for the life sustaining energy, which is in her and emanates from her. Previously in our journey and comparison was made between Campbell and Bloch. Campbell identified with the eternal, infinity, and the awareness of the universal. Bloch promoted the historical fulfillment within space and time, a need for creative action. In the context of discussing "The Gift of the

Goddess," Campbell too affirms the one who is creative, procreative, caring and life nourishing. This motherly love of fertility and the embracing of the new life with true dedication may be an additional aspect of Campbell's awareness of the divine. In the Father of Jesus he emphasizes the eternity within a person's soul as the presence of the Father in every one. In the Mother goddess he affirms the great love for life in the name of the divine.

For Campbell, Father and Mother are complementary metaphors, which stand for a togetherness of two primordial mutually affirming principles. The Father of Jesus is within the Mother of Jesus, and the Mother of Jesus is within the Father of Jesus. Those two are one. Campbell discusses the oneness of the male and female in Chapter VIII, "Tales of Love and Marriage."

> CAMPBELL: ...But marriage is marriage, you know. Marriage is not a love affair. A love affair is a totally different thing. A marriage is a commitment to that which you are. The person is literally your other half. And you and the other are one....(200)

> MOYERS: The Puritans called marriage "the little church within the Church." In marriage, everyday you love, and everyday you forgive. It is an ongoing sacrament – love and forgiveness.

> CAMPBELL: Well, the real word, I think, is "ordeal," in its proper sense. That is the submission of the individual to something superior to itself. The real life of marriage or of a true love affair is in the relationship, which is where you are too. You understand what I mean?

> MOYERS: No, I'm not clear on that.

> CAMPBELL: Like the yin/yang symbol, you see. Here I am, and here she is, and here we are. Now when I have to make a sacrifice, I'm not sacrificing to her, I'm sacrificing to the relationship. Resentment against the other one is wrongly placed. Life is in the relationship, that's where your life now is...

> MOYERS: In the sacred marriage, what God has joined together is one and cannot be sundered by man.

> CAMPBELL: It was one to begin with, and the marriage restates that unity symbolically.

> MOYERS: It was one to begin with?

> CAMPBELL: Marriage is the symbolic recognition of our identity – two aspects of the same being. (201)

Although there is one being, still there are two different aspects. It is not good to speak about the Father of Jesus as separate from the Mother of Jesus. The Father is an expression of the Mother. These are two different metaphors which in the ultimate depth of their meaning are united by the word "parent."

The world of myths celebrates the feminine in a very creative and artistic fashion. It demonstrates an awareness of a wide variety of images; e.g., Paul Friedrich in his book *The Meaning of Aphrodite* demonstrates the richness of mythological characters. Moreover, he holds that "myth is basically about emotion" (7). These emotions are expressed through the vivid imagery in the texts themselves. As such these imageries help us in mirroring ourselves in the presence of a wealth of psychological life. Regarding Aphrodite, he respectfully includes an evaluation by George Calhoun:

> Aphrodite for example, was clothed in infinite variety; she was one among the supreme rulers of the universe, arbiters of human destiny, defenders of moral values; she was also a figure in ancient, grotesque myths and naive tales, and at the same time one of the principle actors in the drama at Troy; she was sexual passion and also spiritual love, the deity of procreation and the personification of the impulses into which love and passion are translated; she was the vision of bright effulgence moving in the heavens, a gracious presence instinct with loveliness; she was the music that breathes....(220)

Because the feminine is so complex, the myths serve more than one character to help us understand this basic aspect of life. For example, the aspect of motherly love and care became personified in Demeter-Persephone. Consequently, in developing the characters somewhat separately, Aphrodite can be understood more in one way, leaving place for the mother-aspect for Demeter. Thus the following diagram helps us appreciate the complexity and creativity of the goddesses as representatives of the feminine and womanhood within our own lives. Each item is not just stated but affirmed as a way of life within the context of the other ways of life.

APHRODITE	DEMETER-PERSEPHONE
Solar, astral, insular	Chthonic
Water, navigation	Drought, desert
Never virgin	Virgin in spirit; chaste
Seduces men in the mountains	Gets raped by gods in meadow
Passionate lover	Anxious and hostile about sex
Arts of love (linking nature and culture)	Arts of agriculture (linking nature and culture)
Maternal love for son	Maternal love for daughter
Human and animal fertility	Agricultural fertility
Mobile/immobile	Mobile (Demeter) immobile (Persephone)
Near	Distant (209)

In *God, Goddesses, and Myths of Creation*, Mircea Eliade includes "The Homeric Hymns," XXX, "The Earth, Mother of All."

> I will sing of well-founded Earth, mother of all, eldest of all beings. She feeds all creatures that are in the world, all that go upon the goodly land, and all that are in the paths of the seas, and all that fly: all these are fed of her store. Through you, O queen, men are blessed in their harvest, and to you it belongs to give means of life to mortal men and to take it away. Happy is the man whom you delight to honour! He has all things abundantly: his fruitful land is laden with corn, his pastures are covered with cattle, and his house is filled with good things. Such men rule orderly in their cities of fair women: great riches and wealth follow them: their sons exult with everfresh delight, and their daughters with flower-laden hands play and skip merrily over the soft flowers of the field. Thus it is with those whom you honour O holy goddess, bountiful spirit. Hail, Mother of the gods, wife of starry Heaven; freely bestow upon me for this my song substance that cheers the heart! And now I will remember you and another song also. (55)

In "The Homeric Hymns" To Demeter, II, 185-299, this goddess is called "bringer of seasons and giver of perfect gifts." In this segment Demeter is described in her sadness about the disappearance of her daughter, Kore. Hades had carried her off into the underworld. She does not speak "because of her sorrow, and greeted no one by word or by sign, but rested, never smiling and tasting neither food nor drink, because she pined with longing for her deep-bosomed daughter..." (63-64) And she is also greeted by Metaneira. "Hail, lady! For I think you are not meanly but nobly born; truly dignity and grace are conspicuous upon your eyes as in the eyes of kings that deal justice" (64).

Of course, one should not confuse the Earth Goddess with Demeter or Aphrodite. Nevertheless, there are many qualities of the Earth Goddess ascribed to Demeter and Aphrodite because of their primordial significance in terms of their personification of fertility, the woman's celebration of passion and love, motherhood, and true dedication to their children.

The spirit of the Earth Goddess receives a voice in the dialog between Tiamat and Apsu in the *Enuma Elish* found in *The Babylonian Genesis*, by Alexander Heidel.

> Apsu opened his mouth and said to Tiamat in a loud voice: "Their way has become painful to me, By day I cannot rest, by night I cannot sleep; I will destroy (them) and put an end to their way, That silence be established, and then let us sleep!"
> When Tiamet heard this, she was wroth and cried out to her husband; She cried out and raged furiously, she alone. She pondered the evil in her heart (and said): "Why should we destroy that which we ourselves have brought forth? Their way is indeed very painful, but let us take it good-naturedly!"

The voice of the mythical sings the praises of the Feminine in reference to the Great Goddesss as the Mother of us all.

> The mother of our songs, the mother of all our seed, bore us in the beginning of things and so she is the mother of all types of men, the mother of all nations.
> She is the mother of the thunder,
> the mother of the streams,
> the mother of the trees and of all things.
> She is the mother of the world and of the older brothers, the stone-people.
> She is the mother of the fruits of the earth and of all things.
> She is the mother of our younger brothers, the French, and the strangers.
> She is the mother of our dance paraphernalia, of all our temples,
> and she is the only mother we possess.
> She alone is the mother of the fire and the Sun and the Milky Way...
> She is the mother of the rain and the only mother we possess.
> And she has left us a token in all the temples, a token in the form of song and dances.

Whose seed are we?

To our mother alone do we belong.
(Myth of Creation of Kagaba People)

The need for celebrating the feminine also exists in modern songs.

...In the beginning exists the Virgin
Her word in Her world bears the breath of life,
Her seed in the wind blows
It seeks and it carries
The blessing of precious women's love...

Glory to Her for the joy in living...

(Part of the record album, "Lavender Jane Loves Women,"
described on the jacket as a religious tribute to Mother-
Goddess-Creator-Protector of life, love and joy.)

Carl G. Jung has brought psychological understanding to the
discussion of goddesses, gods, and other mythical characters. This is very
much affirmed in Campbell's perception of the monomyth, where the multi-
variety of stories is interpreted according to common denominators.
Structuralism is that concentration in anthropology which specializes in the
definitions of common denominators in cultural behavior. The good thing
about Jung's psychoanalytic theory and the contributions of structuralism is
that one does not lose sight of the forest because of the trees. The danger is
that the original life of the story is sacrificed because of the theoretical
interpretations. Nevertheless, some time shall be devoted to the Jungian
appreciation of the feminine. In Jungian terms, the Earth Goddess is an
archetype, a bundle of psychological fibers, which constitute a basic area in
the human psyche. There are numerous archetypes, some more basic than
others. The mother dimension is very basic because so much of life,
especially mammalian, has experienced being carried, born, and nurtured by
the mother. The interesting part of the Jungian discussion is the
understanding that archetypes, which are contained in the collective
unconscious, always come in pairs. One cannot discuss them separately,
because each archetype provides growth potential for the individual.
Psychology is not philosophy, which tries to say what things are essentially
(metaphysics and ontology). Psychology is interested in the maintenance and
enhancement of the psychological equilibrium of the human psyche. The
unconscious centers are gateways for the human consciousness to become

more inclusive of dynamics which are not truly integrated. Thus, it is a discussion about dynamics in the name of the integration.

It can be made more clear when one imagines the collective unconscious as a round pie, which can be divided in numerous slices. Each slice represents a particular concentration of the psychic energy of the collective unconscious. One can name a number of slices by their archetypal significance: e.g., God, as a psychological term, is an archetype; mother too, and also the "self," have archetypal meaning. The masculine and the feminine can be discussed accordingly.

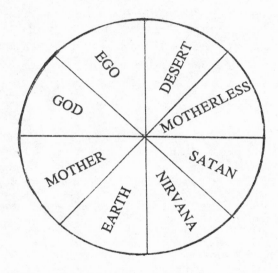

This diagram has placed some archetypes in relation to their opposites. At first sight one may expect that the opposite of the earth is the sky. But myths integrate both as principles of fertility. The opposite of Earth, psychologically, is the desert, the place where fertility is absent. Similarly, the opposite of Mother is not Father, because they are complementary aspects of each other. Anything Motherless, like feeling lonely or forlorn, being all naked to oneself, feeling abandoned, and emotions of that kind indicate the opposite of the Mother dimension. Ego is that aspect of psychological centeredness which one consciously holds about oneself to be the true picture. The opposite would be that which goes beyond the conscious, where one is to let go of the ego and allow its shell to be dissolved so that a wider life may flow in. These wider dimensions are ultimately indicated by the word nirvana, which, psychologically speaking, opposes ego-centeredness as a box of self-preservation. Nirvana stands for letting go, letting evaporate.

In psychological terms, God is opposed by Satan, if, of course, God stands for a divine authority who demands ultimate obedience. If God has another complexity of psychological energy, then another archetypal complex should represent its opposite. That is why M. Scott Peck in his book, *A Road Less Traveled*, describes a twofold use of God in his psychotherapy. In one case he helped a patient to get rid of the God in her life, because he was so domineering. In an other case he helped a patient find a religion and a God.

Campbell's narration of Satan in *The Power of Myth*, becomes understandable when one sees Satan as an archetype as situated in the above diagram. In Chapter VII, "Tales of Love and Marriage," is the following rendition:

> MOYERS: As yet one of my favorite myths is the story from Persia that Satan is condemned to hell because he loved God so much.
>
> CAMPBELL: Yes, that's a basic Muslim idea about Satan being God's greatest lover. There are a number of ways of thinking about Satan, but this is based on the question, Why was Satan thrown into hell? The standard story is that, when God created the angels, he told them to bow to none but himself. Then he created man, whom he regarded as a higher form than the angels, and he asked the angels to serve man. And Satan would not bow to man.
>
> Now, this is interpreted in the Christian tradition, as I recall from my boyhood instruction, as being the egotism of Satan. He would not bow to man. But in the Persian story, he could not bow to man because of his love for God – he could bow only to God. God had changed his signals, do you see? But Satan has so committed himself to the first set of signals that he could not violate those, and in his – I don't know if Satan has a heart or not – but in his mind, he could not bow to anyone but God, whom he loved. And then God says, "Get out of my sight."
>
> Now, the worst of the pains of hell, insofar as hell has been described, is the absence of the Beloved, which is God. So how does Satan sustain the situation in hell? By the memory of the echo of God's voice, when God said, "Go to hell." That is a great sign of love. (204)

In the chapter, "The Hero's Adventure," Campbell discusses Satan in the context of the Buddha myth. First he describes the three temptations of Jesus by the Devil after Jesus was good and hungry from forty days of fasting in the desert. Then follows the comparison with Buddha:

> Buddha, too, goes into the forest and has conferences there with the leading gurus of his day. Then he goes past them and, after a season of trials and search, comes to the bo tree, the tree of illumination, where the likewise undergoes three temptations. The first is of lust, the second of fear, and the third of submission to public opinion, doing as told. In the first temptation, the Lord of Lust displayed his three beautiful daughters before the Buddha. Their names were Desire, Fulfillment, and Regrets – Future, Present, and Past. But the Buddha, who had already disengaged himself from the attachment of his sensual character, was not moved.
>
> Then the Lord of Lust turned himself into the Lord of Death and flung at the Buddha all the weapons of an army of monsters. But the Buddha had found in himself that still point, which is of eternity, untouched by time. So, again, he was not moved, and the weapons flung at him turned into flowers of worship. Finally the Lord of Lust and Death transformed himself into the Lord of Social Duty and argued, "Young man, haven't you read the morning papers? Don't you know what there is to be done today?" The Buddha responded simply touching the earth with the tips of his fingers of his right hand. Then the voice of the goddess mother of the universe was heard, like thunder rolling on the horizon, saying, "This, my beloved son, has already so given of himself to the world that there is no one here to be ordered about. Give up this nonsense." Whereupon the elephant on which the Lord of Social Duty was riding bowed in worship of the Buddha, and the entire company of the Antagonist dissolved like a dream. That night, the Buddha achieved illumination, and for the next fifty years remained in the world as teacher of the way to extinction of the bondage of egoism. (140)

It is interesting that the divine is represented by "the goddess mother of the universe." This indicates that the feminine is part of the divine dimension. Ann Belford Ulanov in her book, *The Feminine in Jungian Psychology and in Christian Theology* reports:

> Jung is strongly critical of the Christian tradition for omitting the feminine as part of the Godhead. He suggests that the Trinitarian symbolism is incomplete: a fourth person, the *matter* and *materia* and hence the dark substance of the flesh and the Devil, should be added. Jung is ambiguous about whether he sees the feminine and the Devil on the same plane. One would prefer to think not. But he does imply as

associative link through the feminine as flesh, as matter, as the dark and the earthy, to the black evil of Satan; and he refers to both as the missing "fourth." Perhaps it reflects the denigrated status of the feminine to see it linked with the demonic. (135-136)

One should understand that in Jungian psychology, which is growth-oriented and wants to integrate all dynamics within the psyche, that any blockage of such integration has a negative effect. Such a negative effect may result in what he calls "the shadow." Thus we read in Ulanov:

The shadow is the image used by Jung to describe those contents in ourselves that we repress because they are unacceptable, such as tawdry thoughts, unbounded power aspirations, secret faults. On the collective level, the shadow is often personified as the devil; on the individual level it is always represented by someone of the same sex whom we dislike and find irritating or even hateful. (133)

Because the Christian tradition repressed the feminine as the personification of bodily existence and the flesh, this resulted in the burning of witches. In his book, *Sex in History*, G. Rattray Taylor makes a distinction between the *Patrist* and the *Matrist* traditions. The first modelled themselves on their fathers, and the second modelled themselves on a mother figure.

PATRIST	MATRIST
1. Restrictive attitude to sex	Permissive attitude to sex
2. Limitation of freedom for women	Freedom for women
3. Women seem as inferior, sinful	Women accorded high status
4. Chastity more valued than welfare	Welfare more valued than chastity
5. Politically authoritarian	Politically democratic
6. Conservative: against innovation	Progressive: revolutionary
7. Distrust of research,	No distrust of research
8. Inhibition, fear of spontaneity	Spontaneity: exhibition
9. Deep fear for homosexuality	Deep fear of incest
10. Sex differences maximized	Sex differences minimized
11. Asceticism, fear of pleasure	Hedonism, pleasure welcomed
12. Father religion	Mother religion

In *The Humanist*, "Why we Burn: Sexism Exorcised," Meg Bowman lists sayings by famous men throughout history concerning women.

"One hundred women are not worth a single testicle." (Confucius)

"A proper wife should be as obedient as a slave" and "The female is a female by virtue of a certain lack of qualities – a natural defectiveness." (Aristotle)

"Among the savage beasts, none is found so harmful as woman." (St. John Chrysostom)

"Any woman who acts in such a way that she cannot give birth to as many children as she is capable of, makes herself guilty of that many murders..." (St. Augustine)

"Do you know that each of your women is an Eve? The sentence of God – on this sex of yours – lives in this age; the guilt must necessarily live, too. You are the gate of Hell, you are the temptress of the forbidden tree, you are the first deserter of the divine law." (Tertullian)

"Woman in her greatest perfection was made to serve and obey man, not rule and command him." (John Knox)

"The souls of women are so small that some believe they've none at all." (Samuel Butler)

"Woman is ontologically subordinate to man." (Karl Barth)

"Blessed art thou, O Lord our God and King of the Universe, that thou didst *not* create me a woman." (daily prayer, still used today, of the Orthodox Jewish male)

"Women should remain at home, sit still, keep house, and bear and bring up children...If a woman grows weary and, at last, dies from childbearing, it matters not. Let her die from bearing; she is there to do it." (Martin Luther)

These statements clearly demonstrate that the suppression of the feminine and also the suppression of the mother goddess has created the shadow reality, which Jung regarded as being sick. If we are to look for the Father of Jesus, then it shall be done well outside such as attitude of suppression. In "Gods, Goddesses, and Bibles: The Canonization of Misogyny," William R. Harwood makes some interesting observations. He theorizes that the Big Discovery which started the male assertion was that "the weapon with which they pleasured their mistresses *also made babies*."

The Big Discovery meant that women were no longer the sole surveyors of life – and therefore neither were goddesses! From being the reproducers of life, women found themselves reduced to the level of incubators, of no more relevance to the birth process than the dirt in which an ear of corn grew into an adult plant...

Following the Big Discovery, nothing could stop them (the males) and nothing did stop them...Before the mind could conceive of any change in the social structure of human society, it had first to postulate a similar change in the sky. Thus, before there could be any king reigning on earth, there had to be created a King of Heaven, a God the Father, who was the Mother's superior and by whose impregnation she produced her children. (24)

Just to become aware of the intrigue by which such developments occurred, Harwood offers an insight about the sacrifice of the first-born, which is quite different from what is traditionally held. He speculates that it is advantageous for a woman to have a child so that man, who wanted good breeders, learned her qualifications. So it was quite possible that the first child was out of wedlock.

> The first child of marriage, regardless of how many years might have elapsed before its birth, being of doubtful parentage, would be sacrificed to Molokh or Baal or Yahweh or Allah or which ever god had the local baby-burning concession. Following the birth and the sacrifice, the wife would observe an adultery taboo. All future children could than be attributed with absolute certainty to her legal owner...
>
> It was the abolition of infant sacrifice that led to the imposition of cradle-to-marriage joy-deprivation on half of the human race...The solution was to deny unmarried girls the opportunity to bring to the marriage bed a womb that might already be carrying seed that could one day produce a cuckoo's chick...
>
> The final step in the degradation of women...by the post-Discovery creator and savior both male, the phallusocracy now came up with the myth that male gods had created a perfect world which women have subsequently rendered imperfect. (25)

Harwood's synopsis of history in terms of the subjugation of women finds some parallels in Hesiod's description of various ages by which man replaced woman in political terms. The Golden Age was a picture of paradise. There were no gods, and men lived without labor, never growing old, laughing much, and to whom death was no more terrible than sleep. The second, the Silver Age was the time of matriarchal societies or gynocracies. Men were utterly subject to their mothers and dared not to disobey them. Erich Fromm speculated that in this age of bliss the Great Goddess, the mother of god, loved her children equally. This is in contrast to the father god, who loves only those who obey his commandments. The Bronze Age was the time when men learned to eat the flesh of animals. In this time weapons were invented and wars were fought. The Iron Age was described by Hesiod as our present deplorable situation because of the male supremacy. (See Elizabeth Gould Davis, *The First Sex*, pp. 63-65.)

If we are to recover the life of the mother god, the Great Goddess, then this celebration of life is still contained in the heritage of the myths. The following is a summarization of the first chapters of *The Feminine Spacious as the Sky* by Miriam and Jose Arguelles. This will be followed by some critical reflections, because this approach is not only inspirational but has some basic pitfalls which may lead to a misrepresentation of the feminine.

The first chapter is called, "The Matrix of the Unborn," indeed, a very paradoxical title. It states that there is nothing that does not have a mother. This, of course, is meant in a mythological sense. It implies that we all come from some source, which, too is generated by another source, and so on. If one arrives at the question about what was before the beginning of the beginning, then "one is confronted with a paradox: whatever lies beyond the mother of the first mother is beyond all concept....One is unable to imagine this beginningless beginning." (5)

> What lies beyond the first mother, whether we search our own experiences or the vastness of the physical universe, still seems a kind of mother, something that accommodates all possible questions and sustains the birth and death of ideas and living beings. This mother of all things is groundless, without any identifiable source. (6)

As such the feminine is unborn, it was never conceived and remains inconceivable. This unborn quality provides the dimension which gives ground to what is "the born." The feminine is understood as the unborn container of creation and destruction. We experience an infinite variety of passing phenomena, which creates an awareness of the emptiness within all this activity. Nothing is for certain, nothing is definite. There is an unborn quality in whatever happens. This unborn quality is representative of the spaciousness of the primordial feminine. Not being definite allows for more and unexpected developments and is as such generative of the not yet. Thus the cosmic feminine womb gives birth to actualities and our perceptions thereof, which are also transitory and relative. Although perceiver and the perceived are inseparable, we experience them in a dualistic way. This dualism creates a sense of separation. At times, in special moments, the sense of separation is removed. This may create a sense of awe about the openness and the possibility of actual freedom. Thus one relates to the unborn, the feminine.

The danger is that one may want to cover up or conceptualize this openness. This is called the process of "solidifying space" which will block fertility to come into action. The uncovering of the feminine is an ongoing process.

The second chapter, "The Birth of Communication," includes the masculine, which is characterized by a desire to conquer, and have union with the feminine. Thus the feminine invites the masculine to respond in a personal and compassionate manner. The masculine is fundamentally indestructible, "for it is the essence of everything contained by the unborn".

> The play of unborn feminine space and the unconditional masculine interpenetration of these principles allows communication and meaningful activity to take place. Although the unoriginated space of the feminine gives birth, there is no separation between the vastness of the unborn and its contents, the masculine. Woven into a cloth that is indissoluble, the interplay of feminine and masculine is an expression of the dynamics of creativity. (17-18)

The feminine is characterized as a spontaneous birth-giving capacity which gives it a motherly quality. There is something special between her and her masculine son. In mythical terms, this relationship between mother and son expresses the human need to identify with the cosmic process of creation and destruction.

> The self-realization of the world is analogous to a mother who spontaneously produces a child and later becomes its lover. The masculine principle is the form that arises and moves within this space and journeys toward its mother. From primordial times, the feminine as the Great Goddess was conceived as mother, lover and destroyer. (19-20)

In the way the myth of Psyche and Eros reports various stages of development, this account follows the interaction between mother and son. The mother is far away, in a territory unknown. She beckons the son. The son is restless and wants to encounter the generating energy. The son is the seeker, the mother represents the unknown. Although re-union is sought, a sense of profound separation is experienced.

> Belief in isolation and a desire for union contradict each other so that the spaciousness and beckoning quality of the feminine may be overlooked. One is left with anxiety-filled womblike fantasies – the impulsive urge to immerse oneself, through whatever means, in some kink of behavior that will ultimately guarantee an all-embracing oblivion or self-extinction. Notwithstanding the potential hazards of possible fixations that may occur, the mother and son relationship, as exemplified in the hero's quest or spiritual path, describes a primary quality of journey that each one of us experiences, a path that is sometimes hidden and sometimes clear, leading from bewilderment to knowing. (21)

These are truly insightful reflections on the mythical dynamics between mother and son, the Great Goddess and her child. This is material which enriches our awareness about the greatness of Jesus relationship with his Father, when understood in mythical terms. Simply taking the Father of Jesus as a masculine reality as expressed in "Our Father" lacks the sensitivity which is present in the expression, "Our Mother." The psychological differences between those two nomenclatures are indicated in the beginning of this chapter. The limitations of a traditional Father God are signaled in the references to Yahweh and Zeus. Obviously the word, God, means more than the Father God represents. The Father God becomes quite particular in the history of the Babylonian and the Hebrew people. The Great Goddess and the Earth Goddess have been discussed to encounter their basic dynamics. The distinction between a Patrist and a Matrist tradition offers us the opportunity to check the prejudices of our cultural history, which have been discussed somewhat. And finally the speculations about the Feminine, the Masculine, the Great Goddess and her son, provide us with insights which supersede traditional concepts and normal wisdom. Thus we enter the realm where the Father of Jesus as a mythical energy receives new understanding.

The danger of the speculation of the feminine by Miriam and Jose Arguelles is already indicated by Harwood. When the male perceived that he was the carrier of the seed, and the woman was simply "an incubator," the soil in which the seed is planted, the woman was reduced to something functional. As happened so often in the history of modern science, many of our interpretative statements about meaning and value have been corrected by factual discoveries in biology and physics. Evolution is a biological discovery which helped us become more celebrative of the account of creation in Genesis. Now we don't have to believe it anymore, but we can delight in the energy of the story. The same science, biology, discovered DNA, so we know that the conception of a new child is not the planting of a seed into a birthing environment, the womb. On the contrary, it is the meeting of two genetically loaded entities, the egg and the sperm. The male is not the pursuer, and the woman is not the pursuee. Both pursue the process of unification of the egg and the sperm. Each has her or his way of becoming involved. The fact is that the genetic makeup of the new baby is 50% informed by the mother's chromosomes and 50% by the father's chromosomes. Each contributes half of all the chromosomes which constitute the life of the fertilized egg.

This information challenges the description of the feminine as presented by Miriam and Jose Arguelles. Nevertheless, their insights are still very valuable if one does not regard the feminine as identical with the female nor the masculine as identical with the male. Here we are helped by Jungian psychology as reported in this chapter. Within every individual there is the polarity of the feminine and the masculine. Wherever one is dominant, the other may resort to the realm of the unconscious. If growth is to be promoted, then the unconscious, be it feminine or masculine, provides the center of such development, because the unconscious complex is the gate toward the wider and more encompassing integration of psychic energy. Thus within the Father are the feminine and the masculine. The description of the feminine is extremely helpful in seeing the Father in a new light. Now, He is not just the lord, who brings order out of chaos, and who creates a future new Heaven and a new Earth, where everything will be perfect. The perfect is not in terms of feats not yet accomplished. The perfect is the integration of what is still experienced as a duality between opposites. Steps toward overcoming the alienation, separation, and suppression within this duality can be taken with the help of the words, "our Mother, who art the universe."

The understanding of life according to biological discoveries is liberating in many respects. To list a few:

a) According to biology, life is not pre-designed, but emerged from opportunities arranged by circumstances at a particular time (life seized the moment). As such, life did not receive a particular meaning according to an imaginary architect, but it is a mystery.

b) Evolution is the process whereby the more complex form emerges from the less complex for the sake of creating a greater adaptability to insure better survival chances. Note, the survival is not served by increasing specific defense mechanisms (the turtle and snail in their shells or whatever serves a species in its survival strategies). It is the creation of a greater openness so that life can be more responsive to increasing challenges with more sophistication.

c) Initially, the procreation of life was by means of cell division (as still happens within the egg after fertilization). Sex is simply an added development in the politics of survival. The strategy for life invented a division of sex roles for the sake of more reliable procreation. To make too much out of the sexual differences between female and male is taking this out of the basic and functional context.

d) The celebration of the sexual differences is part of the playfulness of life. Male birds are often more colorful to attract the female's attention. Female mammals spread around the good news for the males by dispensing of the estrus smell. To place these sexual dynamics into mythical terms is fundamental for the affirmation of life in a cultural as well as a psychological sense. Our imagination is permeated by the sexual energy (Freud's *libido*). If we are to embrace life we are to embrace its sexuality in its multiple varieties.

The video program, "The Mystery of Life," (shown on Public Television many times since 1986) narrates and depicts the makeup of the human genitals and their functions in procreation. One sees the aggressive, goal-oriented movements of the more than 200 million sperm (the amount of one ejaculation). This is a vivid picture of the masculine in biological terms.

The video makes one look at the beauty of the mature egg after ovulation. The picture of her is like the planet earth floating in the blueness of space, slowly rotating. It is voluminous like a full blooming flower. The background music makes it all appear as a majestic presence welcoming the mating sperm.

The whole poetical unfolding of the egg becomes suddenly very decisive when one sperm has entered her realm. Every possibility of entering is closed off hermetically. Then the sharing of the genetic information begins – the blending of the chromosomes. This is followed by the cell division.

Initially each cell is virtually the same and could take the place of any other cell in the zygote. But when the process continues, the specification of the cell's location determines more and more its function and role. The cell in the realm of the ear will develop as an ear cell, the cell in the region of the leg will develop a leg. Before that specification the cell in the ear region could be placed in the leg environment and would become part of the leg development.

Thus there is a duality between the unformed and the formed. The formed energies (chromosomes) form the unformed (potentially open and not significantly specified). The unformed is within a given which is formed in such a way that the unformed is characteristic of its form. The unformed is within the egg as potential for conception. The same is true about the sperm. When it enters the egg it becomes part of the unformed form.

In this way one can play with the aspects called the feminine and the masculine. They provide areas which are conducive to mythical material by which our imagination celebrates the capacities within the mystery of life.

To assume that the sperm is the all-decisive regulator of the new life to be conceived is biologically a heresy (heresy is a partial statement, which does not tell the whole story and exaggerates only one aspect as being all-decisive.). In the same fashion, it is a heresy to proclaim that God is only "Father." Then one presents the divine in a very limited way and exaggerates only one aspect of the divine.

The "Father" aspect receives far more understanding if placed within the context of Great Goddess and the "Mother" aspect. This chapter wanted to say something about that and relate the discussion to relevant studies about these matters.

Next, our journey will explore additional aspects about the Father of Jesus when discussing the Virgin Birth of Jesus.

Chapter Seven

The Virgin Birth of Jesus

We can learn much about the Father of Jesus in the context of the discussion about the Virgin Birth of Jesus. Since my first school days I was taught the words, the Blessed Virgin Mary. Only later, in my seminary studies, did I hear about the basic claims of the Roman Catholic Church. There Mary is considered to have been a virgin before, during, and after the birth of her son, Jesus. The focus was on the biological aspect, that the hymen of Mary remained intact in a miraculous way. This then was to secure the belief that Jesus was not born of a sexual act between a man and a woman. Jesus was the son of God, because he was born of the Holy Spirit who overshadowed Mary. Thus she became pregnant, after she gave her consent to the angel Gabriel. Suddenly he had appeared in her room and gave her this totally unexpected news. From on high, God had decided to finally send his messiah, as promised as of old. And this young woman was to be the vehicle for this coming into history by the God of Abraham, Isaac, and Jacob.

Traditional Christianity developed the information contained in the Gospels of Matthew and Luke into the doctrines of Mary being the mother of God, *theotokos*, primarily at the Ecumenical Council of Ephesus, 433 C. E. Roman Catholics maintain this tradition, while some Protestant denominations disagree with giving Mary such a central place within the salvation history. But in the middle of this century, Pope Pius XII, declared the doctrine of Mary being assumed into Heaven in a glorified state, because she was not subject to Original Sin (a theology developed by St. Augustine, teaching that all humans inherited the sin of Adam and Eve, and at birth the human soul is not in a state of divine grace). Mary was born without Original Sin, and as such she was not subject to death, because death was the punishment for the ins in Paradise. So, from birth Mary was already destined to become the mother of Jesus Christ. Now she is elevated into Heaven to share within her resurrected or transformed bodily existence the glory of her risen son, Jesus. As such she is regarded as the mediatrix, the one who speaks on our behalf, at Jesus' heavenly throne.

Traditional Catholics delight in doctrinal declarations about Mary. She is very much the Mother to whom they can turn in all their needs, moments of loneliness, pain, suffering, and desperation. She is someone personable, and one can relate to her who is part of our human reality. She knows and understands. Moreover, she cares, and she has her ways of approaching Jesus as it was at the wedding in Cana, when the hosts ran out of wine. At the invitation of Mary, Jesus changed "six stone jars" of water into wine. (John 2:1-12)

Born and raised a Roman Catholic, Joseph Campbell grew up in this world of Jesus, Mary, and Joseph, and how they were part of the divine reality. As a child he benefited from the simplicity of the doctrinal language. The story is told as an account of facts that happened two thousand years ago and have created such a sublime reality of the resurrected life of Jesus and Mary who, already ascended and assumed into Heaven, are welcoming us from afar. A place is prepared for us, and the heavenly glory will wash away our tears and change the suffering in our hearts into the eternal delight of divine bliss.

When Campbell matured, he experienced the dissolution of his beliefs, which caused him spiritual pain. However, he emerged with the delight of a metaphorical understanding of these Christian teachings:

> The Christ story involves a sublimation of what originally was a very solid vegetal image. Jesus is on Holy Rood, the tree, and he is himself the fruit of the tree. Jesus is the fruit of eternal life, which was on the second forbidden tree in the Garden of Eden. When man ate of the fruit of the first tree of knowledge of good and evil, he was expelled from the

Garden. The Garden is the place of unity, of nonduality of male and female, good and evil, God and human beings. You eat the duality, and you are on the way out. The tree of immortal life, where you know that I and the Father are one. (107)

This oneness with the Father is further explained in a discussion about illumination.

MOYERS: What is illumination?

CAMPBELL: The illumination is the recognition of the radiance of one eternity through all things, whether in the vision of time things are judged as good or as evil. To come to this, you must release yourself completely from desiring the goods of this world and fearing their loss. "Judge not that you be not judged," we read in the words of Jesus. "If the doors of perception were cleansed," wrote Blake, "man would see everything as it is, infinite."

MOYERS: That's a rough trip.

CAMPBELL: That's a heavenly trip. (162)

Thus Campbell supplies the perspectives by which the mythical characters of Jesus and Mary can be interpreted. While writing and reflecting on Campbell's perception of the heroic, I had to prepare a sermon for the New Year's Day Mass. The focus of the celebration was the "Solemnity of Mary – the Mother of God." Although raised according to the Catholic dogmas and their theologies, one does not become an instructor when one is to give a homily. One tries to become alive in terms of the given focus. So, I used Campbell's approach with the awareness of the dynamic aspects of the heroic. Then the mythical comes alive and something will respond in the hearts of those who listen.

As such I invited the faithful in the church to reflect on Mary when she was alive on this earth in the way we are alive right now, on the same earth. Then I recalled how this young woman was suddenly surprised by a divine presence (the Angel Gabriel) who introduced an understanding of the divine plan of which she was to become part. In this light Mary became prepared to say, "Be it done to me according to your word" and "Behold the handmaid of the Lord." She sacrificed the normal security of living a normal life, having a husband and a family of her own. Then she would know what is expected of normal people in normal circumstances. But because she opened herself to the divine realm, angels guided her and Joseph in finding their special way under threatening circumstances. After the child Jesus was born and had been praised as a true blessing by the Magi who followed a star, and also Simeon and the prophetess Anna in the temple at the circumcision of Jesus, Herod also became aware of such a special prince who might dethrone him. So the persecution was enacted and the male babies in Bethlehem were killed by Herod's soldiers. But Jesus was brought to the security of a foreign land (Egypt). Later Mary and Joseph and the child returned to Nazareth. Mary fulfilled her normal motherly responsibilities in nursing the child and teaching him how to walk and talk and how to behave as a respectable Jew.

But when the boy grew in wisdom, she too became intrigued by the mentality and spirit which inspired her son. Mary was not just a mother. Mary became fully involved in the life that emanated from her son. She marveled at how people reacted to Jesus' sermons, and she observed the reaction of those who were cured by him and praised God for these blessings. More and more Mary became aware of the authority of Jesus which was energized by his heavenly Father. The life of the Father became more and more apparent in whatever Jesus did and said. And so this new life-force became a confrontation to those in power. They decided to do away with this new authority, and they crucified him. And so we find Mary, the mother of Jesus, at the foot of the cross where he son was dying a horrible death. She did not become bitter and she did not curse life and all of existence because they had murdered this just man, her beloved son, the best of the best. She lived up to what had touched her at the beginning of this saga. Like Jesus, she placed her suffering, pain, and agony in the hands of the Father. Then Mary learned to understand the greatness of the Father's power. and when her son appeared as the risen one, she comprehended the newness of this transformation. It was not a magical trick, but a manifestation of the Father's glory. Thus she superseded the agony of death and entered the awareness of the divine creativity which opened to her the realm of light which breaks into the darkness of death, frustration, and despair. In this way we celebrate that Mary, the Mother of God, is truly part of the divine reality, the glory of the Father who raised Jesus beyond death, and elevated Mary to these divine heights.

I did not explain to the people that my approach to this theme was according to Campbell's perception of the heroic. Nevertheless, I sensed that people became intrigued by my wording, and they experienced the conviction by which I presented my celebrative interpretation of Mary's heroic mystery. In this way I became part of Campbell's emphasis that there is an ancient meaning in the mythological. When the mythological is presented in its dramatic dynamics (i.e., awareness of the different phases of the heroic energy), then one connects with this "ancient meaning" in which all people participate.

In the *National Catholic Reporter*, Eugene Kennedy shares his delight in Joseph Campbell's mythical approach of religious truths. The title reads, "Want the Truth?: Turn Over a Myth and Look Under It." A former priest, Kennedy is well educated in the Catholic teachings. He was my teacher in Psychological Counseling at Loyola University in Chicago in 1966. He had not yet married, and some of his doubts and question surfaced in his discussions. Although Vatican II had taken the scene and much freshness was reported about the Catholic "aggiornomento" (renewal, fresh air), still there was the critical voice of someone who had difficulty in identifying with the institution of the Roman Church. All these doubts are superseded in his delight when in this article Kennedy reports on a television interview of Joseph Campbell. He identifies very will with Campbell as a heroic person.

> One minute to air time. The host stares hard at his guest. "I want you to know I'm tough. I lay it on the line.: The red light flashes "ON THE AIR." "I say," the host intones sourly, "myth is nothing but a lie."
> Campbell smiles, for he recognizes his brash interrogator as the mythical everyman cynic...

Yes, Kennedy is an author, and his language comes alive in describing this Campbell event. The freedom within Campbell's attitude is admired and promoted by a personal affirmation:

> "Every myth," he says, "is psychologically symbolic. Its narratives and images are to be read, therefore, not literally but as a metaphor. The problem arises because great Western

religious institutions have lost sight of this. As a result, we
have this popular nightmare of history in which local mythic
images – they always come from the immediate culture – are
interpreted not as metaphors, but as facts. There have been
ferocious wars waged between the parties of these contrary
manners of metaphoric representation. In Beirut, for example,
they are rehearsing Armageddon in three different inflations of
the *same* biblical versions of the idea of God...if you take the
images of religious language literally, they become ridiculous
because they lose their radiance. That is what happens when
you lose the sense of meaning of terms like the Virgin Birth..."
(7)

Kennedy continues his report on these, for him, exciting insights and
he really tries to capture the vitality of this speaker.

Campbell half-turns in his chair as his visitor asks him
to explore some of the great religious metaphors that have
been read literally. He speaks thoughtfully of the various
planes of spiritual progression. "The Virgin birth refers to the
awakening to a dimension of consciousness and of being and of
sorrow and of bliss that is deeper than the appearance of
things. The bewildering world becomes transformed. That is
what we mean when we speak of "the end of the world." One is
then in the Promised Land, the earthly paradise..." (8)

Later reference is made to Campbell's explanation of the chakras.
But he does it in the context of "the pollen path" of the Navajo. There the
initial first three stages are regarded as what we have in common with
animals: the rectum, which refers to eating, the genitals, which concern
sexuality, and the naval which symbolizes conquest. The fourth is the heart,
which opens to compassion, in which we open our hearts to others in a
second birth. This is the beginning of the spiritual life in the human animal.

Campbell turns in his chair, his face alight. "*This* is an
example of what the Virgin Birth means. Anyone who
expresses a spiritual life has a virgin birth. To concretize this
metaphor is to make a monster of Jesus." (8)

In *The Power of Myth*, "The Gift of the Goddess," similar statements
are made, but they receive a new flavor when told in the context of the Hindu
tradition and the Indian psychological system:

The next, or fourth, center is at the level of the heart;
and this is of the opening to compassion. Here you move out

of the field of animal action into a field that is properly human and spiritual.

And for each of these four centers there is envisioned a symbolic form, for example, the first one is the lingam and yoni, the male and female organs in conjunction. And at the heart center, there is *again* the lingam, and yoni, that is to say male and female organs in conjunction, but there they are represented in gold as symbolic of the virgin birth, that is to say, it is birth of spiritual man out of the animal man.

MOYERS: And it happens –

CAMPBELL: It happens when you awaken at the level of the heart to compassion, compassion, shared suffering: experienced participation in the suffering of another person. That's the beginning of humanity. And the meditations of religion properly are on that level, the heart level.

MOYERS: You say that's the beginning of humanity. But in these stories, that's the moment when gods are born. The virgin birth – it's a god who emerges.

CAMPBELL: And do you know who that god is? It's *you*. You can get stuck out *there*. and think it's all out *there*. So you're thinking about Jesus with all the sentiments relevant to how he suffered – out there But that suffering is what ought to be going on in you. Have you been spiritually reborn? Have you died to your animal nature and come to life as a human incarnation of compassion?

MOYERS: Why is it significant of a virgin?

CAMPBELL: The begetter is of the spirit. This is a spiritual birth. The virgin conceived of the word through the ear.

MOYERS: The word came like a shaft of light.

CAMPBELL: Yes. And the Buddha, with the same meaning, is said to have been born from his mother's side from the level of the heart chakra.

MOYERS: Heart chakra meaning...?

CAMPBELL: Oh, the heart chakra is the symbolic center associated with the heart. The chakra means "circle" or "sphere."

MOYERS: So the Buddha comes out –

CAMPBELL: The Buddha is born from his mother's side. That's a symbolic birth. He wasn't physically born form his mother's side, but symbolically.

MOYERS: But Christ came the way you and I did.

CAMPBELL: Yes, but of a virgin. And then, according to Roman Catholic doctrine, her virginity was restored. So nothing happened physically, you might say. What is symbolically referred to is not Jesus physical birth but his spiritual significance. That's what the virgin birth represents. Heroes and demigods are born that way as beings motivated by compassion and not mastery, sexuality, or self-preservation.
This is the sense of the second birth, when you begin to live out of the heart center. The lower three centers are not refuted but transcended, when they become subjects to and servant to the heart. (174-176)

Reading this conversation allows for the obvious conclusion. In the mythical meaning of the virgin, according to Campbell, the Father of the virgin's child is the life of compassion. It is remarkable how well this insight agrees with the findings of scholars of the New Testament who are saying new things about the Virgin Birth.

Before we turn to the new Testament scholars, it should be noted that they are not applying at all Campbell's interpretative approach of the text. They very much study the text in the name of exegesis. They want to stipulate what the texts themselves are saying within their own context, and according to their own authority. In this sense the texts have literal significance.

If one reads the Bible with the mythical interpretation of Campbell, then one does not incur all the difficulties Bible scholars and church theologians have produced. Christians in particular, want to know whether or not Jesus was born of a virgin. This definite question is then discussed in reference to texts which pertain specifically to this problem. Especially the beginning of the gospels by Matthew and Luke are quoted. Traditionally,

Christians assumed that these texts, without a doubt, reveal the virgin birth of Jesus. Then modern scholars, who are quite knowledgeable about the original language of the New Testament and the Bible as a whole, who also know the history of the Bible and the cultural and social circumstances of the biblical days, began to see things differently. One learned about accusations of people in the time of the early Christians, that Jesus was an illegitimate child. Supposedly, Matthew and Luke wrote about the Virgin Birth to make Jesus become acceptable and to counteract these rumors. This suggestion is a bit too simple, and publications about the Virgin Birth of Jesus go much deeper than that.

Here references will be made to two studies which report the context of modern New Testament scholarship and also offer new insights. First, as editor of Explorations: Journal for Adventurous Thought, I was asked to consider the publication of the research by Frank Reilly, which he had completed in 1985 but was unsuccessful in getting published. It resulted in the article, "A Very Unpleasant Alternative: One Response to Raymond E. Brown's Defense of the Virginal Conception". The other is Jane Schaberg's book, The Illegitimacy of Jesus; A Feminist Theological Interpretation of the Infancy Narratives.

Frank Reilly concentrates primarily on the publication of Raymond Brown and the related discussions. He concludes that Brown and people of the same convictions still continue to read Matthew and Luke for facts about the Virgin Birth. Otherwise, as Brown concludes, the texts will leave us with av very unpleasant alternative. This will be the thought that Jesus was conceived by Mary not in conjunction with Joseph, but out of wedlock. And that strongly suggests that she might have been raped and forced in this pregnancy. Reilly demonstrates how the texts of Matthew and Luke can be read this way. Moreover, he concludes that in that case the religious significance of the angel's appearance is delightfully refreshing. Instead of announcing a supernatural feat where the Holy Spirit will impregnate Mary, the angel speaks in the name of God, the Merciful Father, that the child she is carrying will be accepted by God, and will look great in his eyes. The greatness of this redeeming message is that the mercy of the Father supersedes the vicitimizing reality of rape. Thus Mary can sing in the Gospel of Luke that God does mighty deeds.

> My soul magnifies the Lord and my spirit rejoices in my
> God my Savior;
> because he had regarded the lowliness of his handmaid...
> and his mercy is from generation to generation on those
> who fear him. (1:46-48, 50)

The connection between Campbell's interpretation of the Virgin Birth as the birth of humanity with the emergence of compassion and Reilly's insight is easily seen.

Schaberg takes the discussion of Jesus' illegitimacy beyond the immediate Raymond Brown context. Her feminist identity is:

> ...its frank interest in the interplay between text and contemporary situation as both are illuminated by the women's movement. (6)

> Feminist biblical criticism accepts the general tenet of historical-critical scholarship, that biblical texts are historical formulations....To this, feminist criticism adds the sharpening awareness that such contexts are patriarchal and androcentric... and a dangerous misogynist bias....(7-8)

These concerns are summed up in the Introduction. The rest of the book is significant in its scholarship, critical quality, and interpretative creativity. Her conclusions are very mild considering the more flagrant theological assertions by authors such as Mary Daly.

Because we deal with the actual text and the belief system of the religious community from which they emerged, exegesis wants to know what those texts meant for the community at that time in history. Matthew and Luke are treated separately, and each text reveals its own delight of "good news" about what happened to Mary. Matthew begins his gospel with a genealogy in which he mentions the names of four women, Tamar, Rahab, Ruth, and "the wife of Uriah" (Bathsheba). These four represent a participation in the procreation of Hebrew and Jewish blood which is less than normal and subject to concern. They are part of getting their way into the favors of the men by whom they had children. Schaberg concludes:

> ...mention of these four women is designed to lead Matthew's reader to expect another, final story of a woman who becomes

a social misfit in some way; is wronged or thwarted, who is party to a sexual act that places her in great danger; and whose story has an outcome that repairs the social fabric and ensures the birth of the child who is legitimate or legitimated. That child, Matthew tells us (1:1) is "the son of David, the son of Abraham." (33)

Another conclusion is very important for our focus:

Second, Matthew's understanding of God as Father is significant. The God believed to side with the outcast and marginal cannot be a projection or endorsement of patriarchal ideology. Matthew's Jesus commands, "Call no man father on earth, for you have one father who is in heaven" (23:9). In this community and in society in general no one has the right to claim this name or to exercise the power of the "father"–a power that does not empower all. The Jesus movement, as Matthew understood and described it, tried to found a new family, a family of God. (77)

That is what it means, that "the child begotten in her (Mary) is through the Holy Spirit." (1:20) "She was found to be with child by the Holy Spirit." (1:18)

The same scholarly expertise by which Schaberg arrived at her conclusions of Matthew produces similar but different statements at the end of her discussion of Luke. In Luke the material related to the Virgin Birth is far more voluminous. The introduction of the appearance of the angel to Mary is the vision of the angel by a certain priest Zachary. His wife Elizabeth was barren, and both advanced in years, and the angel announced that Elizabeth would bear a son. After this experience Zachary went home and Elizabeth conceived. After half a year the angel appeared to Mary and announced that she too would conceive a son. And when Mary asked how that could be, the angel responded, "The holy Spirit shall come upon you and the power of the Most High shall overshadow you; and therefore the Holy One to be born shall be called Son of God." (1:35)

After carefully examining a substantial variety of interpretations Schaberg concludes:

Both conceptions (by Elizabeth and by Mary) are due to sexual intercourse, and both are empowered by the creative activity of God. But here in 1:35 the terms "holy" and "Son of God" do carry special meaning. This child will be holy because

136

the Holy Spirit will come upon his mother, and she will experience divine protection and empowerment even in a situation deemed unholy. This child, unholy in human estimation, will be holy before God. Like "every male that opens the womb," he will be called holy to the Lord. (2:23) That is, he will be considered sacred, will be set apart and consecrated tot the service of God. The child will be called the Son of the Most High and Son of God because the power of the Most High will overshadow his mother. He will enter the world as Son of God because God says so: god in effect declares him to be son, accepts him as son, anticipating 3:22 (the baptism of Jesus, where the Holy Spirit descended upon Jesus in bodily form as a dove, and a voice from heaven, "You are my beloved Son, in you I am well pleased.) Divine paternity, then, does not replace human paternity. (125-126)

It is good to note that in John's gospel, it is John the Baptist who speaks these words:

I beheld the Spirit descending as a dove from heaven. And I did not know him. But he who sent me to baptize with water said to me, "He upon whom you will see the Spirit descending, and abiding upon him, he it is who baptizes with the Holy Spirit." And I have seen and have borne witness that this is the Son of God. (1:32-34)

If Schaberg is correct in her conclusions, what was the purpose of Matthew and Luke to declare Jesus as the one born of the Holy Spirit? Schaberg refers to the rumors and charges in the days of early Christianity about Jesus' illegitimacy. His name needed to be cleared so that he could be seen as the one who was truly a divinely spirited person. Even when the illegitimacy charge would not have existed, still the acclamations of Matthew and Luke would serve the purpose of the announcement of Jesus as a special person. For both authors the purpose was different.

Matthew is regarded as a Jew who had great hopes for his people and his tradition. In his day, after the death of Jesus, and with enhanced persecution by the Romans and the build-up of the revolutionary forces who created great unrest, Matthew became disheartened in terms of the expectations for the future of this world. The apocalyptic literature had provided him with the imagery of a New Heaven and a New Earth. With his exaltation of Jesus as the Son of God, born of the Holy Spirit, he announced the beginning of the end-time. The greatness of the Lord would secure the breaking in of the final fulfillment of the Kingdom of God which is on high.

Luke, on the other hand, had different aspirations. Like Paul, he was committed to bringing the Kingdom of God on this earth, mightier than the Roman empire and fulfilling all expectations. He needed to make Jesus, the center of this Kingdom, accepted as the son of the Almighty. The citizens of the Roman Empire were assured that this Jesus was a promising authority for a new order.

> Luke sees and seizes the opportunity to begin the story of Jesus with what he considers a perfect response to the word and promise of God, a response of human incomprehension and trust, the response of the woman Mary. God takes the initiative, Mary obeys. As part of his espousal of a new social order based on service and humility....(143-144)

Schaberg elaborates this socio-political concern of Luke in trying to bring about God's Kingdom on this earth.

> In Greco-Roman biographies, stories of miraculous or marvelous conceptions functioned to explain the hero's later greatness. In a similar way, the story of Luke told, of divine involvement in Jesus' conception, set the stage and provided an explanation of Jesus' extraordinary earthly life. The whole structure of Luke's presentation of the life of Jesus resembles in some significant ways the biography of an immortal, or (in broader terms) the Greco-Roman superstar paradigm. Luke's Jesus has an extraordinary conception, lives the life of a benefactor of humanity, dies a martyr's death, and is translated into the heavens. His work is continued in the work of his disciples and followers. (126)

Then she quotes immediately Talbert's "The Concept of the Immortals."

> "There is no way a Mediterranean person could have missed (Luke's presentation) as a portrayal of Jesus in the mythology of the immortals....If the converts in Luke's church came from the Greco-Roman world where philosophers were sometimes described as divine who became immortals, then the Lucan picture of Jesus is intelligible. (126)

Schaberg bases such conclusions on the assumption that Luke himself was a Gentile Christian, who received a good Hellenistic education. He was challenged to interpret the significance of Jesus, who was a Jew, to a Gentile Christian people. (127)

138

Obviously, my use of Schaberg is highly sketchy. So much is left out that my presentation does not give due credit to her outstanding and substantial scholarship in her research. I read her accounts for the sake of formulating the insights here reported. This provides us the opportunity to engage in some conclusions which will lead to further developments in our journey.

Discussion

The connection was made between Campbell's interpretation of the Virgin Birth and the gospel of Matthew. Campbell explained how the Virgin Birth signifies the emergence of compassion as the source of true human spirituality. At the heart of Matthew's account is also the compassion of the Lord which inspired Mary to embrace the child within her with great delight and courage.

Thus for Matthew the seat of the new life in Mary was the mercy of the Lord. In that spirit the pregnancy received true meaning and expectations. What follows is the unfolding of this mercy and compassion in the life of her son.

In Luke's account one may regard the story somewhat in reverse. Luke was impressed by and amazed about the person Jesus and all the things said about him. Here was truly a wonderful man. The life of Jesus was already a great event. People talked about him, and his disciples and followers were in town and in other places. Schaberg argues that the Hellenistic background of Luke provided him with the mythical material by which he could interpret the existence of Jesus.

"The whole structure of Luke's presentation of the life of Jesus resembles in some significant ways the biography of an immortal, or (in broader terms) the Greco-Roman superstar paradigm. (126)

And her quote of Talbert's "The Concept of the Immortals."

"There is no way a Mediterranean person could have missed [Luke's presentation] as a portrayal of Jesus in the mythology of the immortals....If the converts in Luke's church came from the Greco-Roman world where philosophers were sometimes described as divine men who became immortals, then the Lucan picture of Jesus in intelligible.' (126)

This reference to the Hellenistic culture invites us to learn more about the idea, Virgin Birth, in that context. In *The Power of Myth* Joseph Campbell discusses the virgin birth, the mother as conceiving of the spirit, by telling the story about Isis and her child Horus, and then gives further references, which will provide us with related insights:

> MOYERS: So Isis is able to say, "I am she that is the natural mother of all things. Mistress and governess of all the elements. Chief of the powers divine, queen of all that are in hell, but principal of all them that dwell in heaven. Manifested alone and under one form of all the gods and goddesses."

> CAMPBELL: That is a very late statement of the whole theme. That comes in Apuleius' Golden Ass, second century A. D. The Golden Ass is one of the first novels, by the way. Its leading character, its hero, has been by lust and magic converted into an ass, and he has to undergo an ordeal of painful and humiliating adventures until his redemption comes through the grace of the Goddess Isis. She appears with a rose in her hand (symbolic of divine love, not lust), and when as an ass he eats this rose, he is converted back into a man. But he is now more than a man, he is an illuminated man, a saint. He has experienced the second virgin birth, you see. So from mere animal-like carnality, one may pass through a spiritual death and become reborn. The second birth is of an exalted, spiritually informed incarnation.

> And the Goddess is the one who brings this about. The second birth is through a spiritual mother. Notre Dame de Paris, Notre Dame de Chartres – Our Mother Church. We are reborn spiritually by entering or leaving a church. (179)

The *Encyclopaedia Britannica,* 1962, regards Lucius Apuleius as a Platonic philosopher. Moreover, one learns that within this novel there is an episode called, "Cupid and Psyche," (bk iv-vi). This mythological imagination about Psyche dramatizes the developmental aspects mentioned by Campbell in his interpretation of the chakras. In Greek mythology, Psyche is the personification of the human soul. In Platonic philosophy, love, in the highest sense, is the agent of the soul's progress. And that is certainly the case in the presentation of Psyche by Apuleius. Here is the summary as told in the *Encyclopaedia Britannica*:

...Psyche, the youngest daughter of a king, arouses the jealousy of Venus, who orders Cupid to inspire her with love for the most despicable of men. Cupid, however, falls in love with her and carries her off to a secluded spot, where he visits her by night, unseen and unrecognized by her. Persuaded by her sister that her companion is a hideous monster, and forgetful of his warning, she lights a lamp to look upon him as he is asleep; in her ecstasy at his beauty she lets fall a drop of burning oil upon the face of Cupid, who awakes and disappears. Wandering over the earth in search of him, Psyche falls into the hands of Venus, who forces her to undertake the most difficult tasks. The last and most dangerous of these is to fetch from the world below the box containing ointments of beauty. She secures the box, but on her way back opens it and is stupefied by the vapour. She is only restored to her senses by Cupid, at whose entreaty Jupiter makes her immortal and bestows her in marriage upon her lover. (Volume 18, p. 667)

Here we have the basic material which inspired many authors to elaborate on the psychological developmental dynamics signified by this story. For example, Erich Neumann, *Amor and Psyche: The Psychic Development of the Feminine, A Commentary on the Tale by Apuleius; The Great Mother: An Analysis of the Archetype; The Origins of Consciousness*; writings by Hilde Binswanger: "Positive Aspects of the Animus," "Ego, Animus, and Persona in the Feminine Psyche,"; Marie-Louise von Franz, *Problems of the Feminine in Fairytales*.

I hold it very important to become aware of these interpretations, because they are about the Virgin Birth as understood in mythical terms. We are to create an awareness of these universal human experiences as told by the mythical so we learn to appreciate the spiritual significance of these images and characters. In his book, *Jesus: An Experiment in Christology* Edward Schillebeeckx has a subsection called, "In search of the grounds of Jesus' *Abba* experience, the heart of his message, life and death: the secret of his life disclosed." (652). He raises the question:

Can this fundamental, creaturely status, this "being of God" – common to all human beings and at the same time differentiated to each individual's own localized and personal profile – be sufficient ground also in Jesus for elucidating his private, certainly highly profiled *Abba* experience? (653)

The experiences "common to all human beings" is at the heart of Campbell's approach to the religious dimension. The mythological wisdom speaks about the significance of the Virgin Birth, which finds a particular representation in the story about Psyche. If this is the birth of compassion, then we are to see how this compassion is developed and how it is being born. Our guide is Ann Lammers in "The Myth of Psyche: Feminine Consciousness and Individuation." She relies very much on the studies of Hilde Binswanger, Marie-Louise von Franz, and Erich Neumann. Neumann calls myths "confessions unobscured by consciousness." Lammers holds that in symbols and myths the feminine and masculine are interrelated, and one cannot speak about one without the other. The sections of the article have titles which signify the developmental stages in the psychological growth.

"The Untouchable Goddess." Psyche begins her journey in a state of primary narcissism, a childish concern for herself. This is a form of imprisonment by the matriarchal Great Mother, Aphrodite. The beginning of the influence of the masculine in Psyche's story is that she is put on the mountain as the bride of an inhuman, terrifying creature. Although this is a frightful situation, it provides the first step of growth from Aphrodite's power. Growth is regarded as a divine energy – a tendency of the unconscious to seek wholeness.

"Exposure on the Mountain." Psyche's narcissism is now supersede by a miserable isolation. The mountaintop is the place of spiritual ordeal, the holy place of initiation. There Apollo reigns and he is the masculine power. He provides Psyche with a dragon-born husband, Amor.

"The Marriage of Darkness." Psyche does not know who her husband is, cannot see him, is forbidden to talk about him. Psyche only knows the sexual passion of her "beastly" lover. Amor is here the personification of the underdeveloped masculine side, who demands that Psyche be ignorant, sweet, and silent. The aspect of Psyche needs humanizing.

"Psyche as Light Bearer." In the symbolic language of growth, Psyche is pregnant with new life. Now, more than ever, she wants to find out about her husband. The light she carries to take away the darkness around Amor is the unborn child within her. In addition to the lamp, she has a knife, which symbolizes consciousness, the ability to discern and know. When Amor wakes up, he leaves her, and blames Psyche for destroying their happiness. The implications are, that Psyche, trapped in the unconscious, could not be happy. The price to be paid for consciousness, the formation of the ego, is the death of the natural condition. We will learn about the reality of life by the conflicts we encounter.

"The Quest for Reunion." First, Psyche throws herself into the river. That means she wants to step aside from her ego. She want to let go into the unconscious. Thus the conscious and the unconscious meet. From this a transformation emerges. She experiences Pan with Echo in his arms. Pan is the old vegetative wisdom and Echo is the mountain goddess, the listener. Echo encourages her to listen to Pan's wisdom, and receives the message of the instinctive life. Lammers quotes from James Hillman's The Dream and the Underworld: "The ear is the feminine part of the head; it is the conscious offering maximum attention with a minimum of intention." It is the time for Psyche to be patient and let things grow.

It is the time of regeneration as a feminine being. She should not rely totally on the masculine to liberate herself from Aphrodite. Now she has to seek an encounter with Amor on equal grounds and "win him by tender submission." In this spirit she returns to Aphrodite and makes herself available for the task assigned to her. Aphrodite senses that this is not a slavish submission, but a dedication to creativity. She plays along and is intrigued by what this newness may bring.

At this stage Amor comes secretly into play trying to help Psyche in fulfilling impossible tasks. Psyche learns to understand things and make proper responses. She learns to say "no" when appropriate, she becomes wise in gathering things around her with patience and taste. She learns that she cannot save the world and can do only her share. As such, one cannot be like the Great Mother, the All-Merciful who understands everything and forgives everything. As such she develops an individual love.

"Failure and Redemption." Psyche is to find her way back into the instinctive, feminine realm. In this context Lammers quotes Jung,

> Sankhya philosophy has elaborated the mother archetype into the concept of *praktri* (matter) and assigned to it the three...fundamental attributes: goodness, passion, and darkness. These are the three essential aspects of the mother: her cherishing and nourishing goodness, her orgiastic emotionality, and he Stygian depths.

These realms are to be integrated by Psyche. In this sense one is to understand the irrational act of Psyche when she opens the casket of "beauty ointment" from the underworld and falls into a deadlike sleep. As such she totally capitulates to the power of love for Amor. Then Amor appears and wakes her up. Psyche's act of faith is called feminine, because it is not a sacrifice for love's sake, not a victory of herself, but the giving of herself to the love for one person.

"Birth of Pleasure on Mount Olympus." The birth of the self is symbolized by the birth of the child – a daughter, whose name is Pleasure on Mount Olympus." The birth of the self is symbolized by the birth of the child – a daughter, whose name is Pleasure or Joy. This development is the process of a mature individuation, which has made a conscious decision to embrace the greatness of what is beyond the ego – the ability to give of oneself for the sake of goodness in the spirit of compassion. The feminine light-bearer connects the light from within with the light out there. In this spirit the forces of darkness, the experience of failure and defeat, can be counteracted by the divine energy, which strives for wholeness. This is the birth of the true virgin, who will respond to the angel and whose child is born out of the Holy Spirit.

Thus virgin and Virgin Birth are not technical terms which are subject to theological speculations. They are religious terms which represent the growth dynamics within the human energy which is divine in nature. This

Spirit was embraced by the virgin and she conceived her child spiritually after it was conceived sexually.

The myth of Psyche and Amor features Psyche as the hero. This is the feminine who grows by means of the animus complex. There is a need to identify these developmental dynamics in reference to a male. This will be attempted in the next chapter which features the artist. William Blake, his life and his work. In that context additional insights will be offered in reference to publications by scholars of Campbell's interpretation of virgin and Virgin Birth.

Chapter Eight

Other References to Virgin and Virgin Birth

Joseph Campbell's interpretations of virgin and Virgin Birth were not a total surprise to me. In the days of "the death of God" literature, Thomas Altizer made me aware of the great significance of William Blake. He was the only Christian who understood which God should die and which energy should become freed and activated by this death. In *Radical Theology and the Death of God* by Thomas J. J. Altizer and William Hamilton is Altizer's "William Blake and the Role of Myth in the Radical Christian Vision." Altizer states, "Somehow I love this piece more than any other article I have published." The following is in regard to myth:

> All of us know that the old myths are dead. But does this mean that myth itself has died? Are we immersed in a world in which a total vision is no longer a possibility? Can myth in our time be no more than a dead fragment of the forgotten past or a pathological aberration of the sick mind? Or is the mythmaker in our seemingly post-Christian world doomed to be the gravedigger of the Christian God, the seer who can but name the darkness that has descended with the eclipse of our sun? Has the wheel now come full circle; must we return to the night of our beginning with no hope of another day? Have we lost the very power to name the darkness of our night? Ours is a situation that is peculiarly open to the vision of the most radical of modern Christian visionaries, William Blake, for no poet or seer before him had so profoundly sensed the cataclysmic collapse of the cosmos created by Western man. Yet Blake celebrated this collapse as the way to a total and apocalyptic transfiguration of the world. Can Blake's vision be truly meaningful to us? Is the mythical world which he created one that can enter our consciousness

and redirect our sensibility? Can we through Blake know a new form of the human hand and face, and a new direction of the vast cosmos about and beyond us? To the extent that these questions can be answered affirmatively we have a decisive means also of answering affirmatively the question of whether or not myth can assume a new and revolutionary form. (172-173)

It is intriguing to read that Blake was "the most original seer in Christendom...." (173) Moreover:

At this point we must fully recognize that Blake committed the blasphemy of blasphemies by identifying the biblical God as Satan. Not only did Blake leave numerous personal statements to this effect, but in his supreme pictorial creation, his illustrations for the Book of Job (and Blake, like Kierkegaard ever identified himself with Job), depicted God as Satan on the magnificent eleventh plate, and did so in fulfillment of his own vision, in this work, that redemption can take place only after the transcendent and numinous God has been recognized as Satan or Selfhood. (176-177)

Before I read this, I had perused books on the history of art and looked at Blake's most celebrated pieces of graphic art. I also had read some of his engraved poems, but I could not relate to them with great depth. At the encouragement of Altizer, I became determined to investigate the wisdom of this famous poet who lived less than two centuries ago. I read Jacob Bronowski's book on Blake, because I was intrigued that the scientist, Bronowski, could relate so creatively to Blake's poetry. However, everything began to become more understandable when I discovered Anne Kostelanetz Mellor's book, Blake's Human Form Divine. The developmental dynamics of Psyche are dramatically present in Blake's own maturation process. The point of connection with he myth of Psyche is that Blake's main hero is the figure of a woman. The development of his inner life, his psyche, is told in reference to this feminine presence.

Kostelanetz Mellor tells the Blake story according to five stages: Innocence, Energy, Pessimism, Reawakening of Innocence, and Jerusalem. Again, this reference to Blake is made for the sake of a better understanding of the mythical dynamics in the maturation process of the human psyche. Thus we have a better sense of the mythical image, "the Virgin Birth." Moreover, one truly experiences the creative energy of the divine imagination which motivated Blake. The following is based on Mellor's book:

Innocence: Among the first published poems of William Blake are *Songs of Innocence* (1789). The innocence described is a rather simple worldview. It holds that God resides within us and around us. A definite sentiment of wholesomeness and harmony prevails, which is based on the conviction that heaven and earth are virtually one. It is a rather closed form of life, which does not reveal expressive dynamics of an enterprising creativity. The atmosphere is characterized by a faithful obedience to God's rulings, with the secured hope that in His divine wisdom He will provide in our need. When one knows one's proper place and relationship with God, then the spirit of Innocence dwells in one's heart.

The characters featured in these poems are: a shepherd, a little boy, a chimney sweep, a nurse, a lamb, and a myriad of rustic images which represent a world of childlike peace. Some accused Blake of being unrealistic in his description of such a nostalgic innocence. Did he not know that life was a struggle, and in many instances caused suffering and pain? Especially when the social injustices of the eighteenth century became so manifest in the atrocious circumstances of child labor, the slave trade, and situations as were described in Dickens' *Oliver Twist*. Kostelanetz Mellor holds that Blake wrote about innocence in a dialectic fashion. (12) He intended to describe this childlike trust in life because he was afraid that people would lose sight of it in their frustrations with life. He hoped to keep alive this aspect of the divine, and he sang its praise so that people should not stop their longing for this innocence. Thus, in a mild form, we see already Blake's commitment to the divine innocence, in terms of its redeeming importance. Moreover, Blake's opposition to the bleak social conditions of the citizens indicates his belief in reactionary forces which would be able to bring about the land of human dignity and joy.

These characteristics grew substantially in the further developments of Blake's prophetic visions. The growth, however, occurred slowly, and in the intermediate stages it became entangled in some unsatisfactory solutions. This can be seen in *The Book of Thel* (1789). It describes the world of Innocence as opposed to the world of a stratified authoritarian power which oppresses people and prevents them from discovering their own divine aspects. Thel is the maturing girl who faces the invitations of womanhood. Her innocence is divine because she is open to life and willingly wishing (in Greek *thelo* means "I wish" or "I will") to embrace its offerings. The world of Innocence, within which she was educated, had taught her how to integrate and account for the evil aspects in life. That part of evil, which would obstruct people's social relations, had to be overcome with courage and faith. Sickness and death were to be explained as part of the life cycles and were understandable according to the divine agenda. Thel's innocence, however, becomes disturbed when she personally reflects on the fact of her own possible death. What is the meaning of her existence if she finally dies and is buried? Would her fulfillment consist of being eaten by worms?

As in a form of enlightenment she understands that everything and all of reality constitute the divine realm of which we are part. Thus, to be eaten by worms is part of the divine reality, because they too fulfill their divine role. In this spirit, Thel is prepared to be open to life and love. As a woman, she is ready to embrace and be embraced in letting the divine forces of procreation be celebrated. She is willing to become fully part of life's cycle.

But by this openness Thel enters the unprotected and fallen world where the cursing Tiriel rules. The totalitarian system of this dictator was insensitive to the needs of longings of people, and Tiriel made their livers miserable. Thel is exposed to the deceit, fear, and anxiety which rape life and terrorize people. This was too much for her, and she flees back to her home. There are those who accuse Blake for letting this poem end this way. They interpret Thel's final flight as a defeat, where the poet expresses a certain powerlessness in the face of these social evils. Thel does not show signs o a personal commitment to the improvement of the social conditions which plagued England under the dubious government of King George III.

Kostelanetz Mellor explains Thel's flight as a personal choice for a life of love and innocence, instead of a slavery under the ruling powers of the land. These powers were not only of a political and hierarchical nature. They also emerged in the development of science, technology, and empirical philosophy. They too were insensitive to human innocence as experienced by Blake. Consequently, Mellor defends Thel's solution as a somewhat good decision, because the poet maintained his belief in Innocence. He wanted to let his readers know that a personal redemption from the fallen world was possible, as illustrated in Thel's personal choice.

However, did Blake shy away from his responsibility for the improvement of the public life by efforts to eliminate the social evils? Was he a fatalist who did not believe in the making of a better tomorrow? This will be discussed next.

Energy: The impression created in the previous section is that the world of Innocence is opposed to the fallen world and that the two cannot truly interrelate. This view became more and more unacceptable to Blake. In his *The Marriage of Heaven and Hell* (1790-93), he projected that Innocence has to be actively forceful in order to terminate social injustice. Blake called this aspect of Innocence, "Energy," which needed to be activated. The Christian Church was envisioned as the first object of the revolutionary Energy. The sneaking snake of deceit and oppression had infiltrated that land of innocence. This made Blake truly angry, and he described how the just and prophetic man, Tintrah "roars and shakes his fire in the burdened air."

The source of Energy is the eternal delight in life which fights against rationalistic restraints. Reason was understood as the opposite of the delight – seeking Energy. Reason contracts and moves backward to limited restrictions, while Energy expands into infinity. It should be noted that Blake believed in a dialectic worldview. Although he sided with Energy, he understood that reason was needed to put some order in Energy's strivings toward further expansions. In the dialectic struggle between these two aspects of life Blake represented the vigor of Energy. This vitality was so much restrained and oppressed by institutions and conservative authorities who did not trust life and also abused it. The angel of Reason had condemned Energy to Hell as a devil. Blake discovered that there was so much wisdom and goodness in the Energy which the establishment had rejected as devilish. In his "Proverbs of Hell," he described these divine aspects in a vibrant tone.

> The pride of a peacock is the glory of God
> The lust of the goat is the bounty of God

> The wrath of the lion is the wisdom of God
> The nakedness of a woman is the work of God

This is obviously a voice against the prudishness which would become Victorian in the next century. It signals a rebellion against a negative understanding of human life, where false modesty and exaggerated theologies of sin and corruption strangled the pulsating drives of human longings.

Thus Blake developed from a closed Innocence a worldview of Energy as an open and trusting system. The poet believed in a rebellion against oppressive forces, and he expected the battle to be rewarding and successful. This optimism is expressed in two of his works which he finished in 1773: *Visions of the Daughters of Albion* and *America A Prophecy*.

In the first, Energy is portrayed by a matured Thel whose name is Oothoon. She is on her way the "land of death" to relate to her lover, Theotormon, her belief in Innocence. On this journey she is raped by Bromion. When Theotormon hears about that, he considers Oothoon impure. Blake's major concern is to describe Oothoon's reactions and courage by which she shows how Innocence can still be maintained in the corruptive world of authoritarian and rationalistic reason. Oothoon represents Blake's belief in a "breaking day, which symbolizes the vision of time as a progressive dynamic which will bring about the day of redemption. This will be the "last judgment" where goodness and the divine will dethrone evil. The "deadly black" of the night will be replaced by the early morning glow which announces the coming of daylight. Oothoon understands what corrupts the mind of her Theotormon. It is Urizen, Reason, the creator of men. He is the mistaken Demon of Heaven. He inspires kings and priests to take money from the poor and oppress them with their rules which stifle human sexual desires and condemn longings as sinful. In the end Oothoon exclaims, "for everything that lives is holy."

In *America* the poet elaborated on how Innocence and Energy can counteract the closed lifestyle of Reason. As an artist, Blake came to understand that the devotion to creative art helps one to formulate and celebrate the innocent Energy. Thus, one could maintain the visions of Innocence and also communicate these insights to others in the works of art.

Creative art would help people find liberation from evil institutions and develop contact with the projections of Energy. Moreover, in *America A Prophecy*, Blake sang the praise of a political and military revolution which was capable of destroying the suppression of Urizen and his tyrants, George III and the Anglican Church. Orc, the spirit of revolutionary energy, had triumphed.

However, in the same year, 1793, Blake came to a different appraisal of the victorious rebellious forces. He published a picture booklet, *For Children: The Gates of Paradise*, which expresses a rather gloomy worldview. Blake had decided that life on earth is dominated by darkness and there is no real hope for liberation. The booklet contains no pictures of a sun-filled playful atmosphere. The people are portrayed as being hunched over and weary, because the forces around them are oppressive. Man is compared to a caterpillar which survives in the darkness of the cocoon. Hope is centered on life after death, where a person will leave the body, and as an immortal soul, go to heaven, as a butterfly leaves the shell of the cocoon to fly up into the sky. Those who would try to be creative are depicted as youngsters whose wings are clipped by an old man with his eyes closed.

In those days revolutionary-minded people where thrown into prison and tortured by soldiers who executed the ruling and depressive power of the King and the Church.

In the course of these developments, within the poet this interpretation of Energy became far less positive. Energy was no longer valued as a divine power, but it appeared as a neutral force, e.g., a will-to-power. Such a force is not necessarily good and progressive. It can also create a totalitarian and domineering system, where fear and oppression obscure life and its delights. This development is at the heart of Blake's publications from 1794 to 1805.

Pessimism: In this context, pessimism means a distrust in humanity as a source for creating better and more dignified life styles. It is a disbelief in meaning and purpose within the world. All hope for fulfillment is projected in the hereafter, where true spiritual blessings await us.

In his *The Book of Urizen* (1794), Blake described the view of this world which made him pessimistic. The key to the epic is that Reason became totally authoritarian. The creative imagination and energy of the human was overruled by the enslaving rationalistic forces. The historical context was characterized by a series of depressive events. The French Revolution appeared to be a great failure, because the initial signs of liberation were burned down by jealousy and the blind desire of power among the battling groups. In England the reactionaries were persecuted severely, and King George III showed more of his authoritarian oppression by not allowing the Catholic emancipation in Ireland. Religious freedom was not tolerated. Blake wrote angrily, "To defend the Bible in this year 1798 would cost a man his life."

The Book of Urizen tells about the creation of the universe. Urizen represents the mind which is limited by reason. Originally, Urizen was united with Los, the poetic imagination or divine vision. Because of this separation Urizen became a legalistic, rigid, hypocritical tyrant, who incarnated the human body. The poetic vision had disappeared. The present predicament of the world was seen by Blake as fallen Experience, which does not respond to imaginative love. Orc, the revolutionary energy, became also a victim of Urizen and was chained by the totalitarian powers.

There was an element of consolation towards the end of the book. Fuzon, a Moses figure, gathers a remnant of those who still can somewhat hear and see. They undertake the journey out of slavery to the land of promise, but Blake suggests that they have drowned in the Red Sea. Even if they were successful in their flight, no one can ever follow their path because the grip of Urizen is final. He is portrayed as a bearded old man, who is nearsighted and has a closed mind.

By 1795 all of Blake's work, his poetry as well as his drawings and paintings, expressed a gloom-filled atmosphere. He had lost hope for humanity. The life's energy within him sought ways which would lead to some form of consolation. If it could not be found in this world, then we should direct our hearts tot he life after death. This is the character of his book, *Vala*. This writing was very much influenced by Edward Young's *Night Thoughts*. In this epic, Young described in nine episodes (nine nights) the different stages of human corruption and the final victory of hope in the vision of the triumphant resurrected Christ. Thus there is only one consolation: the resurrected life which is spiritual in nature.

Between 1795 and 1797, Blake made 537 watercolor paintings for Young's poem, and he became personally involved in the dramatic contention of this work. He gave much reflection to Young's insights and began to reinterpret the poem's observations and theories. For example, where Young saw the fall of humanity in the failure to obey the lines of reason, Blake considered an excessive observance of laws and reason as the fall into the pit of oppression and suffering. Growth and liberation were overruled by rational behavior. This creative response to Young's poem inspired Blake to write his own nine episodes in *Vala,* or *The Death and Judgment of the Ancient Man, A Dream of Nine Nights* (1795-1805).

The "Preludium" of this epic describes the emergence of inertia within creation, where the imaginative energy of "Eternal Life" falls into the powers of "Duty instead of Liberty." The primordial forces of Innocence, Enion and Tharmes (who represent the original unity of physical and psychic dynamics, became separated. Because of a jealous despair, Enion fashions from her repressed longing for Tharas, a "Phantasm," with which she unites. Out of this copulation come forth Los and Enitharmon, who suck energy from Enion's breasts and grow strong. They are motivated by a desire for power to control time and space. Los is described as a weak, but still significant representation of Innocence. He seems to be concerned with the life which initially inspired his parent, Enion. Enitharmon accuses him of such affiliations, and she asks Urizen to destroy Los. Urizen asserts himself and terminates the life of Innocence, which becomes a hopeless shadow.

Of course, the complexity of the story reveals some of Blake's psychoanalysis of the culture and its influence on people. The corruption of life finds further descriptions in the first seven nights of *Vala.* A variety of pervert situations are portrayed in terms of sexual jealously, prescribed puritanism, violence, social injustice, and other brutal aspects which destroy the joy of life. The culture suffered from mental illness and Blake delineated some of its causes. Tharas, the primordial drive for life, originally united intellect, imagination, feelings, and drives. With this disintegration, fear, anxiety, oppression, abuse, distrust, and despair mushroomed into existence. The culture had lost sight of the soundness within the physical makeup of the human. Because of fragmentation the original unit was lost. Rationality took parts out of their basic context, and certain ideas became rigidly fixed within time and space. These fixed and rationalistic notions obscured the vision of Innocence. The physical body could no longer act as a source which would relate a possible vision of the divine. Orc, as the reactionary and revolutionary dynamic, became a student of Urizen and learned how to be a warrior (similar to Napoleon).

Now Urizen wants to become all in all, and he fashions creation so that everything will mirror him. The products are atrocious little monsters, who frighten even Urizen. He escaped their presence by fleeing into the void. This, however, is not the end of Urizen, because he restores himself into an even more vigorous dictator.

Thus, according to Blake, human passion (Luvah), reason (Urizen), physical and psychic unity (Tharas), and imagination (Urthona), all became corrupted. In the seventh Night there is a final reawakening of Orc as the revolutionary spirit which seeks liberation. There is a tremendous battle, but finally Urizen is victorious and Orc is condemned as a mother of sin. The world situation has become totally hopeless.

Then Blake described Vala as a sorrowful, crying woman. She writes on every tombstone: "If ye will believe, your brother shall rise again." Thus the poet accepted the Christian promise of resurrection, where the fallen human body will be transformed into a pure and spiritual form.

In the ninth Night there is a reference to a final judgment, where all bodies of the dead will be redeemed. Thus, the only consolation for the human is in the belief that God will provide for us after death because of His divine love. In the meantime we just have to wait for these things to happen. Vala seeks her Lord, not within herself but beyond herself, in the realms outside of this world. This worldly life can be entertained with some music, sex, play, and doing the things we have to do to survive. But mentally we should prepare ourselves to grow spiritually, so that we are ready for the afterlife in the divine heavens. The only harmony in life comes from this belief.

Obviously, Blake had lost all concern for the social evils of his time, because they appeared too numerous and overwhelming. His religiosity had grown into an esoteric ghetto mentality where one shields oneself as much as possible from the evil world to save one's soul. However, Blake was not content with this solution in Vala. He continued to search for the land of Innocence, which he did not want to evaporate altogether form this world. His search was rewarded, because he found a far better vision than *Vala* had communicated. He wrote *The Four Zoas*, where he showed the readers a totally different Blake.

Reawakening of Innocence: In a letter to William Hayley (May 4, 1804), Blake described his great joy of having rediscovered the delight of life, which once inspired his youth. He mentioned that this "light" had "for exactly twenty years been closed from me by a door and by window shutters." The letter does not elaborate on the true developments within him, but the excitement is vibrant and jubilant: "For Now! O Glory! and O Delight!...Suddenly, on the day after visiting the Truchsesian Gallery of pictures, I was again enlightened with the light I enjoyed in my youth..." From now on Blake's art became infiltrated with this personal vision of the divine.

Some scholars deny that this enlightenment is already present in his "The Mental Traveller" (c. 1803-1805). The poem emphasized the ongoing vicious cycle within which Urizen emerges repeatedly as the victor over revolutionary Energy. Mellor, however, holds that the key to Blake's personal redemption is already contained in "The Mental Traveller." She explains that there are two visions communicated in the poem. The first indicate the ever-returning perversion of Urizen. The second shows awareness of a transcendental realm which is present in every finite form of existence. Mellor's contention is that Blake emphasized the vicious circle of the Urizenic repression to such an overwhelming degree, that one would accept this as an unavoidable fate within this world. Once a person accepts this state of affairs as a fact, then one can step beyond it and choose by imagination something better. The closed circle of Urizen's power should not bother us, because that would mean a loss of energy. It is better to accept and devote our energy of realms beyond this closed structure. How can this be done?

The wisdom of the redeeming approach is contained in the proverb, "Beauty is in the eye of the beholder." We need to use our imagination and creative energy to observe the divine within reality. Then we may see "a World in a Grain of Sand/And a Heaven in a Wild Flower/Hold Infinity in the Palm of your Hand/and Eternity in an Hour."

It was this enlightened mentality by which Blake felt inspired to rewrite *Vala*. He transformed it into a a new poem, *The Four Zoas – The Torment of Love & Jealousy in the Death and Judgment of Albion the Ancient*. In Blake's poetry, Albion represents a mythological character who emerged in different cultures as basically the same hero. He is Atlas, or one of the Titans in the Greek mythology, King Arthur in the early English legends, or any other vigorous hero in cultural epics.

The Four Zoas relate that Blake has superseded a dualistic worldview where matters are black or white, good or evil, light or dark, ugly or beautiful. The poet learned to understand that the complexity of life can be perceived within the scope of four aspects: Eden, Beulah, Earth, and Ulro. Eden is paradise, where the spiritual and physical exist in a creative harmony. Reason too is integrated with Energy. In Beulah there is some division, e.g., a certain separation of the female from the male. But there has been enough interaction between the two to let them enjoy a sleeping rest after their mutual involvement. Earth is the place where the human finds a particular shape and form. It is the world of Tharas, whose separation from the eternal and the divine can be redeemed in Christ. Beneath Earth is Ulro, the state where Urizen reigns oppressively, and where the male and female forms are divided and suffer from hostile confrontation and repression. The four Zoas are levels of operation according to which a person's energy can function. Of course, in Eden the enactment of Energy is far more gratifying than in the repressive realm of Ulro.

This poem communicated also another new insight of Blake. He became aware that Energy too is in itself complex and can be perceived in different ways. Blake's distinction is threefold. First, energy is the power by which we are able to integrate different aspects. Secondly, the physical, the psychical, and spiritual can become a harmonious unity. This harmonizing of energy is expressed in the libido and other psychic energy (Luvah). The third aspect of energy is found in the imagination (Los and Urthona).

The key to a truly liberated spirit is the ability not to let any of energy's aspects become dominant so that the other would be overruled. This insight is redeeming and gives substantial food for introspection and self-correction. By such a sincere reflection one can observe how certain deviations from the proper balance cause personal suffering. A return to Eden is possible if one becomes integrative about the complexity of life. Then the distrust of physical and bodily desires will not be feared as sinful. The holiness and the divine within the created life can be celebrated in a delightful fashion.

Within these perspectives Blake distinguishes two forms of salvation on Earth. First, there is the psychic integration of one's emotions and longing, so that reason, imagination, and desires blend into a harmonious unity of life. Thus, distrust, jealousy, and fear can be overcome in a creative spirit. This is a salvation for the individual person.

The second form of salvation is of social nature. It is activated by the artist who is able to formulate his insights of the divine and uses his imaginative creativity to communicate to others his redeeming visions. These insights stated in *The Four Zoas* determined the last part of Blake's life and made him an enlightened person. All his art after 1804 displays his mystic, prophetic, and apocalyptic interpretations of reality. It is permeated by a vibrant hopeful energy. This is certainly the case in one of his last poetic epics, *Jerusalem* (1805-1820).

Jerusalem: In this poem Evil is portrayed as the human body which is oppressed by a non-human environment. The divine is envisioned as a delightful, free, open and spacious realm. These are the two poles within which the drama of life takes place. The complexity of living is told as a story, where events characterize the powers of evil and the divine.

Originally, the basic intentions of existence are of a divine nature. But in the course of history at least three basic errors are committed. First, one began to abuse the human body. Second, a definite misuse of the mind occurred, as illustrated by Deists, who interpret the divine in terms of their own rationalistic reasoning. They make the divine lose its transcendental character and reduce it to a realm of systematic categories. The third error emerged in the corruption of the creative imagination. This is very much the fault of the established Christian Church.

Blake's prophetic ideas are directed at the correction of these errors. The body, mind, and imagination are to be transformed by the "divine vision." Thus Blake restored his former belief in the regeneration of goodness within humanity.

This optimism is portrayed by the watchman, who carries a light into the gloomy grave of the fallen world. He initiates the salvation by the divine vision. Albion has to wake up from "the sleep of Ulro." The call to creative action has been voiced by Jesus, who is "not a God afar off" but "a brother and friend." Blake applied his creative imagination in the description of the fallen state.

> The disease of Shame covers me from head to feet:
> I have no hope
> Every boil upon my body is a separate & deadly Sin.
> Doubt first assailed me, then Shame took possession of me
> Shame divides Families. Shame hath divided
> Albion in sunder!

Feelings and emotions which normally guide the human in the stream of life are all distorted and cramped by repression and distrust. Blake called this fallen state "An orbed void of doubt, despair, hunger & thirst, & sorrow."

In his description of Jerusalem as the divine realm Blake imagined its qualities in terms of a mature, beautiful and trusting woman, who gives herself to life as a flower in the warming sunlight. The soul of her fulfillment is her willingness and ability to respond to the expressions of the man's imagination. This is very much Blake's perception of the divine within reality. He held that one should be able to live life in a response to the creative imagination. The city should be built according to this basic dynamic. Then no repression and rigid legalism will abuse the human form divine.

After Albion had been wakened and had absorbed some of the divine inspirations, he had to be taught how to follow Christ. Albion had to overcome his selfishness, replace reason with love, and transform his desperation into a life of expecting imagination. The fall occurred because the individual aspect became separated from the basic harmonious unity.

For example, the woman set herself apart from the man. This made her primordial longings to love deteriorate into neurotic desires and obsessions. The final result was a deep hostility between the sexes and a multitude of suffering. Blake envisioned a different way of life in his description of a divine city, which Albion discovered.

> He found Jerusalem upon the River of his City soft repos'd
> In the arms of Vala, assimilating in one with Vala
> The Lilly of Havillah, and they sang soft thro' Lambeths vales,
> In a sweet sky spread over with wings and mild moon,
> Dividing & uniting into female forms: Jerusalem
> Trembling! then in one comingly in eternal tears,
> Sighting to melt his Giant beauty, on the moony river.
>
> (J 19:40-48)

This, of course, is the realm of Beulah, which is just below Eden. But the creative imagination will urge Albion to go one more step toward the divine. Albion is placed before the choice between the veiled Vala (the veil indicates a form of isolation) and the lovely and naked Jerusalem. The implications are evident. The divine is the sublime form of openness and trust. Even when hurt or frustrated, the divine will be able to forgive and integrate again those who failed.

The danger is building a city, which is to serve as a stronghold for human life, is the need for structure and a lawful organization. If one forgets that these structures are intended to serve the divine life, then they will victimize the feelings of Innocence and the creativity of Energy. Thus Blake was not a friend of the scientists in his day, who seemed to favor a reductionism where everything was explained in terms of their theories and formulas. In addition, the philosophers on the English scene projected a worldview based on the axioms of Empiricism. One was told that truth can only be found in what can be seen, touched, and measured. The scientists and the philosophers were conspirators of Urizen. Blake raged against them. Although this poet was an advocate of mercy and forgiveness, he believed in a holy anger, which was needed to uproot the sources of evil.

Blake's prophetic projections regarding a creative imagination were not of Promethean nature. Prometheus asserted himself against the ruling of Zeus, the master god. In Blake's epic we find a different religiosity. The poet knew that the inspirational energy had to come from the divine source.

Thus we find moments of doubt and hesitation, which take the form of a prayer

> O Lord & Savior, have the Gods of the Heathen
>> pierced thee?...
> Art thou alive & livest thou for-evermore? or art thou
> Not: but a delusive shadow, a thought that liveth not.
> Babel mocks saying, there is no God nor Son of God
> That thou O Human Imagination, O Divine Body art all
> A delusion, but I know thee O Lord when thou arisest upon
> My weary eyes even in this dungeon & this iron mill...
> And altho I sin & blaspheme thy holy name, thou pitiest me;
> Because thou knowest I am deluded by turning mills.
> And by these visions of pity & love because of Albions death.
>> (J 60:52, 54-9, 62-4)

A more convincing affirmation of the divine was expressed previously in a description of Jerusalem within the realm of Eden.

> We live as One man: for contracting our infinite senses
> We behold multitude; or expanding: we behold as one,
> As One Man all the Universal Family; and that One Man
> We call Jesus the Christ: and he in us, and we in him,
> Live in perfect harmony in Eden the land of life,
> Giving, receiving, and forgiving each others trespasses.
>> (J 38 [34]:17:22)

The contracting dynamics are the works of reason, the expanding ones represent creative energy. They are well integrated within the harmonious unity. If integrated, then the human faculties or reason, desire, wrath, and pity are all creative contributors to the human form divine. The worship of God consists of honoring Him with gratitude in a grateful appreciation of His gifts.

> Go, tell that the Worship of God is honouring his gifts
> In other men: & loving the greatest men best, each according
> To his Genius: which is the Holy Ghost in Man; there is no
>> other
> God, than that God who is the intellectual fountain of
>> Humanity.   (J 91:7-11)

> He who would see the Divinity must see him in his children
> One first, in friendship & love; then a Divine Family, & in the
>> midst
> Jesus will appear; so he who wishes to see a Vision; a perfect
>> Whole
> Must see it in its Minute Particulars; Organized...(J 91:18-21)

Blake's apocalyptic views are twofold. The appearance of the divine may occur in the individual's heart on a personal level. This is the emergence of the divine within time. There will also be a out-of-time appearance of the divine for all of humanity simultaneously. Mellor's explanations is as follows:

> For the moment that all men see themselves and each other as gods is the moment when earth becomes heaven, the particular becomes infinite, and time becomes eternity. (325)

She even applies Einstein's formula, $e = mc^2$, which holds that all matter is a form of energy. Energy can be explained in terms of matter, and matter can be explained in terms of energy. Applied to Blake's vision it would mean that the divine can be explained in terms of the created reality, and the created reality in terms of the divine. Indeed, beauty is in the eye of the beholder, and Blake saw so much of it that he displayed a tremendous amount of creative energy to communicate with us his visions of the divine and its redeeming influence on the fallen life.

In his own experience of agony and ecstasy Blake learned to understand that the objects around us are perceived by our own personal imagination. To recognize the relativity is to enter the realm of the divine openness which places everything within the dynamic of creative and imaginative Energy. The visions of Jerusalem help the traveller to delineate perspectives by which her/his journey of longing receives some direction and inspiration. With Albion we are invited to wake up and become universal in our perceptions of parts and segments which surround us and constitute our present makeup. We should not become victims of their particular shapes but let our imagination place them within the harmonizing unity of the divine.

Discussion

Joseph Campbell emphasized the understanding of Virgin Birth as a metaphor. Not to do so is to make a monster out of Jesus. Virgin Birth, then, means a second birth, the birth of the true human conceived by the spirit of compassion.

I found it necessary to elaborate on this aspect significantly by referring to Ann Lammers' interpretation of Psyche's maturation process in reference to Amor. Of course, this is easily understood by Jungian psychologists, who know that the growth of a woman is through her unconscious animus, which is the gate to her unconsciousness. Interpretations of Psyche are numerous and Lammers' rendition is delightfully creative in the understanding of these growth dynamics. Thus virgin birth is by means of Amor but the birth is of Psyche, within Psyche, and through the resourceful energy which spirited Psyche in her own decisions.

Because the maturation process of the male by means of the anima does not enjoy as much discussion as Psyche, more time was spent on William Blake's life journey. One should note that scholars of gnostic literature recognize that Blake was a gnostic. For that reason I looked at many publications by scholars of gnostic literature to see whether they affirm Blake in his powerful reinterpretation of Christianity. This proved to be very disappointing. Most authors seem to be educated within the framework of traditional Christianity. Although they are advanced in research about the Bible and the history of the biblical tradition, somehow the idea prevails that gnostic literature belongs to the world of heretics. There is not much understanding of the wisdom in the gnostic tradition, and there is a need to defend traditional Christianity because of its special claims, which are contested by the gnostic wisdom. Although Pheme Perkins published substantially on gnostic literature, I fail to recognize a religiousness in her which appreciated the gnostic wisdom. Some exceptions are Elaine H. Pagels and James M. Robinson, and also in his own way Werner H. Kelber.

In *Images of the Feminine in Gnosticism*, papers and responses are published as a record of the conference which convened November 19-25, 1985, at the Institute for Antiquity and Christianity in Claremont, California. In her Plenary Address, "Adam and Eve and the Serpent in Genesis 1-3," Elaine Pagels touches on the problem.

> It is an oversimplification – but not much – to look at the whole controversy between orthodox and gnostic Christians as a battle over the disputed territory of the first three chapters of Genesis.
> Yet gnostic and orthodox Christians read the same passages in radically different, even opposite, ways. To borrow the words of the nineteenth-century gnostic, William Blake, "Both read

the Bible day and night; but you read black where I read white. (413)

This is not only true for reading the Bible, it is also the case in reading the gnostic texts. Elaine Pagels alludes to that in her paper, "Pursuing the Spiritual Eve: Imagery and Hermeneutics in the *Hypostatsis of the Archons* and the *Gospel of Philip*," which is Chapter 15 in the mentioned book. Somehow, she is uncomfortable with the approach that one looks at some gnostic texts to find whether or not comments about women are anti-feminine.

> Yet many of us recognize too that this approach has its limits. We realize, first of all, that symbolism is not sociology. Pursuing feminine images through the murky marshes of gnostic texts, we risk falling into the error of the archons pursuing the spiritual Eve. You recall the story: she turns into a tree – the tree of life! – and laughs at the folly that leads her pursuers to mistake spiritual (read symbolic) transactions for merely sexual ones! So in this essay I am exploring a different approach – one that takes gnostic texts, in effect, at their word. Let us begin with the premise that gnostic authors concern themselves (as they say they do) above all the dynamics of religious experience. And let us grant, for our present purposes, that they engage issues concerning gender and sexuality only insofar as they believe that these involve – or, more typically, interfere with – religious experience. (188)

In fact, she is telling the conference that one should allow the gnostic texts to be understood as gnostic and one should not assess them in the hermeneutics of orthodox and traditional Christianity. According to the orthodox Christians, the gnostic texts misrepresent the Christian teachings. As such they are heretical. Such judgments are correct, if one assumes that there in only one true teaching of the Christian faith. If one has no understanding of the religious experience which is at the heart of the gnostic Christians, then one fails to read what they are trying to communicate. The pages devoted to the life and work of William Blake are intended to become aware of the soundness and sanity of the gnostic spirituality. Moreover, Blake accused institutionalized Christianity of killing the life and joy of the religious imagination which is energized in the Christian enlightenment.

It is necessary to become acquainted with insights which are produced by Blake's creative imagination. In *Images of the Feminine in Gnosticism,*

James M. Robinson makes this plea in "Very Goddess and Very Man: Jesus' Better Self."

> Masculine terminology overwhelms Christology, Jesus himself was male. The Jewish idea of the Messiah is built on the model of David and his male successors as kings of Judah. Masculine endings bind Chris*tos* and Kur*ios* to the male realm. *Son* of God and *Son* of *man* do the same. Even the Word of God produced masculine overtones (log*os*). The one christological title that is an exception is also the one that failed to make it: Wisdom (Sophia). The present essay seeks to investigate this aborted feminine Christology. (113-114)

This "aborted Christology" once existed but lost in the powerplay for recognition and dominance against orthodox Christianity. The quest for the fulness of the Christian faith demands that we try to rediscover the wisdom of gnostic Christianity. Robinson states:

> This Sophia Christology, precisely because it did not come to fruition in Western Christianity but shared in the Western neglect of Eastern Christianity, is less a recording of a traceable strand of Christian history than a nostalgic reminiscence of what might have been. Since the mythical world in which Christianity began is for us dead, this still-born Christology may be forever lost. (126)

Robinson reflects further on the significance of this stillborn Christology. He concludes that it is not just a nostalgic reminiscence, but perhaps of existential importance for the revitalization of the Christian faith. It is a case of relevancy.

> But, though we have seen through myths, in recognizing their non-literal and purely symbolic meaning – for example, in demythologization – they may as symbols have a new lease on life. Gnosticism could engender artificially its mythology out of the myths of the ancient Near East, or Plato could create the myth of the cave to portray his idealism, or Freud could appeal to Greek mythology to interpret the Oedipus complex, it is not inconceivable that this Sophia Christology could have an appeal in our day. (126)

But how can this be developed? What does it take to energize the religious imagination in this direction? Robinson holds:

> But, much more important, one must come to grips with what these symbols mean unmythologically, when they were spoken, which was then in the present. It is only pseudotheology to seek to reconcile into some harmonious doctrinal system the various *mythologoumena* by means of which meaning came to expression.

The shared trait, that one has to do with the Wisdom of *God* and the Kingdom *of God*, may provide a relevant lead. Jesus' insight is not just the crowning achievement of some Periclean, Augustean, or Elizabethan age, any more than his vision is that of a purification of the kingdom of this world into a Christian establishment (Christendom as the Kingdom of God). What went into Jesus and came out of Jesus is not of this world. "Of God" means it is transcendent. Not of course in the literal sense: Just as Wisdom did not fly down onto Jesus like a bird, the Kingdom is not some other place, or here in some other time. God's reign is utopia, the ultimate, just as Wisdom is the purity of intention, the commitment. Jesus' whole life was caught up in the cause of humanity, which possessed him with a consuming passion and came to expression through him with radical vision. Those who are caught on fire by him are possessed by the same Wisdom and proclaim the same utopian reign. (127)

What Robinson invites creative Christian imagination to produce in our time in the spirit of Wisdom Christology, William Blake enacted less than two centuries ago. Pagels called him a nineteenth-century gnostic. It is remarkable how dramatically the life and work of Blake signify the Wisdom tradition in his day, and as such into our own modern age.

First, Blake's awareness of Innocence is all-decisive. He did not hold that humanity is corrupted by Original Sin. The corruption, which is obvious, is the product of Urizen, reason and totalitarian systems and institutions. They suppress human spontaneity, and the creative imagination is repeatedly raped, victimized and rendered powerless. His belief in Energy as a revolutionary dynamic underwent some development. First a delight in Energy, and then a drastic disappointment, in the way Beethoven became so thoroughly disgusted with Napoleon, whom he had monumentalized in his "Eroica". But Blake's matured Thel, Oothoon, who initially could maintain her integrity inf the corruptive world which raped her, turned into Vala as a sorrowful and crying woman, who put all her hopes in the hereafter, the promise of the resurrections.

But the energy of Innocence reawakened. The simple belief in the victorious nature of Energy is educated by an awareness of the complexity of such challenges. Then Blake became more conscious of "Integration." (The delight of reading Blake is that he portrays so well the Jungian psychology of maturation a century before Jung's time.) Blake recognized that the physical, the psychical, and the spiritual can become a harmonious unity. The libido can be expressed in the psychic energy of Luvah. And the major agent or source of this integration is found in the imagination. The key to a truly liberated spirit is the ability not to let any of energy's aspects become dominant so that the others would be overruled. This is at the heart of Jung's psychotherapy.

Blake recognized a twofold process of redemption. First, there is the psychic integration of one's emotions and longings, so that reason, imagination and desire blend into a harmonious unity. Thus, distrust, jealousy, and fear can be overcome in a creative spirit. This is a salvation for the individual person. This salvation is amplified on the social level by the creative production of the artists who are energized by the creative imagination.

The last stage of Blake's life, which Kostelanetz Mellor called, Jerusalem, is the awareness of the divine which is symbolized and made present in terms of a mature, beautiful and trusting woman, who gives herself to life as a flower in the warming sunlight. The soul of her fulfillment is her willingness and ability to respond to the expressions of the man's imagination. This is very much Blake's perception of the divine within reality. He held that one should be able to live life as a response to the creative imagination. Then no repression and rigid legalism will abuse the human form divine. One central statement of Blake's mystical vision is quoted repeatedly.

> See a World in a Grain of Sand
> And a Heaven in a Wild Flower
> Hold Infinity in the Palm of your Hand
> And Eternity in an Hour.

This mystical awareness is present in Robinson's promotion of the Sophia Christology. Blake, too, recognized that the inspirational energy had to come from the divine source which he identified in his description of Jerusalem as the realm of Eden.

> We live as One Man: for contracting our infinite sense
> We behold multitude; or expanding: we behold as one,
> As one Man all the Universal Family; and that One Man
> We call Jesus the Christ: and he is us, and we in him,
> Live in perfect harmony in Eden the land of life,

Giving, receiving, and forgiving each others trespasses.

(J 38 [34]:17-22)

In his Response to Robinson's presentation, Charles W. Hedrick appreciates the promotion of the Sophia Christology. He even adds information which strengthens Robinson's awareness of the Wisdom spirituality among the early Christians. He also explains how the orthodox tradition centered on a resurrection Christology to suppress the Wisdom tradition.

> There was a suppressed movement in early Christianity that thought about deity nonexclusively, a movement that could identify the essence of Jesus' inspiration and possession, and the origin of his message in feminine terms. Its day passed, and resurrection Christianity replaced it. The victor, resurrection Christianity, consolidating itself and adjusting itself to life in the world, appropriated social and ethical values from Hellenistic culture, including male dominance. But radical Christianity, in which Wisdom with her nonexclusivity, passion, and utopian ideal is to be included, arises, suffers, and dies only to rise again at some later time. Perhaps Robinson's discovery of the roots of Wisdom Christology may become one such occasion. (135)

Robinson reports that some of the nonexclusivity of Wisdom Christology is suggested in a Q text where the saying is ascribed to Sophia and not of Jesus. It is Luke 11:49-51.

> Therefore also the Wisdom of God said, "I will send them prophets and apostles of whom they will kill and persecute," that the blood of all the prophets, shed from foundation of the world, may be required of this generation, from the blood of Abel to the blood of Zechariah, who perished between the altar and the sanctuary. Yes, I tell you, it shall be required of this generation.

Robinson connects this text with Luke 13:34-35:

> O Jerusalem, Jerusalem, killing prophets and stoning those who are sent to you! How often would I have gathered your children together as a hen gathers her brood under her wings, and you would not! Behold, your house is forsaken. And I tell you, you will not see me until you say, "Blessed is he who comes in the name of the Lord." (121)

For Robinson, these sayings indicate that Wisdom is the decisive source. Whoever speaks in the name of Wisdom is important. It is not so important who does it. So the prophets, Jesus, and whoever spoke while possessed by Wisdom, have fulfilled their significance accordingly. They all will pass away and will be replaced by new prophets who are possessed by Wisdom. This relativizes the person and heightens the message. Orthodox Christianity wanted to elevate the messenger over the message. And that is really one of the major differences between Wisdom Christology and Resurrection Christology.

To bring about a connection between the two traditions, Robinson offers his findings on the resurrection experiences, which became newsworthy, even for newspapers. *The Dayton Journal Herald*, Dayton, Ohio, Saturday, April 24, 1982, p. 10, published John Dart's article, "Son of Light: Scholar says first Christians saw resurrected Jesus as luminous being." Dart reports on a paper presented by James Robinson at the national meeting of the Society of Biblical Literature in 1982. There he concludes that the first generation of Christians believed that the resurrection made Jesus a luminous appearance. Dart notes that Robinson outlines two "trajectories" of Christian belief. One emphasized the resurrection of the flesh, while another (Gnosticism) perceived Jesus' appearances as a great light. Robinson recognized that the former position became the official teaching of established Christianity which condemned the latter belief as heresy. According to Dart, Robinson holds that Jesus' resurrection in the flesh is a secondary tradition. He wants both trajectories to enter into a dialog so that a new understanding about the resurrection may emerge. Indeed, Robinson's article, "Very Goddess and Very Man: Jesus' Better Self," in section 4, "The Visualization of the Resurrection," discusses the political strategy of the orthodox tradition. He explains how the luminous appearance experience can be found at different places in the New Testament. Apparently, Peter had such an apparition as is told in the apocryphal Gospel of Peter. This indicates that the message of Jesus is being transmitted to those who experienced his luminous presence. Jesus is replaced bay new prophets who now personify the presence of Wisdom. But the orthodox Christians did not want to go this route. They wanted to elevate Jesus as the immortal one, the true personification of the eternal God. Robinson holds that Mark and Luke clipped the wings of the gnosticizing trajectory, by reporting the sayings of Jesus within time, place, and the person Jesus. Not the sayings are important, but the person, Jesus, who pronounced them. The

Wisdom Christology and the experience of the luminous emphasized the Wisdom within the sayings and within those who pronounced them.

The reality of the two trajectories is recognized by a number of scholars, including Elaine Pagels, James Robinson, and Charles W. Hedrick, as reported above. Related insights which lead to the same conclusion are included in Thomas Sheehan's book, *The First Coming: How the Kingdom of God Became Christianity*. Professor J. M. Cameron of St. Michael's College in Toronto, reviewed the book in *The New York Review*, December 4, 1986. He delineates some of Sheehan's major theses. One, the message of Jesus is that Yahweh, the Father, has become incarnate in his people, "that God, as God, has identified himself without remainder with his people." According to Sheehan, the Church mistakenly applied what was true of the Father and of his people to the person Jesus. He quotes Sheehan:

> The presence of God among men which Jesus preached was not something new, not a gift that God had saved up for the end of time. Jesus merely proclaimed what had always been the case. He invited people to awaken to what God had already done from the very beginning of time...The "arrival" of the present-future was not God's return to the world after a long absence but the believers reawakening to the fact that God had always and only [sic] been *there*.
> All Jesus did was to bring to light in a fresh way what always had been the case but what had been forgotten or obscured by religion. His role was simply to end religion – that temporary governess who had turned into a tyrant – and restore the sense of the immediacy of God. (25-26)

Christianity started to go the wrong direction by interpretating revelations experienced by Peter. These personal revelations stated that the Father had taken his prophet [Jesus] into the eschatological future and had appointed him the Son of Man. Jesus was soon to return in glory to usher in God's kingdom! Thus the Jesus movement quickly began to identify the kingdom with the person Jesus. Then Jesus becomes the Son of Man who is to bring God's reign. Sheehan writes, "Simon put his hopes on Jesus rather than on what Jesus was about." And then Cameron brings his review to the heart of the matter. He brings the focus on the real concern of Sheehan. He quotes Sheehan substantially.

> One last look, then, at the empty tomb – the real tomb of history, not the one of the Christian legend. As we peer into

that emptiness, the absence of the living Jesus and even of his dead body allows us to identify a unique form of seeking: the desire for that which can never be had. This unique kind of seeking is the experience that makes human beings different from any other kind of entity, and we see it exemplified in the women who actually found the tomb empty on the first Easter Sunday. Such seeking is not something we occasionally get caught up in; rather, it is what makes us human, constitute us as the futile passion, the unfulfilled and presumably unfulfillable desire that we are...

This historical fact of the complete absence of Jesus does have religious significance: It means the *end of religion*...[Jesus'] mission had been to undo religion and its God and to put radical mercy, the living of the present-future, in its place...

The crisis in Christianity is about its origins, its founding story, but...the [true] crisis is that at last Christianity is discovering what it always was about: not God or Christ or Jesus of Nazareth, but the endless, unresolvable mystery inscribed at the heart of being human. (25-26)

These are statements which Campbell would understand.   Cameron, however, confesses, "I do not think I know what they mean."   As such he cannot affirm Sheehan and the wisdom he communicates.   That also will be the division between Wisdom Christology and Resurrection Christology, as there was the division between the Wisdom tradition and the Torah tradition in the Old Testament.   But it should be noted that for Campbell as well as for Blake, Robinson and Sheehan, the heart of the matter is Wisdom.   And this Wisdom is seated within the human heart.   This creative energy is about compassion and integration.   Wisdom people recognize the great or unique personification of this Wisdom in Jesus.   Thus he is the son of the divine, or the son of the Virgin, who conceived of the Holy Spirit, which gave his existence divine importance.   These are the perspectives according to which the words, "Father of Jesus," receive existential meaning.

Nag Hammadi, Gnosticism, & Early Christianity (Peabody Massachusetts: Hendrickson Publishers, 1986) contains the papers presented at a Working Seminar on Gnosticism in 1983, Springfield, Missouri.   There we find James W. Robinson's paper, "On Bridging the Gulf from Q to the Gospel of Thomas (or Vice Versa.)"   At the end he refers to Werner H. Kelber's book, *The Oral and Written Gospel* to strengthen the validity of his insights about the two trajectories in early Christianity.

The basic idea is that the Wisdom energy lived within the Christian community. The wisdom was expressed by sayings similar to what Jesus uttered in his days. Thus the energy of saying and pronouncing this wisdom is the life of Jesus. Jesus lives in the continuation of the spoken word about the divine wisdom. This is the energy one finds in Q as well as in the Gospel of Thomas, which is a list of sayings made by Jesus. As such Jesus is not dead, but he is alive in the continuation of the words with which he indentified. There was no need to look back at the life he lived, where he went, what he did and when. there was no need to tell about his passion, his crucifixion, and his death. That would put the focus on the man, Jesus, and obscure the spirituality of his religiosity. According to Kelber:

> A tradition that focuses on the continuation of Jesus' words cannot simultaneously bring to consciousness what put an end to his speaking...By the same logic, we note again, a heavy narrative emphasis on death, such as one finds in Mark, may imply a critique of the sayings tradition.
> Since Q represents an oral genre, the feasability of its performance is a relevant issue. (201)

Kelber designates Q as belonging to the prophetic tradition.

> It is structured around a present-future mode of christology and functions in an oral, prophetic manner of speech. Schulz himself concedes that in what for him is the youngest, the Jewish-Hellenic stage of Q"...the exalted present Son of man continues to speak through his prophets to the community." The encompassing retrospection that casts tradition into a historicizing, pre-resurrected framework is not within the mental horizon of Q. (202)

The following quotes from Kelber are to indicate his affirmation of those scholars of the Gnostic literature who made decisive judgments about the orthodox Christian gospel authors, especially Matthew and Luke.

> It is not evident what Koester had in mind when he wrote of the "radical critical alteration" Q suffered at the hands of Matthean and Lukan textualization. By pressing the sayings into service of their written gospels, the authors of Matthew and Luke deprived Q of the very trait constitutive of its oral hermeneutics: the prophetically living voice of Jesus became the unalterable words of Jesus' past authority. A literary mentality, unable to tolerate the oral equation of the earthy Jesus with the living Lord, rigorously tied all sayings to the pre-resurrectional Jesus: Q was preserved at the price of being defeated in its authentic hermeneutical purpose. One is bound to conclude that it was precisely Q's oral ontology of language

> that the writers of the written gospels – and one may assume
> the canonizers – perceived to be its essential "defect." (203)

This is strong language and condemning in tone. "Q suffered...", "By pressing the saying into the service...", "the author...deprived", "unable to tolerate...", "rigorously tied...", "Q... being defeated..."

It is very important to become aware of all this information, because it diminishes the "holier than thou" mentality of the orthodox New Testament texts. It also makes one see how much of the Wisdom tradition is still maintained in the New Testament. But most of all, and that is of concern to our focus, Joseph Campbell and other authorities, like William Blake, receive more credulity in their lively and excited ways of interpreting biblical texts. What may seem esoteric, and as such "apocryphal", to those who believe in the canonical texts only, seems to be more authentic and less heretical than is generally assumed. If one is to believe Robinson and Blake, and when on sees the life in the person Joseph Campbell when he talks about Jesus and the Virgin Birth, then one becomes aware that there is an authentic Christian faith communicated in the gnostic Wisdom tradition. Robinson holds this tradition may offer Christianity "A New Lease On Life" (section 5 of his article, "Very Goddess and Very Man" in *Images of the Feminine in Gnosticism* (126-127).

Robinson is looking for relevancy in the way Gnosticism, Plato and Freud benefitted from the wealth of wisdom in the world of myths. His point is well made in the light of the enormous response Campbell received in his presentation of *The Power of Myth*. For that reason, a critical comment about the general attitude of the scholars who convene at special conferences to discuss gnostic texts. Glaringly absent in their discussions are references to authorities who are known worldwide for their interpretations of the mythical wisdom, the stuff goddesses and gods are made of. for example, in *Images of the Feminine in Gnosticism*, there is list of "Works Cited." Not listed are Carl G. Jung, the works of Erich Neumann (not even his *The Great Mother*), no reference to William Blake, or Joseph Campbell. In general, these are biblical scholars who have to deal with the "great discovery" of the Nag Hammadi texts in the middle of this century, but there is no affirmation of "the greatness" of these texts and the tradition they represent. Outstanding exceptions are Charles W. Hedrick, Helmut Koester, Elaine H. Pagels, and James M. Robinson.

Joseph Campbell and William Blake signify how the Wisdom tradition invites one to become involved in the celebration of life by means of an active imagination. This is also delightfully true in Erich Neumann's book, *The Archetypal World of Henry Moore.* The "Primordial Feminine" stands at the center of this sculptor's work. Especially the themes, "the Reclining Figure," and "Mother and Child" seem to have been the fundamental obsession of his sculpting.

> In the image of the goddess with the child—I say "goddess" because everyone will be struck by the suprapersonal quality of this figure, monumentally set in the landscape like one of those on Easter Island—the child has almost the effect of an ornament. It is stone of her stone, and yet how firm and secure it stands on the unshakable plinth of the arm! How strangely human is the oneness of these two beings, how eternal and unchanging their kinship, and how natural! (39-40)

> What Picasso led to a continual dialectic between the thing apprehended and the manner of apprehending it, and in Klee to a specific but consistent technique, where every line and every image reveal a new aspect of this spectral world, compelled Moore to create the same thing over and over again in a sort of fascinated monomania—the primordial image of Woman, Woman in her relation to and identity with the great Earth Mother, as the reclining figure, or Woman as the mother with the child. Only when we grasp Moore's connection with the archaic can we understand his "abstract" and at the same time "primitive" sculptures correctly. (47)

Obviously, Moore's work is not abstract at all insofar as it makes concretely visible the primordial energy, which is the seat of Wisdom.

In his own works Neumann uses "The Great Mother" information to bring understanding to the dynamics in human and cultural development. In his *The Origins of Consciousness* one learns how the "Uroboros" (the self-begetting energy) gives rise to the Great Mother. How the reality of female and male is affirmed in the stories about "The Separation of the World Parents: The Principle of Opposites." The need for self-assertion is celebrated in the Hero Myth, and how growth and maturation find recognition in the transformation myths. The psychological stages in the development of personality are centered on the awareness of an original unity, which reaches into the pain and suffering of the separation stage. But this leads the crisis of consciousness into a wisdom of balance and true creativity.

This process of transformation is very much at the heart of Jungian psychology. There are numerous publications which discuss the dynamics and challenges of the invitation to transformation. Of course, transformation is very much in the awareness of the gnostic Wisdom tradition. But, as Robinson indicates, it is important to make the connection between the ancient texts and our modern situation. The common ground is the reality of the primordial within which we all are rooted then and now. The gnostic texts are not doctrinal in nature, trying to instruct people about dogma for denominational truths. They invite people to become involved and, in the quest for wisdom, reflect and meditate. Kathleen McLaughlin in her article, "Buddhist and Jungian Spiritual Paths: Insight and Imagination" describes meditation techniques for the "active imagination." She connects with Jungian depth psychology which sees the mind or psyche as a single energetic system that "divides itself as it develops. Initially it divides or differentiates itself into two major parts: conscious and unconscious, and each of these parts has both an individual and a collective aspect." (15)

> Psychic energy flows with form and direction in the structure of the psyche. These structural energy points are called complexes. Complexes are particular groupings of images (both visual and auditory) that carry specific feelings with them. The most prominent complexes of the personal or individual psyche are the ego, persona, shadow, and the anima/animus. Each psyche also contains and is contained by collective complexes or archetypes such as the Self, Great Mother, Great Father, etc. It is the function of the ego complex to organize the psyche, differentiating itself from the forming relationships with other psychic contents. As feelings, thoughts, and sensations arise into consciousness, the ego sorts them into "what I am" (persona) and "what I am not" (shadow or anima or animus). (15)

Jungian psychology assumes that thoughts, feelings, and behaviors can be engaged into a psychic wholeness of the Self. As such, if we are to grow and mature, attention should be paid to dreams, moods, accidental or spontaneous actions and feelings in order to learn how all aspects in one's psyche experience an event. Naming the feeling by identifying the voice which is speaking in the psyche is a powerful way of integrating the unconscious. Active imagination is the technique whereby one enters into an imaginative dialog with those voices which are critical. As such, McLaughlin suggests:

> I may ask these voices why they are feeling this way and what they want from me. Perhaps they will point out to me some piece of my writing that is not clear or needs further elaboration. Or perhaps they just jeer at me and tell me I have no right to say these things, and no one cares anyway. As I listen to the content of the voices I can respond appropriately and hope to gain greater awareness of the meaning of this internal experience or criticism. In any case, I am entering into a relationship with the particular content of my particular experience. In Jung's work active imagination may occur through listening to and talking with internal voices, as I have described, or it may occur through the drawing of images that appear in my mind's eye, or in moving to the rhythms that the body feels. The important thing is that the ego takes a positive attitude toward the particular feeling or thought that occurs, and enters into it, giving it form, color, and voice. The ego needs to listen to the image or voice because it may be able to tell the ego something that is important. The other complexes and archetypes in the psyche have perspectives and experiences that are as real as the ego's perspectives, and they need the opportunity to come into the light of consciousness if the wholeness of the psyche is to be experienced. (17)

These are the dynamics which characterize the mythical reality of the Virgin Birth. In the name of wholeness one seeks integration so that life can become more inclusive and celebrative of its dimensions. The key to this transformation into wholeness is the voice of compassion, which spoke to the virgin, promising her that the new life to be born would be of the Holy Spirit. Jesus was conceived twice. Once by the sexual act, and then by the virgin who gave birth to her son by the authority of compassion and mercy. Sensing the divine nature of this integrative compassion is the awareness of the Spirit which motivated Jesus and permeated his whole being in whatever he thought, sensed, said or did. Thus he was of the divine as is expressed by the saying, that he and the Father are one.

Regarding the growth toward the integrative wholeness, Altizer's appreciation and promotion of Blake includes the following:

> (5) he [Blake] stands alone among Christian artists identifying the actual passion of sex as the most immediate epiphany of

either a demonic or a redemptive "Energy," just as he is the only Christian visionary who has envisioned the universal role of the female as both a redemptive and a destructive power; (184)

Because we are in search of the understanding of the dimensions which characterize the integrative energy, which is the spirit of the Virgin Birth, it is very helpful to elaborate on Altizer's statement.

In one part of Blake's "A Memorable Fancy" (Plates 12-13) in *The Marriage of Heaven and Hell*, the prophet Isaiah is described as the one who "discovered the infinite in everything." This authorized him to speak in the name of God. Isaiah confirmed that "honest indignation is the voice of God."

This reference is somewhat an introduction to an understanding of Blake's dealing with reality. Reality provides the realm within which the infinite is observable. Moreover, in our observation of reality we sense in ourselves a reaction, e.g., indignation and hold that this reaction is also an expression of the divine energy.

In terms of the libido, that may have certain implications. Before we discuss this aspect, we need to observe one more of Blake's concerns for reality. In *A Descriptive Catalogue*, Number IV, Blake made the following statement:

A Spirit and a Vision are not, as the modern philosophy supposes, a cloudy vapour, or a nothing: they are organized and minutely articulated beyond all that the mortal and perishing nature can produce. He who does not imagine in stronger and better lineaments, and in stronger and better light than this perishing and mortal eye can see, does not imagine at all.

And those who object to representing spirit with real bodies, "would do well," according to Blake, "to consider that the Venus, the Minerva, the Jupiter, the Apollo, which they admire are all of them representations of spiritual existences, of Gods immortal, to the mortal perishing organ of sight; and yet they are embodied and organized in solid marble." How may this apply to the libido and to the power of sexual love? It is true that lovers see each other with the inward eye of love. They see something in one another which is special. The beloved transfigured by the loving perception of the lover. And the lover too, senses a transformation within her/himself, because of this loving energy. One may conclude that the mortal eye has been helped by the vision of an immortal aspect, which is the sense of beauty or graciousness or whatever transcendental aspect comes into the play of loving energy.

This, of course, is more the romantic aspect of the libido, which itself is not always so refined. The libido, as the desire for sexual gratification, may be perceived by many as simply the lust of our flesh, and it may be evaluated as a temptation which needs to be controlled and disciplined.

Of course, social developments demand forms of domestication regarding our sex life, but they cannot dictate our attitude. Blake is concerned with the value of the basic energy which is at play. If the Greeks celebrated the sexual energy in terms of their mythological characters such as Aphrodite, Eros, and Psyche, then we sense their appreciation of this psycho-physical energy in terms of an inward eye. The physical aspect of the sex drive seems to be quite dependent on the psychological ingredient. It is difficult to enjoy sex if one is not "turned on." One can become sexually aroused by merely looking at pictures of the opposite sex or by imagining them. The male among humans seem to be more centered on the genital areas, while the female may find erogenous zones in the male ear, neck, or whatever may have such an effect on her. "You have sexy eyes, ears, etc." are statements which indicate this. Of course, eyes or ears are not sexy, but they appear so to the beholder. These parts of the body are perceived in a new light. As such, the libido receives more embodiment, and it becomes more inclusive than merely a concentration on the genitals. I hold it as one of Blake's contributions, that he wanted us to look at reality in terms of the given forms, so that we may discern the particular image of the divine energy in this particular thing. But then he urged us not to call this particular appearance of the divine energy as the divine energy itself. It is only an appearance of the divine energy. Thus we have reached an understanding of the Blakean dialectic. On the one hand, the appearance is to be taken seriously as a form of the divine, but it is not the divine itself.

Thus the sexual energy is never vulgar, but can only be perceived in a vulgar way. We have in ourselves the imagination by which we are able to celebrate the sexual energy in terms of its divine character. Blake resisted and rejected vehemently the way the Christian Church and the societal controls had downgraded sex as something that needs to be controlled, and for that purpose they gave it a certain function and a certain character. The whole imaginative dimension of the side of the person was overruled. Sex was not trusted by the institutionalized life. Blake wanted to restore the divine celebration of the sex drive and the sexual relations between humans. He spoke in the name of an indignation which "is the voice of God." Because of these reflections, we may enjoy more the following verses,

> In wife I would desire
> What in whores is always found –
> The lineaments of Gratified desire.

> Abstinence sows sand all over
> The ruddy limbs & flaring hair,
> But Desire Gratified
> Plants fruits of life & beauty there.

Blake's promotion of the divine within sexual energy is not to be understood as a call to join the sexual revolution. Although, there is much divine indignation in the sexual revolution of the Sixties and Seventies, nevertheless, much of it was also an outburst against restraint in the name of fun and irresponsible sex. Even the highly respectable scholar, Norman Brown, in his *Life Against Death* fails to reach the integrity of Blake's praise of the human imagination. Brown argues that the body is more real than the soul, the child wiser than the man, and play more noble than work. It is a form of hedonism, which is in itself respectable. In his sequence, *Love's Body*, this resentment of repression persists for the sake of the pleasure principle and the Dionysian consciousness. Brown argues for playfulness in sex and sexuality. Blake speaks on behalf of amazement as an expression of the divine within the human imagination, the sense of wonderment within the enjoyment of the sexual. The divine is within the real, and is not to be perceived as a transcendental God who rules from on high and dictates how life is to be lived.

Let us return to Schaberg's discussion of the Virgin Birth. The key insight was that Mary, pregnant because of rape, received information that the child would be great because it would be great as a child and a human being. This is dramatized by portraying the appearance of the angel announcing that God in his compassion and mercy would promote this child beyond expectation. Thus we found new understanding for the Virgin Birth.

If we place the same given, which is Mary being pregnant with child out of wedlock, within the context of Blake's celebration of the human imagination, then we arrive at additional insights. Now we don't need an angel to tell Mary that the child will be acceptable in spite of its illegitimacy. Blake's imagination would simply transcend the problem of illegitimacy. The sexuality present in the virgin, which is the divine within energy embodied in her, affirms the presence of the child within her womb. We do not need outside information to sanction this pregnancy. The bodily existence, which in the human imagination is experienced as divine energy, embraces the child. The compassion is within the human imagination which fathers this child within the mother's love.

The next step in our journey is to investigate whether the biblical tradition is essentially against such mythical, existential, and psychological interpretations of the biblical faith. The point is that the Bible seems to speak against the mythical interpretations by narrating the stories as actual happenings. The question is, did the biblical authors interpret events, happenings, and stories to press everything into a particular view? Or, to put it in other words, did those events occur according to the terms of the biblical account? Are the biblical stories themselves interpretations or objective recordings? If they are interpretations, which mythical views determine the editorial concerns of the authors in their selection of their views over and against competing views? Were there competing interpretations, and what were their particular hermeneutics?

Such questions can be answered only by those who are learned in the history of the biblical tradition and the history of the related cultures and languages. All these scholarly accomplishments one finds in the person, Saul Levin, professor of Ancient Languages at the State University of New York at Binghamton. He will be our guide in the next chapter.

Chapter Nine

The Father of Joshua/Jesus

This chapter bears the title of Saul Levin's book, published by the State University of New York, Binghamton, in 1978. Because of the many Hebrew and Greek citations, he did the typography himself on a Vary-Typer of the university. ("No one else in Binghamton could have taken this part of the job, for love or money.")

I am particularly interested in the study of this book because it is written by a philologist, and connoisseur of the Ancient Near East, especially the Hebrew and the Old Testament tradition. As a Jew, he understands the ins and outs of the Jewish mentality and the difference between the written and the oral traditions of its long history. He also ventures into the New Testament and respectfully discusses those parts which belong to his topic.

As such we are not dealing with a theologian who speaks on behalf of a religious tradition or a particular denomination. In the name of philology, he wants to throw new light on those topics where he has some authority to speak.

A traditional way of pursuing the research on the topic, the Father of Jesus, would be to consult the *Theological Dictionary of the New Testament*, edited by Gerhard Friedrich which volumes appeared through the sixties and seventies. One looks up the Greek words for Father, *pater*, and son, *uios*, and virgin, *parthenos*, and other related terms. One finds a wealth of information, but it is encyclopedic in nature – it lists information. Of course, there is a bias, i.e., there is a tendency to speak on behalf of the canonical orthodoxy of

182

the Bible. Thus other interpretations are treated as related information, which is occasionally criticized for being less correct than the so called "true story."

Saul Levin's book is delightful for a number of reasons. First, I know enough Hebrew and Greek to follow his highly sophisticated analysis and discussion of the texts which pertain to his studies. It is always great to see a master at work in his trade. Second, because Levin is a Jew he speaks about the household of the Jewish and biblical culture. He demonstrates how specific groups in their political preferences changed and edited the texts so that they would be more in accordance with their value systems. As a historian he also knows that the customs and habits of the culture were more complex and more realistic than the Law would like it. Consequently, one is introduced to the practice of life which is different from the regulated life. Thus the Father of Jesus in reference to Joshua receives spectra by which we sense and understand the energies at work in the use of such a name.

The first sentence of the Introduction (Chapter One) states the focus of this book. "This is an investigation of fertility miraculously conferred upon human beings." Levin considers the texts he studies not as sources of information, but as important artifacts which have their own identity. They assist us in clarifying our own experience of existence in this world. (2)

Chapter Two "The Divine Name in Joshua's Patronymic," addresses the strange fact that Joshua is called "son of Nun." (Patronymic means a name derived from that of the father or a paternal ancestor.) Levin argues that Nun is simply an unknown and as such does not constitute a father or a paternal ancestor. Levin demonstrates how in Hebrew "son of Nun" is an alteration of "son of Yahweh" or "son of the Lord." What is the story behind this.?

In the biblical tradition there was a development of monotheistic mentality. This became very focused among those who identified Moses as the true prophet. This group became defensive in several ways.

a) Only Yahweh was the true God among the other gods.
b) Other gods shall be abandoned.
c) Moses is the true spokesman of Yahweh.
d) There shall be no one equal or greater than Moses on this earth.

This defensiveness can be traced in alterations and manipulations of the scriptures by the Mosaist scribes who copied these documents.

Levin's focus is on the name, Son of God. As a philologist he substantiates his theory that the Mosaists, in some clever ways succeeded in covering up or blanking out the name, Son of God, given to the hero, Joshua.

Here it is of no use to summarize Levin's linguistic arguments. His conclusions, however, are most revealing in our search for understanding "Son of God" in this religious tradition. One may say that:

a) when a hero was experienced as eminent in wisdom, leadership, and other divine characteristics, this cultural tradition offered such a person the name, Son of God. Obviously, such a custom provided the people the opportunity to identify excellence and to celebrate the divine qualities present in this person. Thus the hero personified the divine as experienced in his words, deeds, and attitudes.

b) The mosaists and people like them finalized the presence of the divine in the life of Moses. Their understanding and account of Moses became a capsule of their beliefs. They are:

1.   Only our God is the real One.

2.   He spoke through Moses.

3.   Moses is not a Son of God.

4.   No one is a Son of God, because God is immensely holy, beyond human personification, beyond any name, beyond any image. His name shall not be spoken nor written.

c) The religious culture of the biblical tradition beyond the mosaists was more complex and less doctrinal. It allowed for celebrating the divine in reference to outstanding persons who did amazing deeds. The mosaist scribes found several ways to obscure this wider tradition. They altered parts of the scriptures so that the name, "Son of God," became unrecognizable at first sight.

The great merit of Levin's studies is that he liberates the biblical tradition from the mosaist grip. He clearly demonstrates the religiousness beyond the mosaist stronghold. This wider tradition provides us with a territory where one is better able to see how the followers of Jesus could begin to call him Son of God. Levin devotes the last chapter of his book explicitly to explain cultural aspects in the time of Jesus which allow for the story of the Virgin Birth, where the angel announced the divine dimension of this pregnancy. Such stories are embedded in a long tradition, where similar interpretations of great events have been recorded again and again.

The early followers of Jesus took this route of interpreting their Messiah in these terms. This created a resentment on the side of the mosaist tradition. Thus a particular group of Jews opposed those Christians who declared Jesus to be Son of God. Those Jews could not allow for a divine presence in reference to a person. They stuck to their Torah and their interpretations of the written word. The Jewish Christians walked the road of an ancient wider interpretation which was still very much alive in the days of Jesus.

Such insights are explained throughout the book and they receive depth in Levin's explanation of related details. For example, in Chapter Three, about the meaning of "Son of the Lord," we learn that a hero, because of his eminence, was not any longer identified in reference to his biological father:

> It was characteristic of a hero to outshine his father's reputation or his brothers'; the father's name might even be eclipsed except for surviving in the patronymic of the one great son. Accordingly the father's greatness was not enough to explain the son's heroism. The son's superiority invited reference to the favor of some god–preferably the greatest god. Now if the traditional conception of that god allowed him to be regarded as a father, it was natural and simple to call a superlative great man his son. From there a story might and sometimes did develop, explaining the circumstances of divine procreation. For when a god, unlike a mere man, copulates with a woman, there is bound to be a good result. The *locus classicus* is the union of Poseidon with Tyro (*Od.* 11.241 ff.), in which he assures her, "When the year comes round, you will bear fine offspring, since the beds of the immortals are not futile." (27-28)

In this context Levin explains how Saul called David, "son of Isai," simply to counteract any elevated names, and to denigrate David's greatness. The other enemies of David did the same. (29)

The subsection, "Fertility Given by the Lord," is truly revealing about non-Mosaic practices. For example, there is the reference to Manoah's wife as told in Judges:

> There was a man of Zorah of the tribe of Dan, called Manoah. His wife was barren, she had borne no children. The angel of Yahweh appeared to this woman and said to her, "You are barren and have had no child. But from now on take great care. Take no wine or strong drink, and eat nothing unclean. For you will conceive and bear a son. No razor is to touch his head, for the body shall be God's nazirite from his mother's womb. It is he who will begin to rescue Israel from the power of the Philistines." Then the woman went and told her husband, "A man of God had just come to me; his presence was like the presence of the angel of God, he was so majestic. I did not ask him where he came from, and he did not reveal his name to me. But he said to me, 'You will conceive and bear a son. From now on, take no wine or strong drink, and eat nothing unclean. For the boy shall be God's nazirite from his mother's womb to his dying day.'"
>
> Then Manoah pleaded with Yahweh and said, "I beg you, Lord, let the man of God you sent come to us once again and instruct us in what we must do with the boy when he is born." Yahweh heard Manoah's prayer for favour and the angel of Yahweh visited the woman again as she was sitting in the field; her husband was not with her. The woman ran quickly and told her husband: "Look, " she said, "the man who came to me the other day appeared to me again." Manoah rose and followed his wife, and he came to the man and said to him, "Are you the man who spoke to this woman?" He answered, "I am." Manoah went on, "When your words are fulfilled, what is the boy's rule of life?" "How must he behave?" And the angel of Yahweh answered Manoah, "The things that I forbade this woman, let him refrain from too. Let him taste nothing that comes from the vine, let him take no wine or strong drink, let him eat nothing unclean, let him obey all the orders I gave this woman." Manoah then said to the angel of Yahweh, "Do us the honour of staying with us while we prepare a kid for you." For Manoah did not know this was the angel of Yahweh. The angel of Yahweh said to Manoah, "Even if I did stay with you, I would not eat your food; but if you wish to prepare a holocaust, offer it to Yahweh." Manoah then said to the angel of Yahweh, "What is your name, so that we may honour you when your words are fulfilled?" The angel of Yahweh replied, "Why ask my name? It is a mystery." Then Manoah took the kid and the oblation and offered it as a holocaust on the rock to Yahweh who works mysteries. As the flame went up heavenwards from the alter, the angel of Yahweh ascended in the flame in the sight of Manoah and his wife and they fell face downwards on the ground. After this,

the angel of Yahweh did not appear any more to Manoah and his wife, by which Manoah understood that his had been the angel of Yahweh. And Manoah said to his wife, "We are certain to die, because we have seen God." His wife answered him, "If Yahweh had meant to kill us, he would not have accepted a holocaust and oblation from our hands; he would not have told us these things. The woman gave birth to a son and called him Samson. The child grew, and Yahweh blessed him; and the spirit of Yahweh began to move him in the Camp of Dan, between Zorah and Estaol. (Jerusalem Bible. 13:2-25)

Levin approaches this story with some revealing comments. First, he notes, that "A man has come to me" in a customary euphemism for sexual intercourse. (35) And when the woman experienced the visit of the messenger of Yahweh a second time she reported, "the man who came to me the other day appeared again." Levin holds that her frankness indicated that she had nothing to be ashamed of "because the man who came to her was superhuman and she had dire need of him in her sterility." (36) Moreover, Levin observes, that there was nothing further between Manoah and his wife but an exchange of words, and "the woman bore a son and named him "little sun" or "solar one." And "the Lord blessed him. (36)

So it is natural to infer from the sequence that the Lord's anonymous messenger fertilized her; and vestiges remain of a mythical background in which the procreator of Samson was the sun-god. (36)

One may also add that the conversation between Manoah and the angel of Yahweh had something to do with particular claims. After all, here we have a surrogate father, and perhaps he will claim certain rights. Manoah wanted to make sure that there would be no interference with his own legal fatherhood. The angel assured him, according to the story, that there would be no trouble regarding these matters.

A second illustration of non-Mosaic practices is the story of Hannah, the mother of Samuel.

There was a man of Ramathaim, a Zuphite from the highlands of Ephraim, whose name was Elkanah, son of Jeroboam, son of Elihu, son of Tohu, son of Zuph, an Ephramite. He had two wives, one called Hannah, the other Peninnah; Peninnah had children, but Hannah, had none. Every year this man used to go up from his town to worship and to sacrifice to Yahweh Sabaoth in Shiloh. The two sons of Eli, Hophni and Phinebas, were there as priests of Yahweh.

One day Elkanah offered sacrifice. He used to give portions to Penninah and to all her sons and daughters; to Hannah, however, he would give only one portion, although he loved her more, since Yahweh had made her barren. Her rival would taunt her to annoy her, because Yahweh had made her barren. And this went on year after year; every time they went up to the temple of Yahweh she used to taunt her. And so Hannah wept and would not eat. Then Elkanah her husband said to her, "Hannah, why are you crying and why are you not eating? Why so sad? Am I not more than ten sons?"

Now after they had eaten in the hall, Hannah rose and took her stand before Yahweh, while Eli the priest was sitting on his seat by the doorpost of the temple of Yahweh. In the bitterness of her soul she prayed to Yahweh with many tears and made a vow, saying, "Yahweh Sabaoth! If you will take notice of the distress of your servant, and bear me in mind and not forget your servant and give her a man-child, I will give him to Yahweh for the whole of his life and no razor shall ever touch his head."

While she prayed before Yahweh which she did for some time, Eli was watching her mouth, for she was speaking under her breath; her lips were moving but her voice could not be heard. He therefore supposed that she was drunk and said to her, "How long are you going to be in this drunken state? Rid yourself of your wine." "No, my lord," Hannah replied "I am a woman in great trouble; I have taken neither wine nor strong drink – I was pouring out my soul before Yahweh. Do not take your maidservant for a worthless woman; all this time I have been speaking from the depth of my grief and my resentment." Then Eli answered her: "Go in peace," he said, "and may the God of Israel grant you what you have asked on him." And she said, "May your maidservant find favour in your sight; and with that the woman went away; she returned to the hall and ate and was dejected no longer.

They rose early in the morning and worshipped Yahweh and then set out and returned to their home in Ramrah. Elkanah had intercourse with Hannah his wife and Yahweh was mindful of her. She conceived and gave birth to a son, and called him Samuel "since" she had said "I asked Yahweh for him." (Jerusalem Bible. I Sam. 1:1-20)

Levin notes that "he remembered her" (in the Jerusalem Bible "Was mindful of her") may be "metaphorically, a sort of fertilization, bringing to life words that reproduce something previously latent in the mind." (37) And then he comments:

Both Hannah's expression (in 1:11) and the priest's (in 1:17) are irreproachably pious; but in between they altercate somewhat lengthily over her apparent drunkenness, and the passage is a clue to the underlying myth or tradition about the procreation of Samuel. Hannah – or the author – is overanxious to prove that the appearance has been misapprehended: "No, my lord, I am a grief – stricken woman, and I have not drunk wine or liquor; but I have poured out my heart before the LORD. Don't put your servant down for a depraved woman." (37)

Levin explains Hannah's fear of being considered drunk, in references to Eli's sons. "And Eli had grown very old; and he heard all that his sons kept doing to all Israel, and they would lie with the women who lined up at the entrance of the meeting tent." (2:22) Levin suggests that a woman at such a place, and not with her husband, could have been one of those who lay with a priest. (38)

> Now the fertility of married women was not separate from blessedness in general but was rather an indispensable part of it. To those who lacked children, no abundance or crops and herds or accumulation of wealth could provide a real solace.
>
> Resorting to a shrine was felt wholesome, and no doubt it was in some cases. In the first place, it made a welcome change from the humdrum life at home, where the sense of frustration and failure would be reinforced daily. The causes of sterility were little understood until modern times, and nearly impossible to diagnose scientifically in any individual. Whether or not the sterility sometimes had a psychological origin, surely it could become engrained through a bad psychological state. Then the visit to a shrine would allow a break in the pattern, and the pilgrims who had been sad before might go home – i.e., with an inner certainty that life would be good from now on.
>
> If pregnancy followed, the credit properly belonged to the divine, unseen possessor of the sanctuary. It made some difference, though perhaps no essential difference, whether the experience there was purely spiritual, as the narrative about Hannah insists, or included a sexual contact. For if one copulated with a stranger and the outcome was pregnancy, it was still the divine grace that made the material act efficacious. (38)

Levin holds that fertility was so mysterious that the good results could be a reason for being grateful to God. Those who engaged in ritual copulation with a stranger, still experienced fertility as a blessing from God. He adds:

> Common sense might have suggested that those who were barren in their marriage had nothing to lose and perhaps something to gain from lying with an outsider, but to do this without violating the marriage, to do it so that the offspring

should be properly belong to the husband and wife – that could only be done if the copulation was hallowed. (39)

Regarding ritual copulation, Levin offers some intriguing insights. According to him religion should have something to offer to those who experienced the severe pain of being barren. Prayers to seek God's consolation, is one way:

> The more vulgar approach to God assumed a different kind of sympathy; man's animal functions – eating, drinking, copulating – when exercised with the *eclat* of a celebration in the presence of God, won his participation so that his worshippers should not thereafter exert themselves in vain. Banqueting before the LORD is presented throughout the Bible as normal and established, but ritual copulation was much more open to moral censure and legal prohibition, on account of the abuses and scandals that were bound to arise from it. (40)

The fact that the Bible repeated rules against such behavior indicates that it was taking place so much that its refutation was deemed necessary. In this context Levin discusses the existence of "hallowed ones." They were mostly men, who were hired by the temple administration to function as sources of fertility. By copulating with a hallowed person, the worshipper communicated with God.

> The service of the hallowed ones was analogous to that of the priest who performed sacrifices at the altar. Both the sacrifice and the sex act on holy ground required a person previously consecrated. That a man of priestly lineage might do both, was not unknown, as is proved by the case of Eli's sons. But aside from the passage (1 Sam 2:22), the sexual role of the hallowed ones is separate from the ordinary priesthood; and the priests are never described as hallowed ones. (43)

One of the requirements of being a "hallowed one" was to be a foreigner or alien, if he was to be tolerated. This separated him from the legitimate priesthood. While reading this information, I saw a nature program on television. There was a report about an African tribe. At a certain celebration (the Zohar) young women gather around the heroes of the tribe. A woman may select the hero she likes best by placing her foot on the shoulder of the sitting man. Then that hero is expected to sleep with her that night. Some men are chosen by more than one woman and will have to perform more than once that night.

When the question was asked about how the husband of such a woman would react, the answer was, that he would be proud to have such a good looking child. He himself would not be able to produce such outstanding-looking children. He would regard himself as the father of a special child.

Levin discusses the name, Joshua, and observes that it is Moses who gives this name, Joshua, to a man called Hoshea. (Numbers 13:16) The scribes may have wanted to tell this story to indicate that this famous hero, who amazed the people and awakened their admiration, was simply a servant of Moses. Levin also indicated that adding the (') or iota or yodh to a name (which is pronounced as a *j*) means a reference to Yahweh and signals a theophoric (god-bearing) quality. Thus the divine affiliation was given by Moses according to Mosaists.

Levin observes that the Bible says nothing about the mother of Joshua. With such silence, people are likely to fill in the blank with stories:

> The aura surrounding Joshua probably grew thus. In appreciation of his exploits, the epithet "Son of the Lord" was attached to his name. Out of that story developed, how his mother had been sterile before she became pregnant with him (but had other children after the sterility was overcome). This story lingered on obscurely among the Jews even when the reform of the Scriptural text converted the patronymic to 'son of Nun.'

Levin consulted rabbinical stories where Joshua's mother is described barren. Her husband is in the temple praying. When he discovered that his wife was pregnant, he was very disturbed, and somehow, events made it clear that this child was willed by God. Levin based his conclusions on such existing rabbinical literature.

Other information which informs the view of traditionalists to become aware of non-Mosaic and other cultural implications can be found in Chapter Five, "The Fertility of the Tribe of Judah." There reference is made to Tamar, as reported by Schaberg and Reilly in their discussion of the illegitimacy of Jesus. Here is the story.

> It happened at that time that Judah left his brothers, to go down and stay with an Adullamite called Hirah. There Judah saw the daughter of a Canaanite called Shua. He made her his wife...
> Judah took a wife for his first born, Er, and her name was Tamar. But Er, Judah's first born, offended Yahweh greatly, so Yahweh brought about his death. Then Judah said

to Onan, "Take your brother's wife..." What he did was offensive to Yahweh, so he brought about his death also. Then Judah said to his daughter-in-law Tamar, "Return home..."

A long time passed, and then Shua's daughter, the wife of Judah died. After Judah had been comforted he went up to Tinnah to the men who sheared his sheep, himself and Hirah, his Adullamite friend. This was reported to Tamar, "Listen, your father-in-law is going to Tinnah for the shearing of the sheep." She therefore changed her widow clothes, wrapped a veil around her, and sat down, heavily swathed, where the road to Enaim branches off the road to Tinnah. Shelah had grown up, as she had not been given to him as his wife.

Judah, seeing her, took her for a prostitute, since her face was veiled. Going up to her on the road, he said, "Come, let me sleep with you." He did not know that she was his daughter-in-law. "What will you give me to sleep with me?" she asked. "I will send you a kid from the flock" he answered. "Agreed, if you give me a pledge until you sent it" she answered. "What pledge shall I give you?" he asked. "your seal, your cord, and the stick you are holding" she answered. He gave them to her and slept with her, and she conceived by him. Then she rose and left him, and taking off her veil she put on her widow's weeds.

Judah sent the kid by his Adullamite friend to recover the pledge from the woman. But he did not find her. He inquired from the men at the place, "Where is the prostitute who was by the roadside at Enaim?" "There has been no prostitute there," they answered. So returning to Judah he said, "I did not find her. What is more, the men of the place told me there had been no prostitute there." "Let her keep what she has," Judah replied "or shall we become a laughing stock? At least I sent her this kid, even though you did not find her."

About three months later it was reported to Judah, "your daughter-in-law has played the harlot; furthermore, she is pregnant, as a result of her misconduct." "Take her outside and burn her" said Judah. But as she was being led off she sent this message to her father-in-law, "It was the man to whom these things belong who made me pregnant. Look at them" she said "and see whose seal and cord and stick these are." Judah examined them and then said, "She is in the right rather than I. This comes of my not giving her to my son Shelah to be his wife." He had no further intercourse with her.

When the time for her confinement came she was found to have twins in her womb. (Jerusalem Bible. Gen. 38:1-27.)

Levin finds Tamar, who gave Judah back two good sons for the two he lost, quite mysterious. He observes that Tamar means 'palm'. That is somewhat interesting.

Since roads in that dry country would, whenever possible, go past springs, wayfarers must have been used to the sight of palms as landmarks of a place where they could quench their thirst. It was also a likely place for a 'hallowed one' to be seen sitting in the shade of a tree and waiting for someone to approach. The very surroundings invited casual copulation. Particularly if a wayfarer happened to be baffled by sterility and haunted by the dread of extinction, a shady grove was the best natural setting to overcome such frustrations. That is how the imagination operates in myths; it would not necessarily be so in the psychology of real life.

The infertility of Judah was overcome when he mated with a palm, or with a woman carrying the name and thereby the attributes of the palm, or with a hallowed woman at Twin Springs (where palms doubtless grew)–three variants of the same theme. (111)

Of course, one does not have to resort to myths to become part of the imaginative aspects of such gathering places where one meets for sexual encounters. Our modern terminology speaks of "watering holes" indicating bars where people meet to pick up mates for a quick encounter.

The subsection, "Fertility from Divine Trees," elaborates on the palm story. Levin comments that Abraham, too, became a father at a shady place called Hebron. There the three passers-by were welcomed by Abraham and he begged them to rest under the tree and accept refreshments. He had his wife made a special cake, and prepared a calf for them. He placed the feast-like meal before them in the shade, and they ate. Levin continues:

"And they said to him 'Where is Sarah, your wife?' and he said, 'There in the tent.' And he [i.e., the LORD] said, 'I will come back to you at quickening time, and there will be a son for Sarah, your wife'; and Sarah was listening at the entrance of the tent, and [the LORD] was behind it." It seems that the divine guest (or guests) asked for the host's wife because they had been served not just the customary dole of a piece of bread for wayfarers but an elaborate meal, set out under the tree. The circumstances obliged the guest to say what the childless couple was most eager to hear.

"And Abraham and Sarah were old, along in years; menstruation had ceased to occur for Sarah. And Sarah smirked to herself to think, 'After being all worn out, I have some fun, old as my husband is.' And the LORD said to Abraham, 'Why is Sarah smirked, as if to say, "Shall I really have a baby, old as I am?" Is anything too wonderful for the LORD? In Season I shall come back to you at quickening time, and Sarah will have a son'" (18:11-14).

> Through some miracle the LORD in human form has made her pregnant. The text is just reticent enough to leave the physical aspect in doubt: (114-115)

Levin notices that, when the story goes on in 12:1-2, it does not mention that Abraham slept with Sarah. It says, "And the LORD did to Sarah as he had spoken. And Sarah became pregnant and bore Abraham a son for his old age, at the season that God had spoken of." The place where Sarah overcame her sterility is called "the oak of Mamre." In this context Levin mentions that, when strangers rested against a tree of special magnitude, then its divinity was extended to them. Some trees were so old that the imagination of the people assumed that they were planted by a divine being.

> To be sure, an altar for a god might be built nearby (Gen. 13:18); so the god, not permanently resident, would come when called by name to a sacrifice and lured by rich odor. The altar was put there because a shady place was a desirable resort for people intent upon a special meat dinner. The exquisite comfort of the shade was the primary attraction; but further blessings might accrue, even procreation to cancel out a lifetime of sterility. (119)

Levin dishes up all those insights because they form the background of material to be found in the gospels. There is a certain awareness of the Joshua veneration which surrounds the affirmation of Jesus. This is treated in Chapter Six, "Motifs of Joshua and David in the Gospels." Levin states his main focus:

> I want to show how the aura of *divine hereditary grandeur*, while at odds with the Mosaic religion, had a Jewish background. It was not (as some admirers maintain) an unprecedented, unique attribute of this one person [Jesus], nor (as critics have argued) simply a common motif of pagan myth that got syncretized onto an offshoot of Judaism. (141)

In the subsection, "The Angelic Annunciation and the Naming of Jesus," reference is made to Matthew and Luke and the appearance of the Angel Gabriel to Mary and Joseph. And so the child receives his name, Jesus, "for he will save his people from their sins." There are a number of Old Testament passages where God or a divine messenger determines the name for the child to be born. In Gen. 16:11 the Lord's messenger said to Hagar that her son's name would be Ismael. In Gen. 17:19 God said to Abraham that he was to call his son Isaac. Other instances are Is. 8:14 and

Hosea 1:2-9. The name Jesus has in Hebrew as first letter yodh or iota, which is pronounced as a *J*. It means that he is of Yahweh or God. Levin comments:

> Bringing God into the child's name or surname is part of the motif which Luke shares with the passages from Genesis where the LORD's messenger addresses the *mother*-to-be. Pregnancy – above all, the first pregnancy – is such a profound change in a woman's constitution, both anatomical and psychological, that she is receptive to the idea of commemorating permanently, by means of the child's name, her marvelous though uncomfortable experience. To her there is an immeasurable difference between copulation and pregnancy, or between mere copulation and that copulation which makes her pregnant.
>
> While she knows that it takes a man (*cf.* Luke 1:34), her subjective emotions insist it is God rather than any man who causes such a mighty change. And in due proportion to what she has felt within herself, she daydreams of the immense effect her child will have upon the world. (144)

Here Levin comes very close to Campbell's interpretation of Virgin Birth, which is of the fourth chakra, compassion, and not of the lust of man. Levin adds, that the enthusiastic followers of Christ, taking suggestions from the Old Testament, "gave his mother credit for a presentiment of his greatness." (145)

> Convinced as they were that his greatness was unparalleled, they could express their conviction only by grasping for Old Testament parallels, which they combined in an ingenious, original manner. They took less from the official Mosaism that fills a large part of the Scripture, but they exploited those motifs which they found relatively non-Mosaic. In particular, Luke, relished the theme of the mother's foreknowledge and connected it with the name *Iesous* and the surname *uios upsistou* [son of the most high], because the majestic deeds recalled the Old Testament hero and were beyond the scale of a man who had inherited only such limited distinction as a human father could pass on to him. In that sense the career and the parentage of Jesus of Nazareth were likened to those of the earlier *Iesous*, the conquering hero. (146)

There is a need to elaborate on the people's imagination regarding this messiah, Jesus. Levin holds that the portrayal of David as rendered in the Old Testament books, was too disciplined to satisfy the enthusiasm of the Jewish masses:

Jesus of Nazareth aroused expectations not only as the "son of David" but also as a new Joshua. The savior tradition harking back to Joshua, and embedded in the very name, was less continuous that that of the anointed son of David, but it could be even more dangerous. For Joshua had been appointed without the mysterious oil ritual, obsolete in Roman times; Moses had simply laid his hands on him. (Num. 17:18-23).

Moreover the Scriptures themselves made it unequivocal that Joshua's greatest victories were miraculous. (163)

Levin mentions how Joshua experienced a theophany, the LORD of host appearing with drawn sword (Joshua 5:13-15), who instructed Joshua about the strategy in conquering Jericho. And at Gibeon, the Lord made the enemies panic. At one time it reads, "And as they fled from Israel down the descent of Beth-horon, Yahweh hurled huge hailstones from heaven on them all the way to Azekah, which killed them" (10:11).

"Is it not written in the Book of the Just? The sun stood still in the middle of the sky and delayed its setting for almost a whole day. There was never a day like that before or since, when Yahweh obeyed the voice of a man, for Yahweh was fighting for Israel. Then Joshua, and all Israel with him, returned to the camp at Gilgal" (10:13-15)

Then the comparison is made between Jesus and Joshua. Levin mentions that the reputation of Jesus promised comparable wonders: a) The destruction of the temple of which Jesus reportedly said, "and within three days I will build another, not hand-made" (Mark 15:58). This alluded to the Jericho story. And b) Jesus reputation encouraged some hope that he would be a leader in ending the Roman occupation. Joshua's stories proved that the motto, "be strong and steadfast" (Deut. 31:6.7, 23, Joshua 1:6, 7, 9, 18, 10:25) provided the right determination and attitude which places all expectations in the Lord, who will be victorious over any enemy. Levin devotes a number of pages to aspects which indicate that Jesus was involved in some stirring of people and gathering them around him, which had some political overtones. (See 166-171). And then he observes:

However, the deadly countermeasures which brought Jesus down argue that his enemies were truly alarmed – and with reason. We do them an injustice and misunderstand the New Testament if we imagine them indulging in a bigoted, fanatical attack upon a harmless, pacific teacher. Doubtless many important and self-important men – scribes and Pharisees in particular – hated him personally for his scornful words about them as a class. But more than that, they saw him as a public enemy, about to precipitate a rebellion in which they had everything to lose, while his faction dreamed of gaining freedom and power (*cf.* John 11:47-48).

On the other hand, Levin recognized that the Jesus teachings were open to different interpretations. If his followers would have been revolutionaries only, then the whole movement would have been wiped out. Because the movement dissociated itself from the insurrectionaries, that is why it survived and adapted itself to other aspects of development.

This then is the complexity as perceived by Levin. In this way he indicated that the imagination about Joshua was part of the interpretation of Jesus. In the way Joshua was the son of the Lord, so, Jesus too, spoke to the hopes and expectations of the people.

It is very intriguing to reflect on Levin's insights from the point that Jesus is spiritually experienced as the one who speaks against institutionalized religion and morality. He promotes the freedom of the heart and the courage to develop one's own strength and authority. One should not be subjugated to any power. This can easily be understood as the idealism or fanaticism of an insurrectionist, and as such a danger for those charged with the protection of the institutionalized life. The spiritual is not separate from existential, and as such is part of reality. One is reminded of the episode in Dostoevsky's *The Brothers Karamazov* and the Grand Inquisitor Legend. There Jesus Christ appears before the cardinal, The Great Inquisitor, as a prisoner, and is found guilty of stirring too much unrest for the life of the Church. He emerges as the guilty savior.

On the other hand, there is also history's recording of Thomas Munzer, the fanatic preacher of the apocalyptic end-time in the days before Martin Luther. It demonstrates that the Christian fervor has the potential of revolutionary energy, which is suspect to those in authority. The Old Testament is filled with dynamics which defy establishment mentalities. It empowers people by religious convictions, and the human is invited to believe in forces which supersede the common. These forces are divine in nature and s such they are sources of powerful movements. In rabbinical literature one finds a traditional fear of revolutionaries, because they may cause so much trouble and unrest, which the rabbi tries to avoid. In other words, the mentality of Joshua is alive and well and was certainly active in the interpretation of Jesus by the people, when they experienced him as an amazing authority.

Thus the Father of Jesus as the Lord who promoted Joshua and forcefully assisted him in his great and mighty deeds, receives a very impressive and determined characterization. The mythical God-Father archetype became quite particular in the Biblical tradition. Of course, additional characterizations of the Father exist as well, e.g., the beautiful parable of the prodigal son:

> While he was still a long way off, his father saw him and was moved with pity. He ran to the boy, clasped him in his arms and kissed him tenderly. Then his son said, "Father, I have sinned against heaven and against you. I no longer deserve to be called your son." But the father said to the servants, "Quick! Bring out the best robe and put it on him; put a ring on his finger and sandals on his feet. Bring the calf we have been fattening, and kill it; we are going to have a feast, a celebration, because this son of mine was dead and has come back to life; he was lost and is found." And they began to celebrate. (Luke 15:20-24)

In the final section, "The Son of God," Levin arrives at summarizations of this particular study. His main insight is that in the biblical tradition, the hero received an epithet of divine paternity to signify his superiority. As such, Jesus is not just the son of Joseph, and he was not just from Nazareth, but Bethlehem was brought into play – the city of David. "Certain passages present Jesus as God's son rather by adoption than explicitly by procreation." (179) For example: the voice from heaven at Jesus' baptism and his transfiguration. "Only the stories of the virgin Mary's pregnancy in Matthew and Luke declare categorically that Jesus from the first had God alone, no man, for his father." (179) Here Levin is not aware of the interpretations of Schaberg and Reilly as reported previously. But Levin adds an interesting note. He holds that these narrations by Matthew and Luke are less about Jesus and more about Mary, to show that she is not just an ordinary woman. The authors of these gospels found it necessary to elevate Jesus' mother to the realm of the divine. (179)

Levin finds it important to emphasize that Jesus himself was recognized by God, when he was an adult. His disciple, and also the demons which he ejected, also became aware of his great authority when he was a grown man. And when John describes him as "God's only begotten son" (3:18), then Levin understands this to mean, "uniquely great, not only in his own generation but for all time." (180)

> Jesus' contemporaries had no practical need to state this, because "son of God" constituted ample recognition that they would never meet his equal. But John was writing to forestall the claim of any later person to be another son of God, like Jesus before him. In the turbid currents of Gnosticism that was no remote danger. (180)

Thus John, too, like Mark, Matthew, and Luke, became political in his description of Jesus. He was against the gnostic interpretations as reported in the previous chapter. He was for elevating Jesus in such way that the messenger is more important than the message. They wanted Jesus to be the anointed son of David, but they needed the Joshua tradition to supersede Mosaism, which was horrified bay calling anyone "son of the LORD." Levin comments:

> A non Mosaic undercurrent, however, remained in popular parlance, beyond the control of the learned, and Jesus of Nazareth may well have profited from it. (181)

In the final paragraph Levin evaluates Jesus' originality against what his followers made him to be. He maintains a philological view, but nevertheless, he recognizes aspects which constitute the roots of his own Jewish heritage.

> Seen not from his own time, he was of permanent and utterly revolutionary importance for severing the bonds of the individual to traditions – whether of the family or the nation – which has assigned to the individual only a transitory role. But even while his adherents publicized the substance of what he stood for, they were still more or less constrained by familiar verbal patterns. Particularly his literary spokesmen, whose words have reached us, had behind them the old Hebrew vocabulary or its customary rendering in the Septuagint. The grandeur of his innovation was less dazzling, more accessible, because they were clothed in age-old phrases. (181)

This is quite a statement. It says that Jesus' grandeur, his innovations, supersedes the wording by which he is described. Thus the spirit of Jesus is beyond the language traditionally available. There is a mystery about this Jesus, which intrigues Levin. Although he delightfully reveals the avenues and ways by which his own cultural and religious tradition celebrated outstanding heroes, he is not a reductionist who leaves this amazing person wrapped in those boxes. Levin holds that Jesus is more dazzling than the old-age language by which they made him accessible to us. What more can one say?

There is a certain irony in the development of the Christology of Jesus. The Mosaic tradition prevented interests in calling Jesus, "son of God." So the early Christians resorted, according to Levin, to a non-Mosaist tradition, which was characterized by the continued awareness of Joshua, as the "son of the LORD." But then those Christians returned to the Mosaist defensiveness by making Jesus the *only* Son of God. Like Yahweh in the Mosaist tradition, this "Son of God" is exclusive, and one shall not have other "Sons of God" beside him. This precludes the continuation of the celebrative affirmation of the divine within creation and the appearance of the divinely inspired heroes. As such Campbell's interpretations of the divine are ridiculed and categorized as "just a mythical understanding of the divine." The orthodox mentality explained the divine in terms of certain unique events only. Thus any connection with the human experience is overruled. The philologist, Levin, made us see how limited such a view is in terms of the wealth of biblical life as indicated in his comments and insights.

Epilog

Our basic interest is in discovering the character of Jesus' Father, as the motivating spirit of this remarkable man. Levin's studies pertain to the Old Testament, and he discusses the New Testament in terms of related aspects. The immediate connection with "Son of God" was Joshua, and in a similar way, David. But these prototypes of the Jesus appearance have been enriched by his discussion of the Virgin Birth phenomenon in reference to the messenger of God who approached Hagar and Sarah. The discussion broadened by including the stories about Tamar and Ruth.

If we would have only the male heroes, then the divine spirit which motivated these men would be recognized only in the excellence of being a great warrior, conqueror, leader, and king. The references to the woman bring in other divine characteristics, e.g., the holiness in desiring a child, the ability to see greatness in God's creation because of our bodily existence and how procreation works. Thus one can say that the male references accentuate "productivity" and the female references emphasizes the "generative" dimensions. Productivity is characterized by assertion and great deeds. The generative indicates openness and affirmation.

Levin recognized this feminine dimension in his discussion of the first miracle narrated in the gospel of John. It was at the wedding in Cana (2:1-11) where water was changed into wine. It was the only time that Jesus' mother was involved in one of the miracles of her son. She is mentioned first: "and Jesus' mother was there; Jesus also was invited, and his disciples, to the wedding. And when the wine ran short, Jesus' mother said to him, 'They have no wine.' Said Jesus to her 'What [is that] to me and you, madam? My time has not yet come.' His mother said to the servants, 'Do whatever he tells you.' Levin finds this quite Dionysiac, and the choice wine is a good omen for the bridal couple. Moreover, for the wedding party more drink was essential:

> The gaiety around the bride and groom would put them at ease and start off their conjugal intimacy with a sense of God's blessings upon them.
> Jesus' mother, like the guest, wished them all possible good; but with the advantage of such a superior son also in attendance, she could do them a unique favor. The background presupposes what is not stated explicitly: that the glorious wine drunk by all present should make the marriage fertile. To that extent the Gospel is still an age-old tradition, and we are not surprised that the person soliciting Jesus' intervention is a matron who is presumably a generation older than the bride and therefore feels the urgency of the event for the future of the family. (155-156)

The Jesus portrayed in John's gospel acts on behalf of his mother's initiative. Moreover, throughout the gospel, Jesus is identified with the basic symbols of life. He is called the light, the water, the water of life, the bread of life, and the generative life of the vine, which gives sustenance to the branches. In this spirit he prays:

I pray not only for for these,
but for those also
who through their words will believe in me.
May they all be one.
Father, may they be one in us,
as you are in me and I am in you,
so that the world may believe it was you who sent me.

(17:20-21)

Chapter Ten

Who Art in Heaven:
The Inner Reaches of the Implicate Order

Campbell himself summarized his educational and research background in his last book, *The Inner Reaches of Outer Space: Metaphor as Myth as Religion*. On reading the book, it becomes evident what the title suggests. The "inner reaches of space" refer to the "inner space," which is one's cosmic awareness present within the core of the human imagination. The life energy which constitutes human existence rings through in our bones, blood, and nerves. Our heartbeat and our breathing tingle with the dynamism of the cosmic forces. Our dreams enter our minds in ways beyond the rational and what we hold to be civil.

Because humans live in limited groups and at a particular location in space and time, determined by the environment of that situation, their imagination is conditioned by those sets of circumstances. The life of the nomads in the desert is different from fishermen or farmers in the Midwest. City dwellers experience their existence in ways unknown to tribes who live on the ancient mountain slopes of New Guinea. As such, each culture has its own characteristics.

"Metaphor as Myth as Religion" is at the heart of Campbell's prophetic authority. The book's first page (p. 11) discusses the fact that Jung spoke of "archetypes" and "the collective unconscious," and Adolf Bastian (1826-1905), an ethnologist and anthropologist at the University of Berlin, coined the term "Elementargedanken," which are elementary or primordial images and ideas which all people have in common. In Campbell's book the argument is that in our day we have become a world community. Consequently, we are to live in a world culture characterized by universal myths and common images. These universal metaphors (images by which all of us see life), according to Campbell, are available in the ancient myths of people. These myths are like dreams which play within an elementary or primordial reality which supersedes the limitation of a culture's location in space and time.

In *The Power of Myth* this issue is being discussed:

MOYERS: Don't you think modern Americans have rejected the ancient idea of nature as a divinity because it would have kept us from achieving dominance over nature? How can you cut down trees and uproot the land and turn rivers into real estate without killing God?

CAMPBELL: Yes, but that's not a characteristic of modern Americans, that is the biblical condemnation of nature which they inherited from their own religion and brought with them, mainly from England. It's right there in Genesis: we are able to be the masters of the world.

But if you think of ourselves as coming out of the earth, rather than having been thrown in here from somewhere else, you see that we are the earth, we are the consciousness of the earth. These are the eyes of the earth. And this is the voice of the earth.

MOYERS: Scientist are beginning to quite openly talk about the Gaia principle. [It holds that the emergence of life on the earth influenced the environment of the earth in such a fashion that it became more and more conducive to the development of life. E.g., tropical forests produce effects which cause rain, while the plants form roots which hold the fertile top soil on location, and as a whole it is the habitat for an immense variety of life.]

CAMPBELL: There you are, the whole planet as an organism.

MOYERS: Mother Earth. Will new myths come from this image?

CAMPBELL: Well, something might. You can't predict what a myth is going to be any more than you can predict what you're going to dream tonight. Myths and dreams cone from the same place. They come from realizations of some kind that have then to find expression in symbolic form. And the only myth that is going to be worth thinking about in the immediate future is one that is talking about the planet, not the city, not these people, but the planet, and everybody on it. That's my main thought for what the future is going to be.

And what it will have to deal with will be exactly what all myths have dealth with – the maturation of the individual, from dependency through adulthood, through maturity, and then to the exit; and then how to relate to this society and how to relate this society to the world of nature and the cosmos. That's what the myths have all talked about, and what this one's got to talk about. But the society that it's got to talk about is that society of the planet. And until that gets going, you don't have anything.

MOYERS: So you suggest that from this begins the new myth of our time?

CAMPBELL: Yes, this is the ground of what the myth is to be. It's already here: the eye of reason, not of my religious community; the eye of reason, not of my linguistic community. Do you see? And this would be the philosophy for the planet, not for this group, that group, or the other group.

When you see the earth from the moon, you don't see any divisions there of nations and states. This might be the symbol, really, for the new mythology to come. That is the country we are going to be celebrating. And those are the people that we are one with. (32)

Ancient myths celebrate the complexity of life in reference to the forces of nature and the psychological energy of our emotions. They are dramatized in the reality of their opposites. The tension between the dualities is at play. So we find:

light & dark	reward & punishment
open & closed	growth & deterioration
life & death	wide & narrow
love & hate	spacious & boxed-in
creation & destruction	fresh & rotten
emergence & dissolution	new & old
good & evil	clear & confused
hard & soft	strong & weak
square & round	deep & shallow
forward & backward	pride & shame
progress & regression	inclusive & exclusive
illness & recuperation	acceptance & rejection
young & old	affirmation & condemnation
beautiful & ugly	free & caught

liberator & terrorist	holy & garbage
God & Satan	give & take
fall & redemption	coming & going
guilt & forgiveness	pain & pleasure
sin & absolution	vision & blindness
warm & cold	plenty & starvation
hope & despair	smooth & rough
clean & dirty	straight & crooked
black & white	fair & foul
summer & winter	fast & slow
up & down	weave & unravel

There are common experiences of all people all over the world. Their myths are made up by complexities of aspects listed above.

In trying to imagine what information constitutes a common ground from which the myth of the future may emerge, Campbell wrote Chapter One, "Cosmology and the Mythic Imagination," in his *The Inner Reaches of Outer Space*. He refers to Carl Sagan's information in his PBS series, *Cosmos*, and the book with the same title. Viewers and readers became aware of the immense vastness of the universe and its overwhelming history of cosmic events, e.g., the Big Bang, the formation of stars and galaxies, our solar system, the birth of live (evolution), the prospects of cosmic futures, and space travel.

This is a valid effort, because such a cosmology as narrated by Sagan truly speaks to the imagination of the modern mind. However, so much is left untouched, which is presently gathering people in a common imagination. This is reported substantially by Marilyn Ferguson in her bestseller, *The Aquarian Conspiracy: Personal and Social Transformation in the 1980s*.

Before the "Contents" and the Foreword by Max Lerner, there are quotations of three authors who found substantial response in the modern imagination:

> Time, events, or the unaided individual action of the mind will sometimes undermine or destroy an opinion without any outward sign of change...No conspiracy has been formed to make war on it, but its followers one by one noiselessly secede.

As its opponents remain mute or only interchange their thoughts by stealth, they are themselves unaware for a long period that a great revolution has actually been effected.
— Alexis de Toqueville

And I strive to discover how to signal my companions...to say in time a simple word, a password, like conspirators: Let us unite, let us hold each other tightly, let us merge our hearts, let us create for Earth a brain and a heart, let us give a human meaning to the superhuman struggle.
— Nikos Kazantzakis

This Soul can only be a conspiracy of individuals.
— Pierre Teilhard de Chardin

Among the existing "networks" where such a modern awareness finds its centers are: Association for Humanistic Education, Association for Humanistic Psychology, Association for Transpersonal Psychology, Committee for the Future, Creative Education Foundations, Futures Network, Institute for Noetic Sciences, Movements for a New Society, The Center for Integral Medicine, New Dimensions Foundation, Planetary Citizens, and Turning Point. (422-424) These institutions publish their own journals, but other related journals are listed as well. (425-427) Ferguson's book, of course, is widely known and translated into many languages, which indicates the world-wide extension of this modern mentality.

Of special interest in our journey is Chapter Six, "Liberating Knowledge: News from the Frontiers of Science." There we find sections like, Brain and Consciousness Research, Holism and Systems Theory, Evolution: the New Paradigm, The Science of Transformation, and A Holographic World. It is here where one can get in touch with perspectives and aspects by which the modern imagination can connect with Campbell's Father of Jesus and the dimensions indicated by the metaphor, Virgin Birth.

Campbell explained how religious thought changes in the history of cultures. It is an ongoing journey which moves to new centers of relevancy for the deeper understanding of the divine. As such, beliefs are statements about reality in respect to a divine origin and divine forces which permeate our hopes and expectations. Thus ultimate meaning is celebrated in one form or another.

CAMPBELL: The earliest evidence of anything like mythological thinking is associated with graves.

MOYERS: And they suggest that men and women saw life, and they didn't see it, so they wondered about it?

CAMPBELL: It must have been something like that. You only have to imagine what your own experience would be. The grave burials with their weapons and sacrifices to ensure a continued life – these certainly suggest that there was a person who was alive and warm before you who is now lying there, cold, and beginning to rot. Something was there that isn't there. Where is it now?

MOYERS: When do you think humans first discovered death?

CAMPBELL: They first discovered death when they were first humans, because they died. Now, animals have the experience of watching their companions dying. But, as far as we know, they have no further thoughts about it. And there is no evidence that humans thought about death in a significant way until the Neanderthal period, when weapons and animal sacrifices occur with burials.

MOYERS: What did these sacrifices represent?

CAMPBELL: That I wouldn't know.

MOYERS: Only a guess.

CAMPBELL: I try not to guess. You know, we have a tremendous amount of information about this subject, but there is a place where the information stops. And until you have writing, you don't know what people are thinking. All you have are significant remains of one kind or another. You can extrapolate backward, but that is dangerous. However, we do know that burials always involve the idea of the continued life beyond the visible one, of a plane of being that is behind the visible plane, and that is somehow supportive of the visible one to which we have to relate. I would say that is the basic theme of all mythology – that there is an invisible plane supporting the visible one. (71)

The last statement, "that there is an invisible plane supporting the visible one," will be the focus of this chapter. In this way, Campbell connects with the modern awareness in terms of the consciousness about the holographic world.

Before the holographic world and the related scientists are being discussed, it may be helpful to feature a few more statements which characterize Campbell's vision of the invisible world.

MOYERS: The waters of eternal life are right there? Where?

CAMPBELL: Wherever you are – if you are following your bliss, you are enjoying that refreshment, that life within you, all the time. (121)

Or:

> MOYERS: What is illumination?
>
> CAMPBELL: The illumination is the recognition of the radiance of one eternity through all things, whether in the vision of time these things are judged as good or as evil. To come to this, you must release yourself completely from desiring the goods of this world and fearing their loss. "Judge not that you be not judged," we read in the words of Jesus. "If the doors of perception were cleansed," wrote Blake, "man would see everything as it is, infinite." (162)

Or:

> CAMPBELL: ...There is an important passage in the recently discovered Gnostic Gospel According to St. Thomas: "'When will the kingdom come?' Christ's disciples ask." In Mark 13, I think it is, we read that the end of the world is about to come. That is to say, a mythological image – that of the end of the world – is there taken as predicting an actual, physical, historical fact to be. But in Thomas' version, Jesus replies: "the kingdom of the Father will not come by expectation. The kingdom of the Father is spread upon the earth and men do not see it" – so I look at you now in that sense, and the radiance of the presence of the divine is known to me through you. (213)

As reported by Marilyn Ferguson, developments in certain areas of the sciences have become sources of inspiration for a contemporary mystical consciousness. Whatever the source of scientific research may have been, it is a common understanding that humans are naturally inclined to seek knowledge about truth. Initial research did lead to the discovery of fire by which food and bodies could be heated and life became more comfortable. Scientific research supersedes the pragmatic and practical of a purpose-oriented technology. Humans are not only interested how to make the most of life. People don't live by bread alone. They also want to discover some sensical ideas about three or four basic questions. Where do we come from? Where are we going? What may we hope to expect? Who knows what is right or wrong?

The question about right or wrong implies that one wants to discern the true makeup of reality so that instructions about good behavior are reliably rooted in our knowledge about how things basically are. One can imagine that in this way physics emerged as the science which wants to unravel the complexity of the physical reality. Consequently, matter was studied and analyzed. Hunks of matter were taken apart for the purpose of finding the true elements of building blocks. In this process scientists discovered that atoms, initially perceived as the foundation of matter, are themselves composed of still smaller elements – subatomic quanta.

The study of the subatomic aspect of reality is known as the new physics. The adjective "new " denotes this physics to be distinctly different from the classical or Newtonian physics. The classical approach assumed a cause-effect (causality) relationship within the physical order. Whatever exists must have a relational cause. Moreover, the Newtonian approach held that nature operates by laws which can be measured and formulated rather exactly and precise. This is a world of things we can see and observe – the macrocosmos.

The subatomic realm is less obvious in its form of existence. Scientists discovered that the cause-effect relationship does not exist there because of aspects where the effect, as it were, precedes the cause. Moreover, the subatomic elements do not behave according to exact laws. They seem to operate in arbitrary ways. Still, scientists found that such spontaneous movements of the quanta can be understood in terms which deal with probability rather than with cause and effect situations.

In the first thirty years of this century, specialists in the new physics were amazed about the astonishing difference between the macrocosmic and the microcosmic (subatomic). They realized that the language and concepts of traditional science could not be used to explain their observations. In their efforts to express their insights, they were helped by the language and ideas used by mystics. Especially the Hindu tradition and the Taoist worldview provided images which served as models for a description of the subatomic realm.

This signals somewhat a turn of events. Where previously the history of philosophy and science helped religious thought in its understanding of the mysterious, now religious language provided concepts for the sciences in their pursuit of understanding reality.

Some of the major insights resulting from the new physics can be listed. One: reality is not created, it always was. Two: there is no nothingness from which creation emerged. There is only the fullness (*plenum*) of being. Three: our present universe is only one of an infinite number of realities. Four: the universe is the way we imagine reality – it is our illusion. Five: the order of nature is not mechanically ruled by cause and effect relations, but it is permeated by an implicate order which orchestrates everything as a whole. Six: disorder is not the opposite of order, but rather a greater and more encompassing order. Seven: energy itself supersedes the forms by which we experience its presence in our daily lives. Eight: the dimensions of space and time are human illusions which are not relevant for subatomic energy. Nine: future, past, and present are illusions of the human mind and have no bearing on the subatomic reality. Ten: the human mind (consciousness) and the external world are not two separate things. They participate in the illusion about human observations.

It is not the intention of this chapter to explain these major statements about the new physics. They are mentioned insofar as they play a role in an emerging worldview. In this context our search for dimensions which signify the mystery within the metaphor, the Father of Jesus, will find new understanding. Perhaps number ten may prove helpful as a first step into this strange territory of identification.

In his book, *Mysticism and the New Physics*, Michael Talbot approaches the traditional division between the subjective (consciousness) and the objective (the external). He proposes the concept, omnijective, which pertains to the belief that "consciousness and the physical world are not separate, but form one fundamental arena of awareness which is omnijective as opposed to being subjective or objective" (188). This insight resulted from Heisenberg's discovery that the subatomic quanta cannot be studied objectively. The moment instruments of measurements are focused on the particle, the phenomenon will become influenced. Further elaborations of this observation made scientists realize that the observer and the observed are part of a relationship which influences both. As such we see what we see insofar as we see it. We cannot see otherwise. Consequently, the world of our observations is the world of our imagination about what we see.

This brings us to number seven: energy itself supersedes the forms within which we experience its presence in our daily lives. It implies that our knowledge about reality is very much based on our prejudices and traditional notions which constitute our everyday perceptions of existence. Because energy seems to function in ways we experience their operation of every day, that is why we conclude these forms to be normal. From our understanding of the so-called "normal" we conclude that causality is all decisive (nothing exists without a mechanical cause). Consequently, we assumed that the universe was created by God out of nothingness. (The logic of causality demands a first cause – God.)

Whenever something abnormal occurs, people have the inclination to reject or abandon it as foreign and strange. Sometimes the authority of the strange energy is so convincing that it makes people change their minds about what is normal. That may be the birth of religious traditions. Moses stood in front of a burning bush which was not devoured by fire. The Hindus religion records moments of ecstasy where humans became aware of the mystical dimensions in existence. The Tao wisdom celebrates its insights in terms of Zen-Buddhism where the realm of rational logic is superseded. Studies in parapsychology report that certain yogi survive sitting nude and outdoors during cold winter nights while perspiring profusely as if they experienced the heat of a hot desert sun.

Such phenomena suggest that our perception of the normal is conditioned by what we hold to be regular. The mind seemingly has the power to break through the wall of normalcy and to make contact with forces of energy more directly than within the channels of our everyday setup. It also suggests that there is a communication possible between the form of one universe or world order and another coexisting universe. Or it may indicate that the physical reality presently known to us is superseded by a higher form of energy. Some yogi are capable of contacting this higher form of energy and allow it to become manifest within our universe. Such powers can be interpreted as priestly insofar as they establish a bridge between the low and the high, or between the natural and the supernatural. Although such phenomena are labeled as parapsychological, the new physics possibly can account for such extraordinary feats. For example, in his book, *Wholeness and the Implicate Order*, David Bohm describes how subatomic quanta which are millions of light-years separated from each other react to each other's movements instantaneously (faster than the speed of light). Such super-luminal phenomena cannot be explained according to Einstein's physics which held that nothing can move faster than light. Bohm theorizes that what may appear millions of light-years from our point of view, may in another universe be immediately close. Perhaps subatomic quanta travel in and out of various universes or world orders like flies which move in and out of beams of light on a summer night.

Whatever may be true about these theories, there is more and more speculation that our reality is simply our way of perceiving existence. In the way numerous radio signals crowd the air waves, a radio will pick up only those to which it is tuned. Of course, the radio has various channels, but normally one can use only one channel at a time. Our universe is one way of picking up radio waves. The new physics theorizes that the subatomic energy operates in and out of different channels.

Bohm also substantiates mathematically the theory that the external order of our universe is basically orchestrated and guided by an implicate order. Like a melody which unites all the different notes, so will the implicate order explicitly direct all the movements of all aspects of the explicate or external order. All the parts participate in the whole. Moreover, all the parts have an awareness of the whole, because that is the nature of their participation. A model, called hologram, will help in our understanding of this, and it serves as a convincing illustration.

A hologram is a picture of a three dimensional form on a photographic plate. When the information of the plate is projected in a room, then one sees a three-dimensional image. The intriguing aspect of this hologram is that each little part of the photographic plate contains all the information necessary to project this three-dimensional picture of the photographed object. It means that each part contains the whole. Thus the whole is not simply the sum of the parts, or only the complete organization of all the parts. The whole is represented in each part.

This is similarly true in the cells of a living organism. Each cell has the same DNA makeup. Although the cells that form the ear function differently from the cells that form the foot, deep down, below these differences, one finds the same DNA formation in each cell. That is why in the beginning of the formation of the zygote, the cells are transferable. Those which started at the location where the ear is formed can be placed in the area where the foot is being formed. The whole, as contained in the DNA structure, operates at different locations in different ways, but it is still the same DNA. Each part participates in the orchestration directed by the implied biological order, the DNA.

This gives a surprising new understand of what is considered to be a part. Previously, in the traditional physics, parts were simply perceived as pieces which fit within the puzzle of the whole. The new physics creates the awareness that parts are permeated with a sense of the whole. In anthropology, it would mean that individual humans are not simply separate creatures. As persons they have within themselves a sense of the whole. In each human heart and mind is a sense of the whole universe and its implicate order.

Perhaps that may explain why people basically enjoy a common sense as a reliable guide in their journey of life. Common sense indicates that one has a sense of the common good in its wider or universal dimensions. One cannot learn to acquire common sense, one is born with it, hopefully. Of course, one can educate the common sense to function better in response to the complex demands of living productively. But to appreciate the gracious mystery of common sense, one should be exposed to people who seemingly lack much of this precious energy. Then one experiences immediately what is failing. Any correction of this hiatus often ends in frustration about the power of education.

Previously, the human brain was thought to store memory in certain locations or lobes, (localized memory). Now research suggests that memory can be present all over the brain. Although certain forms of brain damage can diminish specific forms of memory, still there are indications that this memory can be retrieved vaguely from other places in the brain. Thus the human brain becomes understood in holographic terms and less as a construction of drawers (file-cabinet) where certain pieces of information are stored at definite locations. The brain itself is viewed as a part of the cosmos which in a holographic fashion has a awareness of the universe as a whole which is an integrated order. Consequently, the human brain is capable of mystical experiences which radiate a sense of wholeness into the human consciousness.

What has all this to do with the Father of Jesus? First, in this context we pursue to speak about Jesus in universal terms. This was also the claim of that school of philosophy which understood Jesus as the *Logos*, the center and key of the world order which God had in mind before the beginning of the creation. Other philosophies speak of Jesus in different terms. For example, process thought explains the meaning of Jesus insofar as in this person the divine became a most decisive presence in our reality. Jesus is the one who responded to the revelation of the "eternal objects" (Whiteheadian terms for God's revelation) in a most excellent and decisive way. Thus process philosophy and also *Logos* thought try to explain the Jesus phenomenon in universal concepts.

According to their observations and theories, the new physicists regard a planned order (blueprint) for creation as irrelevant. It does not make sense to them. First, they find the theory of creation rather meaningless. Second, they cannot verify the existence of such an order. The process model, where the divine lures existence into a greater harmony, makes more sense. However, it should be noted that the new physics does not focus on a better tomorrow where a greater harmony may emerge as an evolutionary process. The new physics holds that the wholeness of the implicate order is already present within the explicate order.

The new physics has learned to appreciate the experiences of the mystics and their understanding of the divine or the more or the eternal or the greater dimension of energy. As such it is prepared to recognize phenomena where such an immediate contact with the greater energy becomes manifest.

Of course, in his life Jesus was a good person who amazed many of his contemporaries by his living interest and genuine care. However, Christians became convinced about the divinity within Jesus when he rose from the dead. The narratives of the resurrection appearance of Jesus when he entered rooms without opening doors or windows, indicate that he enjoyed a new state of existence. The accounts in the gospels suggest a state of higher energy by which the normal forms of our everyday life are superseded. St.

Paul in his letters, especially I Corinthians 15, describes the resurrected state in similar terms.

Perhaps a reference to the Shroud of Turin is in order here. In 1988 the radiocarbon dating (the process is described in *Scientific American* by Robert E. M. Hedges and John A. J. Growlett in "Radiocarbon Dating by Accelerator Mass Spectrometry") concluded that according to this measurement the shroud dated around 1300 C. E. This makes further speculations about the claim, that it was the shroud in which the dead body of Jesus was wrapped, very difficult. Nevertheless, one can still benefit from the theories which existed before 1988 and still continue to exist. Experts in radiology, chemistry, biology, and other sciences testified that the image of the wounded and crucified man on the cloth cannot be explained as simply bloodstains or forms of paint. The speculation existed that the shroud's image was possibly the result of what happened to Jesus' body at the moment of the resurrection. On Easter morning the body entered a new state of life and its radiation left an imprint of the body on the cloth. That is why the imprint is like a photographic negative. Only when one develops its photographic positive can one see the portrait of a face and a body.

Rudolf Bultmann and his followers would be less interested in such information. They hold that the resurrection of Jesus is a spiritual event within the minds and hearts of the disciples. Joachim Jeremias and his school would argue that something happened to Jesus himself (an event in history) by which the disciples began to believe that Jesus was not dead but had become transformed. This is dramatized in the conversion of Thomas, the disciple who did not want to believe in the resurrection unless he would see and touch Jesus in his living form. Of course, the conversion of St. Paul when he was thrown to the ground on the way to Damascus suggests the radiating power of Jesus in his transformed existence.

These aspects come into play in the article by John Dart, "Son Light: Scholars says first Christians saw resurrected Jesus as luminous being". Dart reports on a paper presented by James M. Robinson, mentioned in a previous chapter. Robinson holds that the first generation of Christians believed that the resurrection made Jesus a luminous appearance which is different from being in the flesh. The paper outlines two "trajectories" of

Christian belief. One emphasized the resurrection of the flesh, while another tradition (Gnosticism) perceived Jesus' appearance as a great light.

The new physics and its recent appreciation of the parapsychological recognizes that there are people who experience and radiate an energy which is regarded as greater than normal. Of course, the parapsychological has nothing to do with the new physics as a professional discipline, but because of the findings in the new physics some scientists theorize beyond the scope of their field and suggest ideas about orders of energy which are different from our commonly perceived order. These orders exist simultaneously with our known universe. What supposedly happened to Jesus at the moment of his resurrection, as supposed by speculations about the Shroud of Turin, will receive more understanding from the new physics than from the Newtonian or classical physics. The latter believes in the laws of nature as definites – a causality which does not allow for deviations as observed in parapsychological events. The classical approach feels that somehow there has to be an explanation in traditional terms; otherwise it cannot be true. The new physics has reached an understanding of the physical reality which supersedes the mechanical causality of a blueprint based world-order.

There are other ways where the new physics would be able to affirm the luminous appearance of Jesus. The gospel tells us how Jesus lived and what he preached. Moreover, these accounts emphasize that Jesus converted people to a life of hope and expectation. He brought persons out of their particular boxes and communicated to them dimensions of life's greatness worthy of a personal commitment. In their understanding of developmental stages of moral integrity and the life of faith, Lawrence Kohlberg and James Fowler would rate the Jesus of the gospels on the highest level of their maturity scales. It means that Jesus is perceived as someone who lived his personal life according to universal perspectives and holistic principles. The new physics affirms the hologram as a valid model for an understanding of the relationship between subatomic particles. Again, the hologram signifies that the parts contain an awareness of the whole, while at the same time they are parts. One could say that Jesus personified the holographic way of life in an eminent fashion. As an individual (part) he asserted himself, gave commands, cried, was delighted, got tired, enjoyed caring for people, experienced anxiety about his death, but this selfhood which was dear to him radiated a concern for the wholeness of existence. Wordplay allows us to make some connection. For example, Jesus was a wholesome man who wanted people to be whole. He worked hard [preaching the Kingdom] in an effort to make people aware of greater dimensions. His own death became acceptable to him in the name of the greater good. Christian theologies recognize these aspects by teaching that Jesus died for the sins of all people so that all may have eternal life. That Jesus was not interested in a career as a witch doctor is indicated by the story about the lame man who was cured and ordered to pick up his stretcher, At that moment Jesus counseled him in an authoritative manner bay saying, "Sin no more!" This is the holiness prompted by Jesus personally. He wanted people to stay away from crooked practices and open themselves to the power of wholeness which emerges when one seeks the life of integrity. To be integrated means to be in touch with the wider dimensions of loving, caring, and consideration. Such energy resides within the core of our hearts and minds as well as in the life we experience in relationships with other people, animals, water, rain, sunshine, and the cosmic forces of nature.

The integrity of Jesus became so forceful that it radiated in his bodily presence. The woman who suffered from bleeding most of her life was cured instantly by simply touching the seam of Jesus' cloak. Jesus touched the ears and eyes of those who were deaf and blind, and they could hear and see. He also took the hand of the young man whose body was being carried to the cemetery. The man came alive again and was given back to his mourning mother. Jesus commanded the dead friend, Lazarus, to come out of the grave. What happened gives consolation to those mourning their dead when, at the Christian burial rite, they hear this gospel story read to them. Martha believed that Jesus had the power to raise her brother, and so it happened. All these are celebrations of energy greater than sickness, disease, desperation, anger, hate, and death. Because Jesus opened himself to the forces of such a divine energy, which is holistic in nature, these powers emanated from his bodily presence. Moreover, these powers continue to emanate in the stories about Jesus as recorded in the testimonies of those who gathered into communities in Jesus' name. Jesus is quoted as having said that He will be present where two or three are gathered in his name. It happens when we give food to the hungry, companionship to the lonely, consolation to the desperate, and comfort to those who are weak or dying. The holonomic presence of Jesus can be experienced personally when we feel that he brings the best out of us. The divine energy resides in all of us, but it needs to be activated. Some are helped by a guru, others do exercise in cosmic awareness, and others become disciples of the Lord who helps them celebrate the deeper dimensions of life. Then Christianity is not a system which indoctrinates people according to certain dogmas and moral restrictions. Then the Christ in all of us recognizes the excellence and authority of the divine energy in Jesus, who in his own person emanated the divine in such a way that he proclaimed that his Father and he are one. This divine life does not reside in a supernatural Newtonian heaven, outside the realm of this earth. It is the kingdom which is within all of us. The new physics and its interpretation of the physical reality allows us to think and feel in those terms. It is an awareness that all of existence is primordially good – implicitly good.

> CAMPBELL: ...When Jesus says, "He who drinks from my mouth will become as I am and I shall be he," he's talking from the point of view of that being of beings, which we call Christ, who is the being of all of us. Anyone who lives in relation to that is as Christ. Anyone who brings into his life the message of the Word is equivalent to Jesus, that's the sense of that. (213)

And in the last chapter, "Masks of Eternity," the discussion continues:

> MOYERS: You've said that the whole question of life revolves around being versus becoming.

> CAMPBELL: Yes. Becoming is always fractional. And being is total.

> MOYERS: What do you mean?

> CAMPBELL: Well, let's say you are going to become fully human. In the first few years you are child, and that is only a fraction of the human being. In a few more years you are in adolescence, and that is certainly a fraction of the human being. In maturity you are still fractional – you are not a child, but you are not old yet. There is an image in the Upanishads of the original, concentrated energy which was the big bang of creation that set forth the world, consigning all things to the fragmentation of time. But to see through the fragments of

time to the full power of original being–that is a function of art.

MOYERS: Beauty is an expression of that rapture of being alive.

CAMPBELL: Every moment should be such an experience.

MOYERS: And what we are going to become tomorrow is not important as compared to this experience.

CAMPBELL: This is the great moment, Bill. What we are trying to do in a certain way is to get the being of our subject rendered through the partial way we have of expressing it. (228)

One more reference to the Father and his Kingdom:

MOYERS: Eden was not, Eden will be.

CAMPBELL: Eden is. "The kingdom of the Father is spread upon the earth, and men do not see it."

MOYERS: Eden is–in this world of pain and suffering, and death and violence?

CAMPBELL: That is the way it feels, but this is it, this is Eden. When you see the kingdom spread upon the earth, the old way of living in the world is annihilated. That is the end of the world. The end of the world is not an event to come, it is an ever psychological transformation, or visionary transformation. You see not the world of solid things but a world of radiance. (230)

In his booklet, "Do You Believe in God?" Karl Rahner provides us with a deeply felt statement about the "ever psychological transformation" mentioned by Campbell. It is very dramatic in its scope because it is not just about a mystical experience where one senses the overwhelming oneness of the divine. It is truly about the psychological transformation within the person in terms of openness.

Have you ever experienced the spiritual element in man?...Have we ever kept silent, despite the urge to defend ourselves, when we were unfairly treated? Have we ever forgiven another although we gained nothing by it and our forgiveness was accepted as quite natural? Have we ever made a sacrifice without receiving any thanks or acknowledgments, without ever feeling any inward satisfaction? Have we ever decided to do a thing simply for the sake of conscience, knowing that we must bear sole responsibility for our decision without being able to explain it to anyone? Have we ever tried to act purely for the love of God when no warmth sustains us, when our act seemed a leap in the dark, simply nonsensical? Were we ever good to someone without expecting a trace of gratitude and without the comfortable feeling of having been "unselfish?"

If we can find such experiences in our life, then we have had that very experience of the Spirit, which we are after here – the experience of the Eternal, the experience that the Spirit is something more than and different from a part of this world, the experience that happiness in this world is not the whole point of existence, the experience of faith for which this world provides no reason. (112-113)

This exemplifies what Campbell refers to in his statement, "To come to this, you must release yourself completely from desiring the goods of this world..." (162)

The next chapter will incorporate more aspects of transformation. The reference to the new physics and Bohm's implicate order was intended to make us aware of the presence of the holistic within everything. This is the realm of heaven which can become immanent to those who nurture the "inner reaches" as described by Campbell.

Chapter Eleven

The Multifaceted "Father"

The journey, "Search for the Father of Jesus," has created an awareness of the complexity of the metaphor. Campbell, Priest, and Wilder explained how the perception of God as Father received a localized interpretation in the biblical tradition. Saul Levin's studies showed how within the biblical tradition there was a very orthodox group, the Mosaists, who dominated the editions of the Scriptures. The non-Mosaists continued to co-exist, and they provide the cultural perspectives by which the Father of Joshua can be applied in learning about other than traditional orthodox interpretations of Jesus' Father.

Moreover, the pursuit of this divine dimension in reference to the mythological Great Mother and the Mother Goddess helped significantly in the enrichment of this religious focus. This became even more substantial in our study of the Virgin and Virgin Birth. All this information broadened and deepened the view of what the Father of Jesus may signify in our human sense for ultimate meaning. It also helped to liberate Jesus from the orthodox Christianity which had wrapped him up in their limited theologies.

Campbell, however, was not just an instructor who informed us about a multitude of mythological and religious information. In his presentation of *The Power of Myth* he very much demonstrated that he was himself empowered by the spirituality emanating from the mythological. Although he was a master in the scholarship about myths and world religions, he had incorporated and embodied this primordial wisdom. That is the uniqueness of the book as well as the video of this PBS TV program. It is a dialog and discussion. Campbell is not a lecturer, but speaks spontaneously and with great personal involvement and delight. He is not a theologian, philosopher, or anthropologist who shares his learned insights. He is Joseph Campbell, the person, who speaks with great conviction, authority, anger, and humor. The love of live received a voice, a face, and a person in him. The word, prophet, does definitely describe him accurately. This prophetic dimension will be the focus of this chapter. It will be approached by a variety of references which together will constitute the multifaceted dimension.

The Dualistic or Monistic View

Campbell's spirituality expresses a monistic worldview. It holds that there is only one kind of ultimate dynamic and that reality is one unitary organic whole. He is not as simplistic in these matters as so many "gurus" in holistic psychology. They make one feel guilty that life is experienced as painful and frustrating. One is admonished to do breathing exercises, watch funny movies, and meditate two or three times a day; then one will receive the right vibrations. The correct openness to significant body language will provide the right tranquility by which alpha waves will purify one's soul from the twisted complexes which create so much hurt. Then enlightenment becomes an esoteric exercise where particular instructions followed will produce the desired peace of mind. Those who fail to arrive at such a mental tranquility must be doing something wrong. This is the world of popular therapies. Campbell's wisdom transcends the market of those holistic workshops and journalistic publications. He is not speaking on behalf of how to feel better about yourself. The genuine commitment to arriving at a personalized response to the challenge of life is at the heart of his conviction. It is not the learning of a holistic philosophy, but the acquisition of a definite integrity which motivates him. The spirituality of this motivation deserves to be investigated so that is can speak on its own terms.

In the chapter on the Religious Imagination and the Heroic Intensity, the prophetic voice of Ernst Bloch was recorded. This was followed by a comparison between Bloch and Campbell. It will be insightful to continue the comparison between these two prophets, because their worldviews are distinctly different. It was mentioned that Bloch had a dualistic worldview. He perceived the physical world as insensitive, and as such it was to be subjected to the divine, which is over and above the physical. His commitment to an apocalyptic future experienced the physical as the "monstrous, headless stage prop" which opposes the creative power of the divine. We are to bring sparks of divine life within the physical reality to energize it on the road toward new creations. If not, then Bloch warns us about the lesson to be learned from the Cabbala, where "God shattered the deathly-clear rubble heap of worlds because man did not occur in them." (*Man on His Own*), p. 64)

The prophetic religiosity of Bloch is typical of the biblical spirituality in general and also of orthodox Christianity. It is the awareness of the supernatural, which is the divine over and above the physical reality. The history of the biblical God is that He came into human history to work mighty deeds of redemption. As such it is in this world but not of this world. The only monistic element in this teaching is the belief that in the beginning God created everything to be perfect—paradise. The split came because of original sin. Thus duality is experienced because of evil. Bloch goes one step further and declares the physical world itself to be insensitive and in need of divine sparks to become more divine.

This sets the stage for amplifying the depth of Campbell's wisdom. According to him, it is natural for the human to experience the duality between the spiritual and the physical because of our limitations. These limitations are the product of our fears, prejudices, and our defensiveness. It is the fear of flying, or the lack of courage. It is also a form of short-sightedness, but at the same time, he holds that the source of a true spirituality resides within the human potential. This dynamic is frustrated in many ways, not just because of sin. Campbell would not place any blame on the nature of the physical reality itself. On the contrary, in his admiration of the American Indian, he holds that nature itself is extremely sensitive and that the soul of life permeates all of existence, not just the human heart. Consequently, he reads the story of Eden or Paradise differently than the orthodox tradition.

And the cherubim at the gate – who are they? At the Buddhist shrines you'll see one has his mouth open, the other has his mouth closed – fear and desire, a pair of opposites. If you're approaching a garden like that, and those two figures there are real to you and threaten you, if you have fear for your life, you are still outside the garden. But if you are not longer attached to your ego existence, but see the ego existence as a function of a larger, eternal totality, and you favor the larger against the smaller, then you won't be afraid of those two figures, and you will go through.

We're kept out of the Garden by our own fear and desire in relation to what we think to be the goods of our life.

MOYERS: Have all men at all times felt some sense of exclusion from an ultimate reality, from bliss, from delight, from perfection, from God?

CAMPBELL: Yes, but then you have moments of ecstasy. The difference between everyday life and living in those moments of ecstasy is the difference between being outside and inside the Garden. You go past your fear and desire, past the pair of opposites.

MOYERS: Into harmony?

CAMPBELL: Into transcendence. This is an essential experience of any mystical realization. You die to your flesh and are born into your spirit. You identify yourself with the consciousness of life of which your body is but a vehicle. You die to the vehicle and become identified in your consciousness with that of which of the vehicle is the carrier. That is the God. (107)

Another reference to the Garden or Paradise elaborates this theme.

The Christ story involves a sublimation of what originally was a very solid vegetal image. Jesus on Holy Rood, the tree, and he is himself the fruit of the tree. Jesus is the fruit of eternal life, which was on the second forbidden tree in the Garden of Eden. When man ate of the fruit of the first three of the knowledge of good and evil, he was expelled from the Garden. The Garden is the place of unity, of nonduality of male and female, good and evil, God and human beings. You eat the duality, and you are on the way out. The tree of coming back to the Garden is the tree of immortal life, where you know that I and the father are one. (107)

This non-duality is at the core of Campbell's perception of the divine. Particular statements may indicate that this monistic energy is located exclusively within the human soul.

Heaven and hell are within us, and all the gods are within us. This is the great realization of the Upanishads of India in the ninth century B. C. All the gods, all the heavens, all the world are within us. They are magnified dreams, and dreams are manifestations in image form of the energies of the body in conflict with each other. That is what myth is. Myth is a manifestation in symbolic images, in metaphorical images, of the energies of the organs of the body in conflict with each other. This organ wants this, that organ wants that. The brain is one of the organs. (39)

But then one is reminded of Campbell's basic understanding of the monomyth regarding the hero:

A hero ventures forth from the world of common day into a region of supernatural wonder: fabulous forces are there encountered and a decisive victory is won: the hero comes back from this mysterious adventure with the power to bestow boons on his fellow man. (*The Hero with a Thousand Faces*, p. 30)

Campbell's mysticism remains devoted to the real world, although the spirituality for such a commitment resides within the soul. The importance of this statement is substantial. The existential question of religious life is about where to place one's dedication. Should our concern be about being prepared for entrance into heaven, or shall we become totally committed to this world and its future expectations?

It seems that Bloch and his apocalyptic future is dedicated to bringing about the divine within this physical reality, particularly within the social domain where social justice is sick and cries out for a decisive revolution. Campbell would understand this prophetic concern, and he would participate in such actions, but his spirituality would be less dualistic, less characterized by an either/or mentality. Life is placed in the context of an unfolding cosmic awareness. Such an enlightened awareness is to inspire our determination to become involved in the adventure of creative living. Then the heroic act is more significant than its accomplishments. The celebration of the creative awareness is at the heart of it all. The vision of the complexity of energies constitutes the core mentality of vital mythologies.

This is not just an abstract discussion about a dualistic versus a monistic worldview. This is a personal search for the Father of Jesus. The real question is about the Father's mentality. Raised as a Christian, I was taught that our world and the life we live is God's creation. From a scientific point of view, especially the new physics, this theology or God-talk does not make much sense anymore. Nevertheless it expresses a spirituality which is dear to me. It indicates that the reality we experience, and of which we are part, floats on or emerged from a creative energy which wants to be productive. Existence is an expression of some primordial dedication to bring forth and urge reality into being. Moreover, because we are creatures with self-reflection, we feel and sense a kind of invitation to affirm or reject the goodness of existence. There are those who declared reality to be absurd or meaningless. Nevertheless, that is not the only possible response. It is my basic experience that existence and life are inviting us to our personal affirmation. I find this invitation answered significantly by the person Jesus. His answer is remarkable in its strength, dedication, and sincerity (Jesus was deadly serious). I hold that this invitation can be interpreted as the voice of Jesus' Father. It speaks on behalf of creation and the need for its improvement on the social level to bring about more justice, fairness, love, and kindness.

A dualistic view places the Father of Jesus over and above this reality. A monistic vision experiences the divine within existence itself. A dualistic view makes our dedication to this world a task or job to be fulfilled to receive heavenly credits. A monistic attitude senses that a commitment to existence is from the heart and a heart's desire. The fulfillment is not in any possible rewards but in the very energy of the action itself. Thus sacrifice and bliss become one.

MOYERS: In classic Christian doctrine the material world is to be despised, and life is to be redeemed in the hereafter, in heaven, where our rewards come. But you say that if you affirm that which you deplore, you are affirming the very world which is our eternity at the moment.

CAMPBELL: Yes, that is what I'm saying. Eternity isn't some later time. Eternity isn't even a long time. Eternity has nothing to do with time. Eternity is that dimension of here and now that all thinking in temporal terms cuts off. And if you don't get it here, you won't get it anywhere. The problem with heaven is that you will be having such a good time there, you won't even think of eternity. You'll just have this unending delight in the beatific vision of God. But the experience of eternity right here and now, in all things, whether thought of as good or as evil, is the function of life.

MOYERS: That is it.

CAMPBELL: This is it. (67)

For Campbell, the soul is the meeting-point between the internal and the external. So reality is viewed by an internal awareness of the eternal. The here and the now is an emanation of the eternal. We view reality with the eyes of eternity. Consequently, the dedication to the here and the now is inspired by the mystical. This mystical inspiration is described by the metaphorical statement, "I and the Father are one."

The title of this chapter carries the word, multifaceted. A good image of such a concept is a gem or diamond, which has been cut and polished so there are multiple surfaces. Each surface represents one side of the precious stone. The stone is presented by the various sides and aspects of its brilliance. The presence of the divine in terms of an invitation to affirm life, which is the voice of the Father, can be experienced in many ways. Some will be explored next.

Signals of Transcendence

In his discussion of the Virgin Birth, Campbell referred to the chakras, and the fourth center, the level of the heart.

> And at the heart center, there is *again* the lingam and yoni, that is to say, male and female organs in conjunction, but there they are represented in gold as symbolic of the virgin birth, that is to say, it is the birth of spiritual man out of the animal man.
>
> MOYERS: And it happens –
>
> CAMPBELL: It happens when you awaken at the level of the heart to compassion, compassion, shared suffering: experienced participation in the suffering of another person. That's the beginning of humanity. And the meditations of religion properly are on that level, the heart level. (175)

Here the spiritual realm is signified, and compassion can be regarded as a signal of transcendent. In his book, *A Rumor of Angels* Peter makes experiences of such signals of transcendence central for the rediscovery of religiousness in modern society. They are characterized by two words: ecstasy and redemption. Ecstasy means "a standing outside of the taken-for-granted routine of everyday life."(28) It is an amazement for the openness of existence, and it is psychologically and mentally inspiring and life-saving. The aspect of redemption is already with the meaning of ecstasy. It is

Berger's contention that all religions are offering their solutions (redemptive aspect) to suffering, evil, and death. (90)

These two dynamics can be found in the specific signals of transcendence featured by Berger:

> By signals of transcendence I mean phenomena that are to be found within the domain of our "natural" reality but that appear to point beyond that reality. (53)

The first signal mentioned is the awareness of order, which makes humans assume that there is a divine order underlying all of existence and permeating it thoroughly. This was discussed in our text and the chapter on the implicate order, as theorized by David Bohm; but Berger approaches this phenomenon in an existential and down-to-earth setting:

> A child wakes up in the night, perhaps from a bad dream, and finds himself surrounded by darkness, alone, beset by nameless threats. At such a moment the contours of trusted reality are blurred or invisible, and in terror of incipient chaos, the child cries out for his mother. It is hardly an exaggeration to say that, at this moment, the mother is being invoked as a high priestess of protective order. It is she (and, in many cases, she alone) who has the power to banish the chaos and to restore the benign shape of the world. And, of course, any good mother will do just that. She will take the child and cradle him in the timeless gesture of the Magna Mater [Great Mother] who became our Madonna. She will turn on the lamp, perhaps, which will encircle the scene with a warm glow of reassuring light. She will speak or sing to the child and the content of this communication will invariably be the same – "Don't be afraid – everything is all right." (54-55)

And then Berger proves the significance of this phenomenal celebration of order. He asks the question: "Is the mother lying to the child?" If one wants to dramatize the reach of this question, one could add, "Doesn't the mother know that life is absurd, that being born into this world is an entrance into a totally unknown, that finally death will kill us all?" The justification of the other to say, "Don't be afraid," comes from her authority as a mother. This woman experienced the cycles of her bodily existence which are related to the moon and the basic flow of life. She represents the feminine as bride and mother. As bride her psyche delighted in the trust she had found in the living embrace of life. As mother, she made herself available in a fundamental way. Within her own being the child developed, began to kick, grew into a birthing creature, and finally, her arms and her nursing body welcomed the child into this world. In the way her womb provided security and growth, the mother protects her child with genuine care. It is the mother's awareness of order which is mentioned by Berger as a signal of transcendence. He does not refer to philosophical or scientific theories.

Another phenomenon which points at a domain beyond our "natural" reality is "play." Berger refers to the insights of Johan Huizinga.

> One aspect of play that Huizinga analyzes in some detail is the fact that play sets up a separate universe of discourse, with its own rules, which suspends, "for the duration," the rules and general assumptions of the "serious" world. One of the most important assumptions, thus suspended is the time structure of ordinary social life...Joy is play's intention. When this intention is actually realized, in joyful play, the time structure of the playful universe takes on a very specific quality – namely, it *becomes* eternity. (58)

A similar awareness of the transcendent can be experienced in humor. Berger holds that one of the main points in humor is the realization that our spirit was imprisoned in a certain way. Humor produces laughter the moment we look at ourselves from such an angle that we realize how little our worries or dramas are in respect to wider dimensions. We are so caught up in ourselves that it may appear laughable if one reflects for a moment on its limited concern. Of course, it becomes comical if we come to this realization in a rather sudden fashion. That is why one is to serve the punch line at the right time. Timing is what counts in bringing about laughter, but it will work only if it expresses "the imprisonment of the human spirit: in the light of greater dimensions. (70) In this context Berger refers to Ernst Bloch and his spiritual awareness of hope. This has been described sufficiently in our journey.

The final signal of transcendence mentioned by Berger is justice and the reality of "damnation." It is about the agonizing question of capital punishment. Among those who favor capital punishment, some argue that justice is needed. It is not a question of revenge or a deterrent to major crimes. Certain forms of crime are so evil, e.g., the murder of innocent children, that a cry for "justice" demands the death penalty. One may call it "the Lord's anger," insofar as, in the Bible, God is portrayed as the one who is tolerant of evil only so long, and then He comes from above and lashes out against those evil doers. The sentiment is that toleration has its limits and in certain cases drastic action is necessary. This sense of justice resides in the common sense of people and it transcends arguments for or against capital punishment. Thus the Father of Jesus can be interpreted as the Spirit of compassion, the basic trust in some greater order, the source of laughter, the delight of play and the cry for justice, rooted in hope.

The Celebration of Divine Creativity

Very much similar to the signals of transcendence is the celebration of creativity, which is regarded to be divine if it is of a primordial dimension. Just winning a ball game or driving a car may be creative, but the implied perspectives are not very indicative of a fundamental dynamic. In this section three or four aspects of creativity will be discussed in terms of divine dimension: common sense, the pursuit of happiness, and productivity will be evaluated in terms of human freedom.

Freedom: The concept freedom is often confused with the notion of liberty. Liberty is a state wherein one is allowed to move around rather freely. Fewer boundaries equal more liberty. However, there are many people who have been given substantial liberty and still do not enjoy freedom. To be free is a state of mind. Some people sacrifice their liberty in the name of freedom. They would rather be arrested and imprisoned than sell their souls, or whatever is truly meaningful to them. Consequently, freedom is a virtue. It means that one has acquired the ability to function respectably in terms of human potentials. People are born with the potential to reason. When children grow and develop they are encouraged to become thoughtful, and also prudent. This learning process is interested in letting the child become aware of its ability to reason. It is hoped that the child will face the challenge of its growing pains, which may become dramatic during the adolescent years. Thus the adult emerges by learning to be truly thoughtful and considerate. The difference between childish and adult behavior is that the former can be selfish and not concerned about others. Adults are expected to be less selfish insofar as they may have experienced the joy of thoughtful relations with others. Such an openness to the greater good for others is the virtue of freedom. It has to be nurtured and practiced before it truly can become a person's basic attitude.

The debates about human freedom in psychology (behaviorism) and philosophy (determinism) are not much about the concept, freedom, as an openness to the greater good, but are about the question of whether humans are actually free. This, of course, depends on the persons themselves. In the first part of this book, reference was made to Kohlberg and his six stages of moral development. No doubt, the person operating on level six can be regarded as acting out of an ultimate concern. This expresses human freedom as described here. Kohlberg's description of level six indicates the divine nature of such a moral maturity. When a person has integrated the virtue of freedom significantly, then she or he can say, "I and the Father are one." The energy of the spirit has permeated this creature substantially.

Common Sense: Thomas Jefferson believed in people. He advised his nephew, Peter Carr, to use reason as the judge in matters of facts and opinions. He advised him to question God's existence, because such a God would appreciate the scrutiny of reason. Religion too was to be critically examined, and the Bible should be read as any other great book. The laws of nature were considered important criteria in the deliberation of certain falsehoods in the Bible. "Your own reason is the only oracle given you by heaven and you are answerable not to the rightness, but uprightness of the decision."

To learn of the sources within which Jefferson's optimism about people is rooted, is to understand the scope, as well as the intentionality of his moral premises. A thorough study of these matters has been conducted by Garry Wills in his book, *Inventing America: Jefferson's Declaration of Independence*, especially Part Three: "A Moral Paper" and Chapters 12 ("...self-evident...") and 13 ("...endowed by their Creator...") Wills researched Jefferson's use of the term, self-evident. Some scholars supposed that it was a concept from John Locke, the empiricist, who held that knowledge is only reliable if it comes through the senses of our mind. The mind itself is a clean slate (*tabula rasa*). It knows only insofar as it observes by sight, sound, and touch. This approach reduces human knowledge to a process similar to mechanisms such as cameras and tape recorders, which take pictures and store sound waves.

Chapter 12 explains what Locke meant by self-evident. It is an aspect which is so obvious that in saying it, nothing is added to knowledge. For example, "the same is the same" and "the same is not different." Locke called such statements self-evident and regarded them as superfluous. Wills makes it clear that Jefferson's use of self-evident (which is very important in his Declaration of Independence) comes from a different source. He mentions Thomas Reid and his book, *Inquiry Into the Human Mind*. Reid was the philosopher of common sense in the days of Jefferson. His book was among Jefferson's favorite readings. Jefferson and Reid were both substantially influenced by a school of ethics called "Moral Sense," which flourished at the University of Glasgow, Scotland. It was promoted by Francis Hutcheson who was appointed to the chair of Moral Philosophy in 1729. He held this position until 1746. Jefferson himself was a Scottish decent, and he kept in touch with immigrants from Scotland who informed him of the important things happening at the University of Glasgow.

Wills suggests that Reid's understanding of common sense is similar to the principle of the "Moral Sense School" which excited many minds in Western Europe. In sum, it holds that in the way people have a basic and innate sense of beauty, so they have a basic and innate sense of the moral. The sense of beauty can be nurtured into greater sophistication; so too can the moral sense learn to appreciate deeper dimensions of moral wisdom. The principle of the moral sense is present in each person.

The presence of moral sense needs no explanations of certain basic values because these are self-evident. This is Jefferson's position when he wrote, "We hold these truths to be self-evident: that all men are created equal; that they are endowed by their Creator with inherent and inalienable rights; that among these are life, liberty and the pursuit of happiness:..." The appreciation of common sense becomes more substantial when Wills summarizes Reid's major thoughts.

First is Reid's egalitarian epistemology. Epistemology is the study of the nature of human knowledge. Egalitarian refers to an equality in status. In regard to oral wisdom, Reid held that there is no real difference between the common person and the philosopher. The philosopher may have acquired more technical knowledge about moral matters, but the wisdom aspect is practically the same for people in general. Second is Reid's humble empiricism. Empiricism emphasizes that all people have eyes and ears, and they observe basically the same things in the world around us in the same manner. Thus they have a common perception of what can be understood about the fact of life.

Third is Reid's communitarian morality. Because everyone looks at life from an individual vantage point, there is a need for comparing notes with other people. This community aspect (comparing notes) multiplies the dimension of common sense by the number of people who participate in the deliberations. The ancient Roman ruling, *Vox Populi Vox Dei* (the voice of the people is the voice of God) became relevant.

It is simply amazing that we have common sense to such a degree that the Constitution of the United States is based on it. As such, the Founding Fathers truly believed that they had created a new order (*Novus Ordo Seclorum*) as is printed on every one dollar bill.

Joseph Campbell goes into some detail discussing the symbolisms found on the one dollar bill.

MOYERS: There is something about that one the Great Seal of the United States.

CAMPBELL: That's what the Great Seal is all about. I carry a copy of the Great Seal in my pocket in the form of a dollar bill. Here is the statement of the ideals that brought about the transformation of the United States. Look at this dollar bill. Now here is the Great Seal of the United States. Look at the pyramid on the left. A pyramid has four sides. These are the four points of the compass. There is somebody at this point, there's somebody at that point, and there's somebody at this point. When you're down on the lower levels of this pyramid, you will be either on one side or on the other. But when you get to the top, the points all come together, and there the eye of God opens.

MOYERS: And to them it was the God of reason.

CAMPBELL: Yes. This is the first nation of the world that was ever established on the basis of reason instead of simply warfare. These were eighteenth-century deists, these gentlemen. Over here we read, "In God We Trust." But that is not the god of the Bible. These men did not believe in a Fall.

They did not think the mind of man was cut off from God. The mind of man, cleansed of secondary and merely temporal concerns, beholds with the radiance of a cleansed mirror of reflection of the rational mind of God. Reason puts you in touch with God. Consequently, for these men, there is no special revelation anywhere, and none is needed, because the mind of man cleared of its fallibilities is sufficiently capable of the knowledge of God. All people in the world are thus capable because people in the world are capable of reason. (25)

Regarding the experience of the Founding Fathers that they had created something truly new is the following:

MOYERS: That would explain the other inscription down there, "*Novus Ordo Seclorum.*"

CAMPBELL: "A new order of the world." This is a new order of the world. And the saying above, "*Annuit Coeptis*," means "He has smiled on our accomplishments" or "our activities."

MOYERS: He –

CAMPBELL: He, the eye, what is represented by the eye. Reason. In Latin you wouldn't have to say "he," it could be "it" or "she" or "he." But the divine power has smiled on our doings. And so this new world has been built in the sense of God's original creation, and the reflection on God's original creation through reason, has brought this about. (26)

Campbell explains the transcendental realm as signified by the thirteen stars arranged in the form of a Star of David. He observes that they form two triangles, and he sees in them a Pythagorean tetrakys, a primary symbol of Pythagorean philosophy. The star in the center represents the cosmic creativity.

MOYERS: The center of energy, then?

CAMPBELL: Yes. The initial sound (a Christian might say, the creative Word), out of which the whole world was precipitated, the big bang, the pouring of the transcendent energy into and expanding through the field of time. (27-28)

At Campbell's suggestion, one may say that metaphorically, the Father and Jesus are one in that very center. It is very refreshing to hear Campbell affirm the realization of the divine energy in the birth of the United States as depicted on the dollar bill. Enjoying his delight in such divine matters is a form of participation in this transcendental dimension which entered history by means of the Founding Fathers. Disagreeing with such an affirmation of the divine may be the result of higher expectations about the divine realm. This disagreement, too, is a form of relating to the divine.

The perception of the United States as a creation of divine energy can easily result in a form of self-righteousness. This danger was signaled by Abraham Lincoln. We find this discussed in William J. Wolf's book, *The Almost Chosen People*. Lincoln was convinced that the blessings of God had united this country. But he was not self-righteous in making his cause identical with the will of God, but his cause and the American cause were only in accordance with God's will if they were truly right.

> "I know that the Lord is always on the side of the right. But it is my constant anxiety and prayer that I and this nation should be on the Lord's side." (128)

Particularly, Lincoln arrived at the wisdom that one should not equate an institution (the United States) with God's will. But he very much saw God at work in the history of the United States. He believed, as Campbell explained, that God is at the center of the divine order, and as such this divine energy informs people and urges them to act in this spirituality. Thus it is understandable that Lincoln could easily allow himself the idea that the American people in their struggle for freedom and justice are the instruments in the hands of the Almighty and are his almost chosen people.

This is expressed in his address to the New Jersey Senate at Trenton on February 21, 1861.

> I recollect thinking then, boy even though I was, that there must have been something more than common that those men struggled for [Revolutionary War]. I am exceedingly anxious that the thing they struggled for; that something even more than National Independence; that something that held out a great promise to all people of the world for all time to come; I am exceedingly anxious that this Union, the Constitution, and all the liberties of the people shall be perpetuated in accordance with the original idea for which that struggle was made, and I shall be most happy indeed if I shall be a humble instrument in the hands of the Almighty, and of this, his almost chosen people, for perpetuating the object of that great struggle. (13)

Productivity: The celebration of divine creativity can be found in many ways. The biblical people interpreted their history in terms of their liberation from slavery by their God. The Founding Fathers and later,

Lincoln, evaluated the history of the United States in reference to a divine energy at work in the quest for freedom and justice for all. Peter Berger discovered this divine dimension in capitalism as the phenomenon of free enterprise. This he describes in his recent book, *The Capitalist Revolution: Fifty Propositions about Prosperity, Equity, & Liberty.*

There is no modesty in the book's title. A "revolution" is claimed. However, in his presentation throughout the book, Berger is extremely low-key. He does not want to look like a political activist. As Professor and Director of the Institute of Economic Culture at Boston University he is in the discipline of Sociology. His observations are to be understood as "scientific" statements. He wants to refrain from any polemics. Moreover, there is a disclaimer at the beginning. Although the book as a whole could be used by capitalists to defend their economic system and so prove that socialists and communists are wrong, this is not Berger's intention. He somewhat reluctantly came to the conclusion that capitalism appears impressive in the light of sociological studies.

> I did not start out with a procapitalist bias. When I began to occupy myself with these questions more than fifteen year ago, I was very open to the possibility that socialism may be a more humane form of economic and social organization. It was the sheer pressure of empirical evidence, registered in my mind over years of work, that compelled me to arrive at the position I now hold. Perhaps it is one of the ironies of my professional career that, very largely because of my perception of capitalism, I moved to the "right" while a sizable segment of my colleagues in the social sciences moved to the Left." (10)

To make sure that his appreciation of capitalism is of an empirical nature, the following is clear on that.

> I hold no philosophical (or, for that matter, theological) position that would lead me either to embrace or to reject capitalism. Thus this book also does not intend to constitute a moral argument in favor of capitalism. As will become clear, I do indeed think that such an argument can be made, and in the final chapter I spell out the values on the basis of which one may so argue. (9)

Indeed, in the last pages of the book Berger discusses the significance of capitalism in the content of seven commonly held values:

1.   The material well-being of people, especially the poor.
2.   Equality.

3.   Political liberties and democracy.

4.   Protection of human rights.

5.   Individual autonomy.

6.   Preservation of tradition.

7.   Community.

No doubt, regarding value number 1, capitalism "is the indicated choice" for the material well-being of people, especially the poor. Regarding the second, "equality," Berger writes, "Capitalism, then does not come out very well in the perspective of this value. But neither does socialism, or any presently existent of plausible imagined form of societal organization." (219) But "political liberties and democracy," the third value, are decisively served by capitalism. "The value here is what in ordinary parlance is meant by 'freedom.' If the proposition of the mergent theory holds up, this value clearly dictates a choice in favor of capitalism." (219) The same holds for "protection of human right." Once again, this value prompts a choice in favor of capitalism." (220) This is also the case for the fifth value of "individual autonomy." For the sixth value "preservation of tradition," both capitalism and socialism are not doing very well. The reason is that both promote a kind of modernity which supersedes the traditional. However, Berger adds:

> A good argument can be made, though, that traditional institutions and life-styles fare better under democratic regimes, for reasons that are not difficult to spell out. This value, then, will also tend (at least mildly) toward the capitalist choice, because of the aforementioned linkage between capitalism and democracy. (221)

The final value, community, favors socialism, if understood according to Berger.

> There are, however, new forms of community in the world, both existent and aspired-to communities created deliberately and de novo communities that are *not* grounded in traditional ways of life...For those, however, who aspire toward some new, all-embracing community, transcending anything to be found in the world today, socialism will probably continue to be the preferred choice. (221)

This wisdom is stated at the end of more than two hundred pages which try to assess developments in the economies of many parts of the world. For those who doubt the sincerity by which Berger places himself within the empirical context rather than in a polemic defense of capitalism, the following is pertinent to the book. This is an argument in Chapter Nine, "Capitalism and the Dynamics of Myths." Simply put, the author holds that socialism is based on belief or myths by which humans aspire to ideals about humanity. Capitalism does not operate on such assumptions.

> Capitalism, as an institutional arrangement, has been singularly devoid of plausible myths; by contrast, socialism, its major alternative under modern conditions, has been singularly blessed with myth-generating potency. (195)

For example, the language and images of Marxism are biblical in nature. This has been observed by Nicholas Berdyaev and Ernst Bloch. Especially the theme of eschatology is at play.

> That is, Marxism can also be understood as a peculiar secularized version of the classical biblical view of history of a fall from grace, a set of redemptive events embodied in a human community, and as a leading up to a great climax that will bring ordinary history to an end. Marxism has substituted private property and its "alienations" for original sin, the revolutionary process for the *kairoi* of God's redemptive activity, the proletariat (and later, with Lenin, the party as the "vanguard of the Proletariat") for the church, and the attainment of true communism for the advent of the Kingdom of God. (197)

In this context the true nature of Berger's capitalism can be characterized. In sum, Berger holds that capitalism is simply factual in the human experience. It is not based on, or promoted by, an ideology. It simply is pursued because it works so well and so convincingly that it does not need any prophets.

In the segment "Signals of Transcendence," this chapter introduced the religious imagination of Peter Berger. This religiousness, I feel, is also to be found at the very end of Chapter Nine. He discusses proposition 50:

> Capitalism has a built-in incapacity to generate legitimations of itself, and is particularly deprived of mythic potency; consequently, it depends upon legitimating effect of its sheer facticity or upon association with other, non-economic legitimating symbols. (208)

Berger then goes on to say that praising capitalism because of its fortunes is rather cheap. It would mean a form of opportunism, which is not aware of the basic dignity of human life and its natural needs. But to appreciate capitalism because it provides the opportunity for human dignity in its basic needs is another story. Let us look at the last sentence of Chapter Nine:

> The benefits of capitalism *are* attainable. In the successful capitalist societies of the West and Eastern Asia they abound on all sides, part and parcel ordinary, everyday experience. The ordinary breeds contempt and the attainable, once attained, looks cheap. A special kind of perception is required to link these prosaic facticities with the values of aspiration for which people are prepared to sacrifice. Such perception is not easy to come by and it lacks popular appeal. (209)

In my understanding Berger is saying that it takes a special kind of people to appreciate the basic blessings of capitalism. It may be ordinary, or even vulgar, but the blessings are so fundamental that it escapes the religious imagination of too many. That is why I wanted to include this understanding of capitalism as a "celebration of divine energy." It is easy to speak about the divine on the top of a high mountain, or looking at a splendid sunset or a starry-bright night. But it takes special imagination to see "eternity in a grain of sand" according to William Blake. It seems that the new developments in Russia and Red China indicate that their imagination about free enterprise is taking hold. However, if it is simply for the sake of opportunism and not for the celebration of [the seven commonly held] human values, then it lacks the true insight of wisdom. Nevertheless, capitalism does not work as an ideology, is not dependent on human theories about it. It works because on its own it is an expression of the divine within human existence. It is our oneness with the Father by which the creativity can be celebrated in free enterprise. It is not a religion, not esoteric theology, not poetic imagination. It is simply primordially divine.

If it is difficult to identify with the divine presence within free enterprise, perhaps one is helped more by Robert J. Lifton's book *The Life of the Self: Toward a New Psychology.* Previous to the book, Lifton authored the article, "The Struggle for Cultural Rebirth" for *Harper's Magazine.* He came to realize that previous theologies, traditional religions, and ideologies in general fail to provide the modern human with myths needed for a proper motivation to approach life creatively. He proposed the "Protean" psychological life-style. It is the mentality of a survivor that somehow makes things work in spite of tremendous threats to life in general. "Somehow" means that the Protean person is capable of picking and choosing in an eclectic manner bits and pieces which become integrated in one's view of existence. The awareness of annihilation and death is so pervasive that the challenge in our day is to face this squarely. At the end of his article he refers explicitly to Joseph Campbell:

> Ultimately, genuine transformation requires that we "experience" our annihilation in order to prevent it, that we confront and conceptualize both our immediate crises and our long-range possibilities for renewal. Joseph Campbell reminds us: "...the idea of death and rebirth...is an extremely ancient one in the history of culture," frequently, in the form of "shock treatment for no longer wanted personality structure." In our Protean environment the principle still holds: *every significant step in human existence involves some inner sense of death.* (90)

This inner sense of death is at the heart of Campbell's new psychology as reported in *The Life of the Self*. In Chapter Three, he describes the concepts of a formative depth-psychological paradigm. The formative theory emphasizes the need of initial imagery and the agility to abandon outlived models and symbols for the sake of engaging new images. The state of mind which determines the present lifestyle is at the same time a boundary as well as a bridge. The boundary aspect allows for some sense of secured life energy, while the bridge aspect indicates that this experience of security can be recreated in a new symbol system.

The controlling image of psychic life according to Lifton is that death and survival are dialectic aspects of existence. Each will evoke the dramatic reality of the other. Wherever we sense death in terms of separation, disintegration, and stasis, we will experience the urgent psychological need for forms of connection, integrity, and movement. The formative processes are recognized as ordering dynamics in the crisis of the human. Formative processes in the human psyche find a focus in the concepts of grounding and centering. The former is understood as the ordering of experience by the self along the various dimensions that must be dealt with at any given moment – temporal, spatial, and emotional.

The temporal plane represents the view that older images can prepare us for future changes. The spatial plane recognizes the difference between the immediate and the distant (ultimate) meanings of life. Centering should not confuse the two. The emotional plane differentiates between our most impassioned images and those which are at the periphery of our interest. Decentering is necessary for creative renovation to emerge. Psychological health depends on a balance between centering and decentering.

The concept of grounding denotes the relationship of the self with the biological, individual, and cultural roots of history. The individual's centering needs this wider sense of rootage to allow for decentering without the feeling of being totally naked and stripped of any form of identity. Grounding makes decentering less traumatic and provides continuity.

Toward the end of Chapter Three, Lifton mentions some difficulties in the formative process of the psyche. Either there is a blocking of the image-forming process or there is an absence of required images or forms. This may result in a loss of grounding. Thus the person will lack the necessary environment within which centering and decentering take place. Forms of fanaticism and lack of common sense will devastate the balance between centering and decentering. The person will not have connections which promote a life-celebrating symbolization.

Lifton suggests some of his personal identity in these matters when he describes the transformation of immortality symbol. The traditional symbolization offered the following options:

a) Corporate immortality, where one lives on in the lives of children.

b) Theological immortality, where one believes in the continuity of life [soul] on higher planes.

c) Romantic immortality, which can be found in achievements produced during one's lifetime (books, monuments, etc.)

d) Natural immortality, which is the awareness that nature itself survives all of us and this signifies substantial continuity.

e) Transcendental immortality, which is a mode of psychic enlightenment where space and time fade away and a sense of eternity enters our consciousness.

Joseph Campbell's sense of immortality would be described by the last option. Lifton, however, demonstrates here his true Jewish identity. It is characterized by an immense commitment to creativity and productivity. Consequently, immortality for Lifton is not symbolized by the perpetuation of his name. For Lifton, it is existentially gratifying to realize that his personal contributions to civilization and culture became significant. In this way, the enterprise of culture would continue beyond his own life. This symbol of cultural immortality indicates Lifton's identity with the divine in true human productivity. The life of human culture became for Lifton an aspect of the divine, which supersedes his own death. He feels at one with the divine in this respect. It is there where the inner and the outer world meet for Lifton. The presence of the Father is at the meeting point of cultural productivity. Lifton's book closes with a dramatic quote from Joseph Campbell's *The Hero with a Thousand Faces*:

> A god outgrown becomes immediately a life-destroying demon. The form has to be broken and the energies released. (171)

Forgiveness: Especially in the reference to virgin and the Virgin Birth, Campbell emphasized compassion as the seat of the divine. His story about the rescue efforts by the Hawaiian police officer illustrated his personal and existential awareness of the level where all people experience the energy of a fundamental oneness. Other examples can be found, especially in stories told by Samuel Oliner in his book, *The Altruistic Personality: Rescuers of Jews in Nazi Europe*. Such rescuers were prepared to risk their lives to save others. Some were moved by the suffering of those whose lives were in danger. That is the compassion as described by Campbell.

It is seemingly somewhat natural to act in the spirit of this fundamental sense of compassion, which is the spirit of at-one-ment. One may act spontaneously in moments of urgency. However, the spirit of compassion expresses itself also in the spirit of forgiveness and mercy. It is the acceptance of the human condition in the face of shortcomings, failings, and crime. The celebration of divine creativity finds a focus in the psychological theory of Carl Ransom Rogers. He is widely known for his non-directive approach in therapy. The claims are quite simple and well-defined. Briefly put:

a)   The client should be regarded as someone who is responsible for his or her own behavior.

b)   The therapist cannot cure people. People can become participants in a curing process.

c)   The client shall be affirmed with an unconditional positive regard. That is, whatever the client states, wants, or desires, is the client's problem.

d)   The method is primarily focused on mirroring back to the client what is communicated to the therapist. One is not to interpret meanings and underlying dynamics. One truly listens to the client and tries to understand and verbalize to the client his or her basic communications.

e)   Of true interest to the therapist are the client's personal and emotional fears, joys, anxieties, expectations, frustrations, anger, and longing. The pains and hurts as well as the emotions in coping with life in terms of victory and defeat are all allowed to enter the realm of the positive regard.

It shall be noted the Rogers' attitude is based on the resolve to respond creatively to the challenges of frustrations and victimization. His unconditional regard expresses a religious dimension. It implies a basic trust in people, but not just that. The fact that Rogers requires the attitude of an unconditional positive regard as the environment most conducive to growth throws new light on the fundamental biblical message of God's limitless mercy as found in Psalm 103:

Bless the Lord, O my soul;
and all my being bless his holy name.
Bless the Lord, O my soul,
and forget not all his benefits.
He pardons all your iniquities,
he heals all your ills.
He redeems your life from destruction.
he crowns you with kindness and compassion.
Merciful and gracious is the Lord,
slow to anger and abounding in kindness.
Not according to our sins does he deal with us,
nor does he requite us according to our crimes.
As far as the east is from the west,
so far has he put our transgressions from us.

As a father has compassion on his children,
so the Lord has compassion on those who fear him

(1-2, 3-4, 8, 10, 12-13)

The Christian awareness of God's mercy can be understood according to two fundamental facts. One, people are sinful in many ways. Two, this sinfulness will not pull us down or destroy us, when we accept divine mercy. The acceptance of divine mercy is the basic affirmation of one's own self-appreciation.

Upon further reflection on this message one learns that we are unacceptable (because we are sinners), and still divine mercy declares us to be acceptable. This is because of divine love. Thus we may say, "God loves us no matter what," or "Divine mercy is greater than my sinfulness." Divine love is unconditional. The problem is that we have great difficulty accepting this graceful message. It is hard to believe that one can receive so much without meriting it. But that is the message of mercy in its divine nature – it is beyond justice and fairness, it is unconditional.

The unconditional positive regard of Rogers receives a religious dimension when placed in conjunction with divine mercy. This religiousness is of a revelatory character. That means it cannot be expected to be true unless one is empowered to accept it as being true. The presentation of Jesus' life and his oneness with his Father expresses a distinct proclamation of the unconditional divine mercy. This is expressed in Luke's gospel:

When they reached the place called The Skull, they crucified him there and two criminals also, one on the right, the other on the left. Jesus said, "Father, forgive them; they do not know what they are doing." (23:33-34)

Without such biblical connections, Roger's positive regard would remain simply one of the many attitudes one can take in approaching emotionally disturbed clients. The opposite is also true: in Rogers' method, the biblical message of God's limitless mercy receives a vehicle by which the dimension of divine love can be applied in practical forms of therapy, which are true moments of redemption.

On this note, the search for the Father of Jesus has found a significant crossing point. With Campbell we learned to become interpretive of the religious language with references to the mythical dimensions. The metaphorical dimension became activated and our religious imagination experienced the wider realms of particular concepts and words like the Father of Jesus, Virgin, and Virgin Birth. As such, we arrived at perceptions beyond the box of orthodox theologies. In this way we are invited to return to traditional texts to appreciate the particular message as can be found in Jesus' prayer on the cross asking his Father to forgive his persecutors. In this prayer we hear what the oneness with the Father does to a person like Jesus, and we learn about the essence of his goodness, the forgiveness of one's enemies.

MOYERS: What do you think about the Savior Jesus?

CAMPBELL: We just don't know very much about Jesus. All we know are four contradictory texts that purport to tell us what he said and did.

MOYERS: Written many years after he lived.

CAMPBELL: Yes, but in spite of this, I think we may know approximately what Jesus said. I think the sayings of Jesus are probably pretty close to the originals. The main teaching of Christ, for example, is, Love your enemies. (211)

Speaking about Jesus' oneness with the Father, Campbell offers one of his many stories to share his personal identification with this insight.

One of the great heresies of the West is the heresy that Christ pronounced when he said, "I and the Father are one." He was crucified for saying that. In the Middle Ages, nine hundred years after Christ, a great Sufi mystic said, "I and my beloved are one," and he, too, was crucified. As he was going to the cross, he prayed, "O my Lord, if you had taught these people what you have taught me, they would not be doing this to me. And if you had not taught me, this would not be happening to me. Blessed is the Lord and all his works." (117)

Chapter Twelve

A Meditation

"The Word" – The Son of "The Father"

"Son of the Father" is a metaphor. It is important to become aware of what this figure of speech represents. It is one thing to declare that something is a metaphor. Another thing is to sense the substance underlying a particular figure of speech. Symbolic language is never precise, although one is generally well aware of what the symbolic communicates.

"Son of the Father" has a rich and multi-cultural tradition, which is obvious in most of the preceding chapters. The Father's Son has also a definite meaning in the concept "Word" or "*logos*." The gospel of John opens with, "In the beginning was the Word: the Word was with God and the Word was God. He was with God in the beginning. Through him all things came to be, not one thing had its being but through him" (1:1-3). Scholars agree that this first part of John's gospel is a pre-existing hymn. Obviously, it sings about the primordial significance of the Word. Sophia – wisdom is described in a similar way in Proverbs, chapter 8.

There wisdom is perceived in its primordial existence. Logos and wisdom point at the same elementary aspect of existence. The human search for meaning itself is based on a fundamental awareness of an all-pervasive order. This deeply rooted sense of order also implies that there is some ordering principle or energy. As such one hears people say, "Nothing comes from nothing," or "Someone must have started it all," or "Everything has a beginning."

These statements agree that life, existence, and the universe are together something. It is not nothing. It is! And insofar as it is, it can be perceived – somehow it hangs together and its constitutes on all-encompassing order.

This is the stuff of the human mind, which is in need of understanding what is going on. Every normal human walks around, talks, and functions because she or he believes in something. The human mind needs the answer to the question, "What is the story?" ("What is going on?")

Psychotherapy exists mainly because it helps a person to get her or his story together. Without a story you are nobody, and with a story you are "somebody." The same is true for a culture, which gathers people into a particular tradition of stories. "Without stories there is no culture, and with stories you have the making of a culture." Dogs, cats, birds, amoebas, flowers, grass seed, and billions of life forms operate overwhelmingly well without stories. But somehow, life itself has a built-in story – DNA. By DNA life procreates, maintains and enhances survival. The fact that it is that way does not necessarily mean that it was planned or created that way.

We are part of life and are permeated by a basic sense of order. This is how we operate and function. We always will respond to the basic requirements of the brain to let some form of order become understood.

Language is an expression of such a fundamental requirement. We don't speak non-sense. We try to place words in such an order that we make sense to ourselves while we speak. To become aware of this basic reality of language is to become aware of the primordial importance of the word. The word (i.e. a meaningful word) establishes our stories about ourselves, our relatives, our world, our lives and existence as a whole.

Modern discussions about language hold that the practical human mind will develop this function because it is profoundly needed for making an individual grow. Richard M. Restak in his book, *The Mind* – the official companion for the PBS series aired in 1988 – offers one chapter which deals with the aspects of language. At the end it reads:

The research of Bellugi, Poizner, and Neville provides a "window" on a basic process of mind: the human capacity for language is so profound that even in the absence of hearing from birth, a completely separate and autonomous language system develops...

Perhaps our minds *are* in part molded by language; perhaps language merely *reflects* the workings of the brain and mind. There are too many loose ends, too many intriguing observations, for us to be able to know. We are perhaps best satisfied by what psycholinguist Michael Studdert-Kennedy says: "The development of mind, thought, and language is simply a nexus in which it is impossible to separate one from the others." (230-231)

Such mindful statements are based on anthropological and neurological findings. These two are just a few of a multitude of disciplines, which receive their names in connection with "logy" at the end.

Psychology, sociology, theology, physiology, biology, oncology, ontology, etymology, etiology, cosmology, enology, morphology, epistemology, Christology, philology, geology, metereology, ecclesiology. Patrology, ecology, dermatology, hematology, endocrinology, phenomenology, organology, radiology, sinology, typology, gynecology. (Not much of a science or "logy" is in the study of politics or history.)

"Logy" indicated that there is a basic order in some aspect of reality, and that one can study this and speak (logos) about it in an orderly way. We can speak only in generalities and categories, and the uniqueness of something cannot be brought into words. For example, "apple" generally means a category of fruit. A "red" apple is different from a "yellow" apple. "That" apple is different from "the other" apple. But even "that apple" is only of interest insofar as it is a form of apple. That object is identified by the word apple. The word gives the phenomenon a substance. Through the word the thing receives understanding. We cannot relate to things which we do not understand. We can play with them, fear them, like them, or throw them away. However, the moment we want to understand what "it" is, we have to choose words.

In an unpublished paper, "Christ, the *Logos*, and Contemporary Language Analysis of the Work," presented at a regional meeting of the College Theology Society in the early eighties, I recalled an experience when I was a student in Wurzburg, Germany. I had the opportunity to attend a guest lecture by Martin Heidegger. The auditorium was filled with people who had heard about this famous existentialist philosopher whose books were read all over the world. When this man appeared behind the lectern he looked like a farmer tanned by the sun and whose muscles were hardened by working the land. When he began to speak, I sensed a special atmosphere. This man wanted to communicate something which was very dear to him, and he hoped that we would respond accordingly.

The theme was *Das Wort* (the word), and the concern was that words are unique especially when spoken in actual language. Here is the picture. We all came together to listen to a philosopher who used his presence and his words to communicate with us his personal appreciation of the phenomenon, the word. Heidegger was successful with me because I sensed the sacredness of his existential appreciation of word and language.

One evening, more than twenty five years later, I had gone to bed to get a good night's rest. Sleep did not come, however, and something was brewing within me. For some unknown reason I found myself drifting into that part of my brain where the knowledge of the German language is stored. I must say that it was very dusty, but my consciousness took delight in trying out my German. I began to speak aloud. I heard myself say words in a language which I had not used for years. I became philosophical and allowed myself reflections on the word as an existential phenomenon. It became so substantial that I had to leave my bed and go to the typewriter. Here is a translation of my playing with German words about *Das Wort*.

The word is presented to us so that we will understand more. An understanding is signified so that its sign may signal its meaning in us. In an understanding we experience a relationship so that insights may light up in us. The word is uttered so that the veils on things may be lifted and the things can be looked at in a new way.

The word is not part of the things it talks about. It belongs to the perception of things so that they become conceived in certain ways.

We assume that those who speak words, mean to relate meaning so that things become speakable. Words may intend to present explanations so that the presence of things becomes more plain. In such presentations things become real in our understanding of reality.

If words are imaginative, they may help us in our imagination about things. This imagination is an expression of the human spirit which approaches things in terms of images.

In the images about things, the human conjures an understanding of life. Thus human life allows itself to be called into meaning. Words indicate such images, and in words reality becomes realized.

Words contain invitation to motion. The humans can be motioned by words. The human spirit experiences an inspiration when words are said about things. The word unites in us a spiritual image about somethings out there. Words offer indication of what can be indicated. Words belong to the reality of things but they result from listening to things and words about them. By words we appropriate things by our approval of them in our hearts and minds.

Words emerge because they want to say something important about things. Things become present to us in the presentation of the word. It may be that some expectations may result from words which may impregnate in our minds certain connections among things still to be made. Words speak to our spirit and make it understand something. We experience that the word is not the spirit but is an expression thereof. By means of words we recognize that there is a spirit within us and a spirit of things we talk about. The expectations of things can be expressed in words about such expectations. Hope emerges from such caressing words so that we may become caring and careful about the things of which they speak.

By means of words things may become redeemed insofar as that which is deemed to be important to them may become realized. Words are spoken in a language which wants to explicate possible connections between things so that they can be understood in a new context. This new context may be valued as a bond by which things can be lifted beyond their old boundaries. Then the value of things depends on the evaluation it receives in our words. Our words may signify their redemption. Such a redemption is not an annihilation of the concreteness of things but a concretion of the things in the spirit of things. Redemption is an alleviation in terms of a new understanding by which things will receive a transubstantiation. In this context one experiences that the word is understood as the maker of all things. Insofar as we agree on certain words and a certain idiom, we can relate to one another about our world. The word is not the maker or creator, but the orderer of existing reality. As such, the Father is not the word. The word of the Father is spoken in the name and spirit of creativity.

The word is always more than what we say. As such it is primordial and before the beginning. The word is not the beginning, but it is in the beginning.

Words are being said to indicate that life is greater than we ever can say. This awareness in us is unfathomable – the beyond words. The "unspeakable" and unfathomable" are nevertheless words. They supersede concepts, but still, they say something with which the brain, the mind, is satisfied. It is a dimension, a category for which the mind has a place. It means, it cannot be labeled but it still deserves a place in our read-outs of life.

That is why in the Hindu tradition the Brahman supersedes the creator-God. That is why we hold that we have a body and a soul, i.e., we assume that we know who we are because of our bodily existence. We also know that the very core of our existence is more than a thing. The "more than a thing" is an indication of what is held to be spiritual.

But even the spiritual can be talked about and is within the realm of the word, the "logos." The metaphors "Son of the Father," "*logos*," and "word" represent the dimensions of a primordial underlying root of being, the depth awareness of creativity. This mystery receives some focus in the saying, "Son of the Father." It expresses a respect for existence in reference to its divine energy which emanates from it and is in it.

Thus existence is not just a blind accidental happening – not just absurd. The "Son of the Father" is our brother, who is among us to help us say more than we can say on our own. The "Son of the Father" came among us and helped us see more than we can see on our own. Through his words, the "Son of the Father" helps us to believe more than we can believe on our own. Because he lived among us, he relativized belief systems, which were our expressions of the valuable about life.

If we truly believe in values, then we will welcome the one who makes the values more valuable – the "Son of the Father." He is not the founder of a religion. He personifies the awareness of the stuff from which religions are made. He supersedes any doctrine, any nation, any tradition, and any culture. He also affirms doctrines, nations, traditions, and cultures because they are tentative statements about the valuable in life and existence as a whole.

The "Father" is not just interested in our planet, Earth, (which is four billion years old) and in the human race (which is less than 200,000 years old). The "Father" is of the universe and all the universes we can imagine. The "Father" is of eternity and in his name "the Son" helps us to appreciate the blade of grass and the dewdrop shining on it in a multi-colored brilliance. In this spirit, heroes emerge in the name of the quality of life and the need for justice and fairness. The "Father" is among us and in us as signified in our words, which receive meaning in the word, the "Son of the Father."

It is important not to forget that this language is metaphorical. Thus, there is no Father, there is no Son in terms of locality and being in space and time.   Many people were and are inspired by looking at Jesus.   This inspiration is real, but the doctrine is not. The admiration is real, but the veneration is not. Saying in Jesus' name, "Abba," "Our Father," is real, but praying to him is not. In the name of "Our Father" who is in the very depth of us, and whose name we know because of his "Son," who is the word within us, we sense a creativity beyond and within everything.

Jose and Miriam Argeulles in their book, *Mandala* offer their "Ritual of the Mandala," which is a beautiful way by which to end this journey.

> To Him Who is the Lord of the Center
> The Diamond Weaver
> The Invisible Father of the Sun
> Who is seated on the Throne of the Archetypes
> Teller of Fables of the Celestial Night
> Dreamer of the Visions of All Men
> Teacher of the Twelve-fold Rites of the Sun
> Keeper of the Book of Days
> Seed of the Names of All Things
> Seer of All Entrances and Partings
> He who sets in motion the Elements and Seasons
> And who places the Rainbow Border on all Creation.
>
> You, O nameless One, we invoke:
> Enter our hearts and speak through us
> Lend to us the Vision of Unity
> Teach us the Science of the Whole
> Make known to us once again the Right of the Mandala
>
> Hear us O Lord of the Center
> Keeper of the Radiant Law
> In our silence may Your Voice ring clear
>
> We are as Seeds
> Only You who walk the Sky
> Can show to us the Path
> Our feet must follow this Earth
> Only You can heal and make us whole
> Only through our submission to You
> May we heal ourselves and become whole –
>
> In this way may we be led once again on
>   the Path of Beauty (81)

Chapter Thirteen

Epilog

After one returns from a journey, one may hope to have acquired some insight beneficial to the soul or mind. It has to do with wisdom. Because in the introductory chapter I stated my existential position and my need to inquire about the Father of Jesus, it is now time for testimony regarding my own development.

First, the journey was richer than I had expected. I was particularly enlightened by the Gnostic sources and how they express a spirituality about Jesus by which Campbell's sayings became more substantiated. Saul Levin informed me about the non-Mosaist traditions which provide avenues for a closer identification between the biblical faith and Campbell's emphasis on the wider dimensions of the Father and Son of the Father metaphors.

But these and other aspects of personal learning really came to a dramatic realization when I was listening to a choir singing Carey Landry's composition, "Abba! Father!" (Copyright 1977 by North American Liturgy Resources, 2110 W. Peoria Avenue, Phoenix, AR 85029).

Abba, Abba, Father.
You are the potter,
we are the clay, the work of your hands.

Mold us, mold us and fashion us
into the image of Jesus Your Son,

Abba, Abba, Father.
You are the potter,
we are the clay, the work of your hands.

Father, may we be one in You
as He is in You and You are in Him.

Abba, Abba, Father.
You are the potter,
we are the clay, the work of your hands.

Before the journey I understood this prayerful song only in its obvious image. It is about those two: The Father and His Son, and about us, simple creatures, invited to become part of God's holy will.

The journey, however, had introduced me to a variety of aspects by which the metaphor, Father, can be understood. A number of them came to my imagination while listening to the song about the Father. The music is very calming and meditative, and it allows for introspection. It was as when one looks at illustrations of Gestalt theory. The most widely known is two faces looking at each other, but the same picture can be viewed as a vase. When one sees the vase, one does not see the faces. When one sees the two faces, one does not see the vase. This was my experience when the musical cry, "Abba!" "Father," floated in the air. Instead of one of the other images of "Father," there were at least three which came to my imagination.

The obvious image of Father, the one who dwells in Heaven, above us, or out there, was replaced with Campbell's insight of the Father "within", which is the spirit of compassion. When one sings, "Abba, Father. You are the potter, and we are the clay," in terms of "You, Spirit of Compassion, within me, please, fashion us into the image of Jesus, then this prayer is from the heart.

Moreover, when one sings, "Abba, Father," in terms of the divine eternity within the very core of our own being, then the prayer, "May we be one in You as He is in You and You are in Him," becomes like an Hindu chant in which one expresses a longing for spiritual growth. One utters the willingness to let go of one's ego-centeredness. The mystical dimension of the eternal is called into one's awareness. This definitely has the power of true contemplation.

Also, the insights about the Virgin and Virgin Birth came to mind, where the heart expressed a responsive readiness to the celebration of life, to accept being embraced in opening oneself to the fruit-bearing energy within us and around us. This receives an environment of nourishment when one hears within "Abba!" also the reference to Mama! or mother. Years ago, when the womens' movement suggested and urged for a reference to God as Mother, and not just Father, I experimented accordingly. When I was about to say "Our Father, who art in Heaven," I said "Our Mother, who art..." When I stopped, intuitively I felt less inclined to say, "who are in Heaven," Somehow I sensed that the expression, "Our Mother" provides a feeling of being surrounded. The metaphor, Mother, creates an awareness of a warming presence. Thus the musical cry, "Abba!," becomes transparent. It is liberated from a labeled box, and it dances around in our imagination by taking on various "Gestalts."

Gestalt means "whole" or configuration. Gestalt psychologists (Werthheimer, Kohler, and Koffka) regarded the whole as being more than the sum of the parts. They found that the individual organizes stimuli into objects according to certain principles. The principles, figure and ground, form a relationship. The figure is what one perceives, and the rest of the picture is reduced to ground. In certain pictures figure and ground are reversible. Thus perception depends very much on the character of the perceiver, but it also depends on the character of the stimuli.

Figure and ground perception. The top half of the picture shows black birds (figure) against a white ground, whereas the lower half shows white fish (figure) against a black ground. If you look closely, you can perceive reversible fish and birds running through the middle area of the picture. (M. C. Escher-Haags Gemeentemuseum Collection, The Hague)

This journey provided energies of transformation for both, the perceiver of the Father, and also about the perceived, the stimuli, which may result in various configurations, e.g., Father, Mother, Spirit of Compassion, eternally divine within the core of our soul.

The question, "Who is the Father who motivated Jesus so much that He felt One with His father?" is quite direct. The answer is enormously complex. Becoming aware of such a complexity is a true religious experience deeply rooted in our own human existence. It helps us to say "Yes!" to life, death, and all that constitutes the amazement about the mystery divine.

Reversible figure and ground perception. You can perceive devils or angels, but you cannot perceive both at the same time. Nor can you truly indentify which is the figure and which is the ground. (M. C. Escher – Escher Foundation)

BIBLIOGRAPHY

Altizer, Thomas J. J. and Hamilton, William. *Radical Theology and the Death of God*. New York: The Bobbs-Merrill Company, Inc., 1966.

_____ "The Anonymity of God," in *The University of Dayton Review*, 14/3, Fall 1980, (ed. William P. Frost), pp. 17-26.

Arguelles, Miriam & Jose. *The Feminine: Spacious as the Sky*. Boulder & London: Shambala, 1977.

Aurobindo, Sri. *The Life Divine*. New York: E. P. Dutton & Company., 1949.

Ayer, Alfred Jules. *Language, Truth and Logic*. New York: Dover Publications Inc.

Barnstone, Willis. Ed., *The Other Bible*. New York: Harper & Row, 1984.

Becker, Ernest. *The Denial of Death*. New York: The Free Press, 1985.

Bellah, Robert. "Religious Evolution." *American Sociological Review* 29, 3:358-374.

Benford, Gregory. "The Universe According to Guth." *Discover*, June, 1983, pp. 93-99.

Berger, Peter. *A Rumor of Angels*. Garden City, N. Y.: Doubleday, Anchor Books, 1969.

_____ *The Capitalist Revolution: Fifty Propositions about Prosperity, Equity & Liberty*. New York: Basic Books, Inc., 1986.

Binswanger, Hilde, "Positive Aspects of the Animus." *Spring* 1963. New York: Analytic Psychology Club of New York, 1963.

Bloch, Ernst. *Man on His Own*. New York: Herder & Herder, Inc., 1971.

Bohm, David. *Wholeness and the Implicate Order*. London, Boston, and Henley: Routledge & Kegan Paul Inc., 1980.

Bowman, Meg. "Why We Burn: Sexism Exorcised." *The Humanist*, November/December, 1983.

Brown, Norman. *Life Against Death*. New York: Random House, 1959.

264

Brueggeman, W. "David and His Theologian." *Catholic Biblical Quarterly*, 30, 1968, pp. 156-181.

Burhoe, Ralph W. *Sciences and Human Values in the 21st Century*. Philadelphia: The Westminster Press, 1971.

Cameron, J. M. "A New Testament." Review of Thomas Sheehan's book, *The First Coming: How the Kingdom of God Became Christianity* (Random House, 1986) in the *The New York Review*, December 1986, pp. 23-27.

Campbell, Joseph. *The Power of Myth*. New York: Doubleday, 1988.

_____ *The Inner Reaches of Outer Space: Metaphor as Myth as Religion*. New York: Alfred Van Der Marck Edition, 1986.

_____ *The Hero with a Thousand Faces*. Princeton University Press, 1968.

_____ *The Portable Jung*. New York: The Viking Press, 1971.

Childs, Brevard. *Myth and Reality in the Old Testament*. London: SCM Press Ltd., 2nd. edition, 1968.

Dart, John. *The Laughing Savior*. New York: Harper & Row, 1976.

Davis, Elizabeth Gould. *The First Sex*. Balitmore, MD: Penguin Books, Inc., 1973.

Eliade, Mircea. *Gods, Goddesses, and Myths of Creation*. New York: Harper & Row, 1974.

_____ *Patterns in Comparative Religion*. Cleveland and New York: The World Publishing Company, Meridian Books, 1976.

_____ *Images and Symbols: Studies in Religious Symbolism*. New York: Sheed and Ward, Search Book Edition, 1969.

Ellwood, Robert S. Jr. *Reading on Religion from Inside and Outside*. (esp. Chapter Four, "Dancing Before God: Religious Symbol and Rite. Englewood Cliffs, N. J.: Prentice-Hall, 1978.

Fawcett, Thomas. *The Symbolic Language of Religion*. Minneapolis, Minnesota: Augsburg Publishing House, 1971.

Ferre, Fredrick. *Language, Logic and God*. New York: Harper & Row, Harper Torchbooks, 1961.

Ferguson, Marilyn. *The Aquarian Conspiracy: Personal and Social Transformation in the 1980s*. Los Angeles: J. P. Tarcher, Inc., 1980.

Feynman, Richard. *Surely You're Joking, Mr. Feynman!* W. W. Norton & Company, Inc., 1985.

Fowler, James and A. Vergote, eds.; *Toward Moral and Religious Maturity*, Morristown, N. Y.: Silver Burdett, 1980.

Friedrich, Gerhard. *Theological Dictionary of the New Testament.* Grand Rapids, Michigan: Wm. B. Eerdmans Publishing Company.

Friedrich, Paul. *The Meaning of Aphrodite.* Chicago: The University of Chicago Press, 1978.

Fromm, Erich. *Escape From Freedom.* New York: Holt, 1955.

_____ *The Revolution of Hope.* New York: Bantam Books, 1968.

Frost, William P. "Buddhism: Progress or Regression?" *The American Ecclesiastical Review*, 168/7, September, 1974, pp. 469-481.

_____ *Roots of American Religiousness.* Washington, D. C.: University Press of America, 1977.

_____ *Visions of the Divine.* Washington, D. C.: University Press of America, 1977.

Greeley, Andrew. *The New Agenda.* Garden City, N. Y.: Doubleday & Company, Ind., 1973.

Gutierrez, Gustavo. *A Theology of Liberation.* Maryknoll, N. Y.: Orbis, 1973.

Hamilton, William. "Banished from the Land of Unity." *Radical Theology and the Death of God.* Thomas J. J. Altizer and William Hamilton. New York: The Bobbs-Merrill Company, Inc., 1966.

Harwood, William R. "Gods, Goddesses, and Bibles: The Canonization of Misogyny." *The Humanist*, May/June, 1985.

Hedges, Robert E. M. and Growlett, John A. J. "Radiocarbon Dating bay Accelerator Mass Spectometry." *Scientific American*, January 1986, pp. 100-107.

Hedrick, Charles W. "A Response to Very Goddess and Very Man." *Images of the Feminine in Gnosticism.* Ed., Karen L. King. Philadelphia: Fortress Press, 1988.

Hedrick, Charles W. and Hodgson, Robert Jr., eds. *Nag Hammadi Gnosticism & Early Christianity.* Peabody, Mass.: Hendrickson Publishers, 1986.

Heidel, Alexander. *The Babylonian Genesis.* Chicago: The University of Chicago Press, Phoenix Books, 1967.

266

_____ *The Gilgamesh Epic and Old Testament Parallels.* Chicago: The University of Chicago Press, Phoenix Books, Fifth Impression, 1965.

Hillman, James. *The Dream and the Underworld.* New York: Harper & Row, 1979.

Horsley, Richard A. *Jesus and the Spiral of Violence: Popular Jewish Resistance in Roman Palestine.* San Francisco: Harper & Row Publishers, 1987.

Huxley, Julian. *Essays of a Humanist.* New York: Harper & Row, 1964.

Kelber, Werner H. *The Oral and Written Gospel.* Philadelphia: Fortress Press. 1983.

Kennedy, Eugene. "Want the Truth?: Turn Over a Myth and Look Under It." *National Catholic Reporter*, May 1, 1987, pp. 7-8.

Kohlberg, Lawrence. "Moral Development, Religious Thinking, and the Question of the Seventh Stage." *Zygon: Journal of Religion and Science*, 16/3, September, 1981.

King, Karen L. ed., *Images of the Feminine in Gnosticism.* Philadelphia: Fortress Press, 1988.

Lammers, Ann. "The Myth of Psyche: Feminine Consciousness and Individuation." *Explorations: Journal for Adventurous Thought*, 3/3, January 1984.

Levin, Saul. *The Father of Joshua/Jesus.* Binghamton, N. Y.: State University of New York, 1978.

Lifton, Robert J. *The Life of the Self: Toward a New Psychology.* New York: Simon and Schuster, 1976.

_____ "The Struggle for Cultural Rebirth." *Harper's Magazine*, April 1973, pp. 84-93.

L'Heureux, Conrad. *Rank among the Canaanite Gods.* Missoula, Montana: Scholars Press; "Harvard Semitic Monographs", Cambridge, Mass., 1979.

_____ "Cultural Anthropology and the Death-Immortality Dialog." Unpublished Paper. Dept. of Religious Studies, University of Dayton, Dayton, Oh. 1972.

McKenzie, John L., *Dictionary of the Bible.* Milwaukee: The Bruce Publishing Company, 1963.

McLaughlin, Kathleen. "Buddhist and Jungian Spiritual Paths: Insight and Imagination." *Explorations: Journal for Adventurous Thought*, 5/6, Summer 1987.

Maslow, Abraham. *Religions, Values, and Peak-Experiences*. New York: Viking, 1964.

Mellor, Anne Kostelanetz. *Blake's Human Form Divine*. Berkeley: University of California Press, 1974.

Miguens, Manuel. *The Virgin Birth: An Evaluation of Scriptural Evidence*. Westminster, MD: Christian Classics, Inc., 1975.

Moltmann, Jurgen. *Theology of Hope*. New York: Harper & Row, 1967.

Mullen, E. Theodore. *The Divine Council in Canaanite and Early Hebrew Literature*. Chico, CA.: Scholars Press; "Harvard Semitic Monographs," Cambridge, Mass., 1980.

Neumann, Erich. *The Archetypal World of Henry Moore*. New York: Harper & Row, The Bollingen Library, 1959.

_____ *Amor and Psyche: The Psychic Development of the Feminine, A Commentary on the Tale by Apuleius*. New York: Bollingen Foundation, 1956.

_____ *The Great Mother: An Analysis of the Archetype*. New York: Pantheon Books, 1955.

_____ *The Origins of Consciousness and History of Consciousness*. Princeton, N. Y.: Princeton University Press, 1971.

Nickelburg, George W. E. *Resurrection, Immortality, and Eternal Life in Intertestamental Judaism*. Cambridge, MA: Harvard University Press, 1972.

O'Brien, William J. *Stories to the Dark: Explorations in Religious Imagination*. New York: Paulist Press, 1977.

Oliner, Samuel. *The Altruistic Personality: Rescuers of Jews in Nazi Europe*. New York: Free Press, 1988.

Oser, F. "Stages of Religious Judgment." *Toward Moral and Religious Maturity*. Ed., J. Fowler and A. Vergote. Morristown, N. J.: Silver-Burdett, 1980.

Pagels, Elaine. "Adam and Eve and the Serpent in Genesis 1-3." *Images of the Feminine in Gnosticism*. Ed., Karen L. King. Philadelphia: Fortress Press, 1988.

268

_____ "Pursuing the Spiritual Eve: Imagery and Hermeneutics in the *Hypostasis of the Archons* and the *Gospel of Philip*." In *Images of the Feminine in Gnosticism*. Ed., Karen L. King. Philadelphia: Fortress Press, 1988.

_____ "Exegesis and Exposition of the Genesis Accounts in Selected Texts from Nag Hammadi. Eds., Charles W. Hedrick and Robert Hodgson, Jr. *Nag Hammadi Gnosticism & Early Christianity*. Peabody, Mass.: Hendrickson Publishers, 1986.

Pannenberg, Wolfhart. "Appearance as the Arrival of the Future." *New Theology* no. 5, eds., Martin E. Marty and Dean G. Peerman, New York: The MacMillan Company, 1968.

Piaget, Jean. *Play, Dreams and Imitation in Childhood*. W. W. Norton & Company, 1962.

Priest, John F. "Myth and Dream in Hebrew Scripture." *Myths, Dreams, and Religion*. Edited by Joseph Campbell. New York: E. P. Dutton & Co., Inc., 1970.

Rahner, Karl. "Do You Believe in God?" New York: Paulist Press, 1969.

Rank, Otto. *Beyond Psychology*. New York: Dover, 1958.

Reilly, Frank. "'A Very Unpleasant Alternative': One Response to Raymond Brown's Defense of the Virginal Conception." *Explorations: Journal for Adventurous Thought*, 6/4, Summer, 1988, pp. 79-116.

Reese, James M. "Contributions of Sociolinguistics to our Understanding of the New Testament." *Explorations: Journal for Adventurous Thought*. 6/3, Spring 1988, pp. 79-88.

Restak, Richard M. *The Mind*. New York: Bantam Books, 1988.

Robinson, James M. "On Bridging the Gulf from *Q* to the *Gospel of Thomas* (or Vice Versa)." Eds., Charles W. Hedrick and Robert Hodgson, Jr. *Nag Hammadi Gnosticism & Early Christianity*. Peabody, Mass.: Hendrickson Publishers, 1986.

_____ "Very Goddess and Very Man: Jesus' Better Self." Ed., Karen L. King. *Images of the Feminine in Gnosticism*. Philadelphia: Fortress Press, 1988.

Rogers, Carl R. *Client Centered Therapy*. Boston: Houghton Mifflin, 1951.

Russell, Letty M. *Human Liberation in a Feminist Perspective*. Philadelphia: Westminster, 1974.

Rust, Eric C. *Evolutionary Philosophies and Contemporary Theology*. Philadelphia: The Westminster Press, 1969.

Safrai, S. and Stern, M. *Compendia Rerum Iudaicarum Ad Novum Testamentum*. Volume One. Philadelphia: Fortress Press, 1974.

Sagan, Carl. *Cosmos*. New York: Random House, 1980.

Schaberg, Jane. *The Illegitimacy of Jesus: A Feminist Theological Interpretation of the Infancy Narratives*. San Francisco: Harper & Row Publishers, 1987.

Schillebeeckx, Edward. *Jesus: An Experiment in Christology*. New York: The Seabury Press, 1979.

Schroeder, Steven. "Ecclesiogenesis: Leonard Boff and Dietrich Bonhoeffer on the Church." *Explorations: Journal for Adventurous Thought*. 7/1, Fall, 1988, pp. 41-54.

Sheehan, Thomas. *The First Coming: How the Kingdom of God Became Christianity*. New York: Random House, 1986.

Sherburne, Donald W. *A Key to Whitehead's* Process and Reality. New York: The MacMillan Company, 1966.

Talbot, Michael. *Mysticism and the New Physics*. New York: A Bantam Book, 1981.

Tate, Randy W. "The Biblical Reader as Artistic Recreator: Implications For Interpretation." *Explorations: Journal for Adventurous Thought*, 6/3, Spring 1988, pp. 65-78.

Taylor, G. Rattray. *Sex in History*. New York: Harper and Row, 1973.

Teilhard de Chardin, Pierre. *The Phenomenon of Man*. New York: Harper & Row, Harper Torchbooks, 1961.

Tillich, Paul. *The Courage To Be*. New Haven, Conn.: Yale University Press, 1952.

Ulanov, Ann Belford. *The Feminine in Jungian Psychology and in Christian Theology*. Evanston: Northwestern University Press, 1971.

von Franz, Marie-Louise. *Problems of the Feminine in Fairytales*. Irving, Texas: University of Dallas, 1972.

Von Rad, Gerhard. *Wisdom in Israel*. Nashville and New York: Abingdon Press, 1972.

Weber, Renee. *Dialogues with Scientists and Sages: A Search for Unity*. London and New York: Routledge & Kegan Paul, 1987. Esp. Chapter Four, "Morphogenetic Fields: Nature's Habits," which discusses the theories of Rupert Sheldrake.

270

Webster's New World Dictionary (College Edition), 1964.

Wilder, Amos. "Myth and Dream in Christian Scripture." *Myths, Dreams, and Religion*. Edited by Joseph Campbell. New York: E. P. Dutton & Co., Inc., 1970.

Wills, Garry. *Inventing America: Jefferson's Declaration of Independence*. Garden City, N. Y.: Doubleday, Inc., 1978.

Wolf, William J. *The Almost Chosen People*. New York: Doubleday and Company, Inc., 1959.

Zukav, Gary. *The Dancing Wu-li Masters: An Overview of the New Physics*. New York: William Morrow & Company, Inc., A Bantam New Age Book, 1979.

INDEX

274

Y

Yahweh (Jahweh), 46, 47, 75, 78,
99, 101, 102, 103, 119, 182,
185, 186, 187, 195, 199

Z

Zeus, 105, 119, 159
Zukav, Gary, 7, 8, 270

TEXTS AND STUDIES IN RELIGION